# Introduction

The tea towel had a modest birth in 19th-century England. Later, its original form, a small linen square used to dry fine china, gave way to a fine-spun towel embellished with hand-stitched edges.

Even though the English are still known for their penchant for tea, it is no longer commonplace to use tea towels for their original purpose. A tea towel may be used as a teapot cozy or a basket warmer, becoming a prominent detail in the presentation of tea.

The decoration expanded to include commercially printed towels that featured pastoral scenes, calendars and even English monarchs.

Today we love tea towels because we love all things retro, and tea towels bring to mind 1950s kitsch. It seems that our grandmothers' code demanded that they drape tea towels over stove handles, cupboard doors and faucets—and the more unusual the designs the better! Tea towels that were adorned with everything from maps of Paris to dancing fruit were the exclamation point of knickknack decor.

The colorful and quirky projects in this book will add flair to your modern-day kitchen. With 101 to choose from, you can make as many as you need to match the season or to match your mood.

You can purchase a ready-made tea towel to enhance, or you can make your own with our instructions. The instructions given are based on a finished size of 18" x 25", but you may make yours smaller or larger to fit your needs.

What are you waiting for? Get started making a set of tea towels to showcase your personality and color preferences.

# Table of Contents

*Dimensional Dryers,* ***page 81***

*Appliqué Delight,* ***page 70***

# Tea Towel Basics

The designs in this book may be used on purchased tea towels, or you can make your own using the instructions below. The patterns in this book have been designed for use on 18" x 25" tea towels. Pattern adjustments may be required for different-size towels.

The instructions for the individual tea towels reference these instructions throughout the book.

## Finishing Towel Edges

Many of the tea towels shown in this book have a ¾"-finished band along the bottom edge.

To add a band, remove the finished edge of a purchased towel on one short end. If making a towel for use, follow instructions for preparing to add a border in Making a Tea Towel.

Method one creates a double layer on the end with the added band. To make a ¾" band, cut a 2¼" x 19" strip of the fabric you would like to feature on the bottom of the towel.

Measure up ½" from the raw edge of the towel and mark a straight line from one side of the towel to the other. Press under one long edge of the 2¼" x 19" strip ¼".

Center and pin the right side of the remaining long raw edge of the strip along the marked line; stitch ¼" from the raw edge of the strip as shown in Figure 1. Press the strip to the right side.

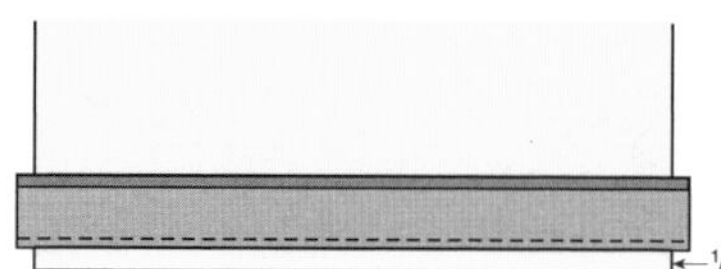


Figure 1

Turn towel over and press each short raw end of the strip under ¼". Turn in short edges again over the back side of the towel to enclose side edges of the end of the towel as shown in Figure 2.

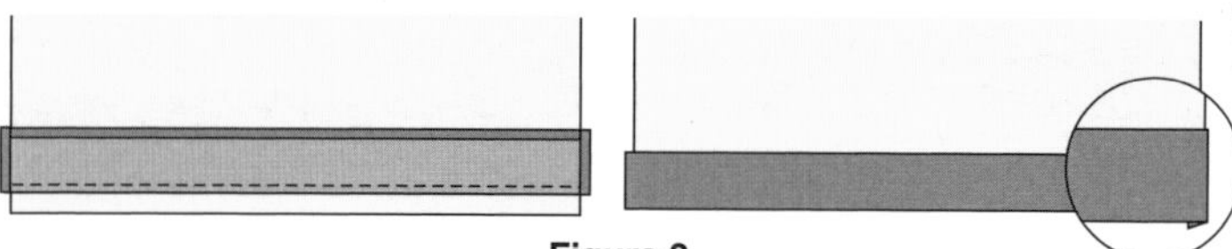

Figure 2

Press the long folded edge of the strip over the back side of the towel to enclose the stitched long edge. Hand-stitch in place on each short end and along the length of the strip on the back side to finish.
See Making a Tea Towel for instructions on making a wider border.

Method two results in a less-sturdy edge of the towel, but is quicker and easier.

Press one long edge of the 2¼" x 19" strip ¼" to the wrong side. Sew the opposite long edge with right sides together along the trimmed edge of the tea towel using a ¼" seam allowance. Press the strip down with seam toward the strip.

Turn in the short ends of the strip to the wrong side ¼" and over the edge of the back side of the towel; hand-stitch in place on the finished-side edge of the towel.

Turn the long pressed edge of the strip to the back side of the towel to cover the seam and hand-stitch the strip in place to finish the edge.

The edges of any tea towel, whether purchased or self-made, may be bound. This method may be used to finish the edges of a tea towel that has a pieced band. If using this method, eliminate turning under the ends of pieced strips and simply trim these ends even with the edges of the towel.

To make a contrasting or coordinating binding, measure the sides to be bound. For example, if the bottom edge has been finished with an added band, the two long sides and remaining end may be bound. This distance is approximately 68" (25 + 25 + 18). Add at least 6" and create a 1½"-wide strip this length. Press under one long edge ¼".

Align the remaining long raw edge with the sides and end of the tea towel, extending binding ½" on the beginning end. Sew all around to the opposite end, mitering corners as shown in Figure 3. Trim excess binding to ½".

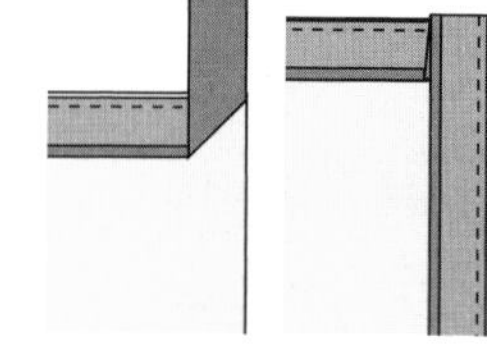

Figure 3

Turn under the ½" excess and then turn the binding to the back side of the tea towel and hand-stitch in place to finish.

Some of the tea towels with pieced bottom bands require special edge finishing. If this is the case, these instructions are given in the chapter or specific project instructions.

## Making a Tea Towel

If you prefer, you may make your own tea towel. It can be any size, but these instructions are to make a towel that finishes at 18" x 25".

To make your own 18" x 25" tea towel, select fabric that will work with the tea towel design you would like to use. For example, if you will be adding an embroidery design from the Embroidery chapter to your towel, the towel background should be a light color that will showcase the design. Most of the sample tea towels in the Embroidery chapter are stitched on muslin, Osnaburg, ticking or gingham fabrics. Refer to the specific instructions with your chosen design for any special treatments required.

The fabrics should be a tight weave, and for the most part, 100 percent cotton or linen. Depending on its final use, a tea towel should be able to withstand washing and drying.

You will need ¾ yard of fabric for the basic tea towel. Cut a 19" x 26" rectangle from the fabric.

Turn under ¼" all around and press. Turn under again ¼", press and stitch to hem.

If adding a band to one narrow end, it would be easier to add it before hemming the basic towel. In this case, deduct the measurement of the finished band plus ¼" from the 25" length. For example, if you want a 2" finished band, cut the basic towel rectangle 22¾".

Cut the strip for the 2" finished band 4½" wide; this includes twice the size of the finished band (2" x 2) and ¼" seam allowance on each long side (½" total).

Add the band to the basic towel before hemming following the instructions for Finishing Towel Edges on page 4. Hem the edges, press the long edge of the band ¼" to the wrong side and turn to the back side of the towel 2" and hand-stitch in place to finish. ❖

# Meet the Designer

Trice Boerens has worked for many years in the quilting, needlework and paper industries. Along with designing projects for best-selling books and kits, she has also worked as a photo stylist, an art director and a creative editor.

The designs for this book were inspired by treasures that she uncovered in antique stores, flea markets and attics.

House of White Birches, Berne, Indiana 46711 Clotilde.com

# Piecing

## General Instructions

At the soul of American art is the charming artistry of fabric piecing. A pieced (or patchwork) quilt deserves its place alongside such favorites as a wing chair, a tilt-top table and a hurricane lamp. This beloved technique is adapted to create tea towel borders and medallions.

### Fabric

Choose 100 percent cotton fabrics that are preshrunk, soft to the touch and colorfast. For a subtle effect, use colors that are close in hue and value. Since the pattern pieces required to make the designs in this section are small, choose fabrics with small motifs or patterns.

### Supplies & Tools

- Scissors or shears—Make sure these are sharp and feel comfortable in your hand.
- Pencil or fine-line permanent marker
- Air-soluble or water-soluble pen
- Template material—tracing paper, or lightweight plastic or cardboard
- Straight pins—Longer pins with a thin shank work best for patchwork piecing.
- Thread—all-purpose thread to match fabrics

### How to Begin

Mark fabric with a pencil or air-soluble or water-soluble pen. The ink from the air-soluble pen will disappear after several days. The ink from a water-soluble pen will disappear when the fabric is spritzed or blotted with water.

All seams on patchwork designs are ¼". The patterns given feature a solid cutting line to indicate cutting, and a broken line to indicate stitching. The ¼" seam allowance is included on these patterns.

Use tracing paper or lightweight plastic or cardboard to make templates from the pattern pieces given. Place the template material on the pattern and carefully trace along the cutting line with a pencil or fine-line permanent marker. Label each template with the corresponding letter; cut along the marked lines.

If using tracing paper, it may be glued to a piece of lightweight cardboard, such as that used in cereal boxes, and then cut out to make a sturdy template.

Trace around the templates on the right side of the appropriate fabrics as directed in the instructions for the chosen pattern, for number and color to cut. Accurately cut out the pieces on the marked lines. If a piece should be reversed, cut the reverse pieces by turning the template over or by layering two fabric pieces with wrong sides together to cut two pieces at one time with one being reversed.

To sew, pin the fabric pieces right sides together, matching along raw edges, and stitch ¼" from the edge. Trim threads and press seams flat to one side—usually toward the darker fabric.

### Preparing Towel for Piecing

If using a purchased towel, remove the bottom hemmed edge. If making your own tea towel, do not hem the bottom edge.

Fold the towel in half along the length and crease to mark the center.

### Finishing Towel Edges

Press under each side edge of the pieced band ¼", turn to the back side of the towel and hand-stitch the folded edge in place.

Press the bottom edge of the band under ¼"; turn 1" to the back side of the towel. Hand-stitch in place on the back side to finish. ❖

# Piecing Pleasures

## Project Note

Refer to Piecing General Instructions (page 4) to prepare tea towel for piecing and to finish edges.

### Pinwheel

## Materials

- 1 purchased or self-made towel in desired color
- Assorted fabric scraps
- 1" x 19" B strip coordinating solid fabric
- 2¼" x 19" C strip coordinating fabric

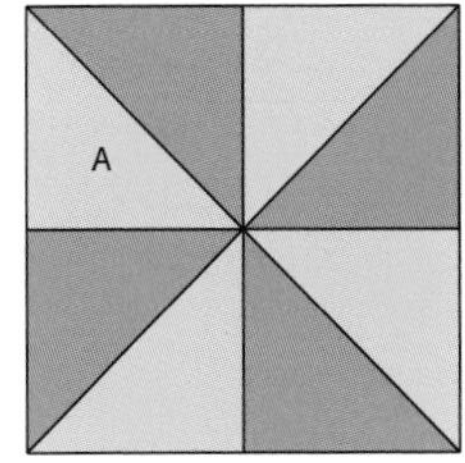


**Pinwheel Block**
Make 5

## Instructions

**1.** Prepare towel for piecing. Prepare A template using pattern given on page 12; cut as directed.

**2.** Select two sets of four A pieces; join one triangle from each set to make an A unit as shown in Figure 1; press. Repeat to make four units.

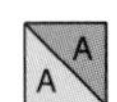


**Figure 1**

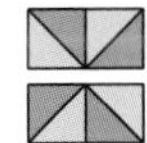

**Figure 2**

**3.** Join two units to make a row; press. Repeat to make two rows. Join the rows to complete one Pinwheel block referring to Figure 2; press. Repeat to make five blocks.

**4.** Join the five Pinwheel blocks to make a strip; press.

**5.** Cut two ¾" x 4⅛" scrap strips. Sew a strip to each end of the block strip; press. Trim strips even with the top and bottom edges of the block strip.

**6.** Center and sew the B strip to the top edge and the C strip to the bottom edge of the strip; press.

**7.** Measure up 4⅝" from the bottom edge of the tea towel; draw a line from side to side. Center and place the pieced strip right sides together with the towel with the B edge aligned with the drawn line and stitch as shown in Figure 3.

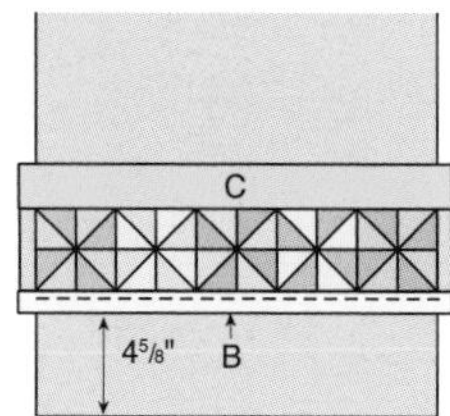


Figure 3

**8.** Press the strip to the right side. The C strip will extend below the bottom of the towel. Finish edge.

**Pinwheel**
Placement Diagram 18" x 25"

## Nine-Patch

### Materials

- 1 purchased or self-made towel in desired color
- 1 fat quarter each lavender and aqua solids
- 1 fat quarter each light and dark blue prints

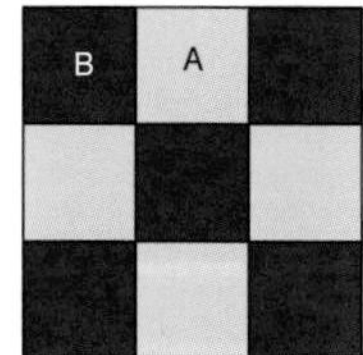


**Nine-Patch Block**
Make 3

### Instructions

**1.** Prepare towel for piecing. Prepare templates using patterns given on page 11; cut as directed.

**2.** Sew an A square between two B squares to make a row; press. Repeat to make six B-A-B rows.

**3.** Repeat step 3 with a B square between two A squares to make three A-B-A rows.

**4.** Sew an A-B-A row between two B-A-B rows to make a Nine-Patch block as shown in Figure 4; press. Repeat to make three blocks.

Figure 4

Figure 5

**5.** Arrange and join the Nine-Patch blocks with the C and D pieces to make a pieced strip as shown in Figure 5; press.

**6.** Cut one 1½" x 19" E strip and one 4" x 19" F strip from the light blue fat quarter. Center and sew the E strip to one long side, and the F strip to the remaining long side of the pieced strip; press.

**7.** Measure up 7" from the bottom edge of the tea towel; draw a line from side to side. Center and place the pieced strip right sides together with the towel with the E edge aligned with the drawn line and stitch as shown in Figure 6. Press the pieced strip to the right side. The F strip will extend below the bottom of the towel. Finish edge.

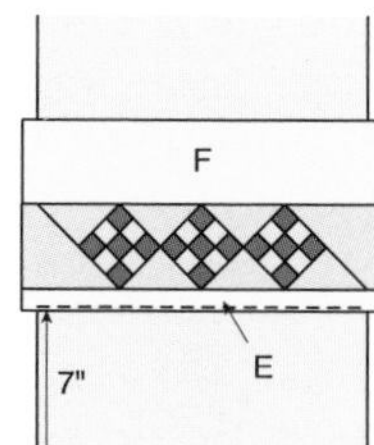


Figure 6

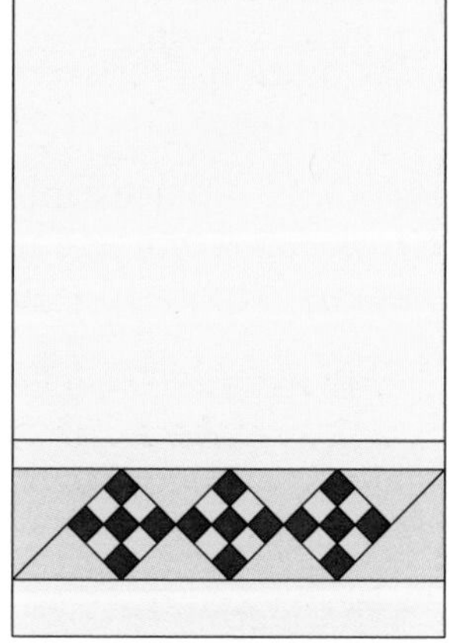

**Nine-Patch**
Placement Diagram 18" x 25"

## Butterfly

### Materials

- 1 purchased or self-made towel in desired color
- Fabric scraps: violet, white, blue, cream, magenta and lavender solids; green and light blue prints; and magenta dot
- 2¼" x 19" F strip pink print for binding
- 6-strand embroidery floss: magenta and blue

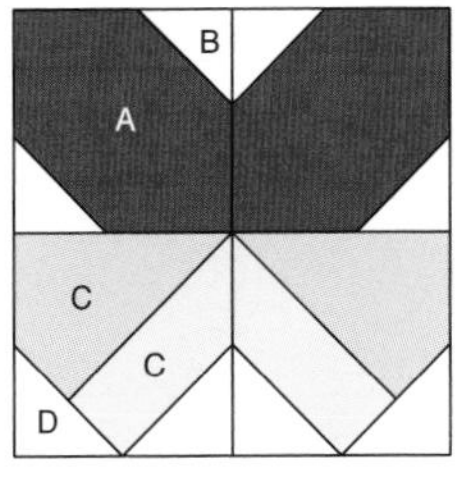


**Butterfly Block**
Make 3

## Instructions

**1.** Prepare towel for piecing. Prepare templates using patterns given on page 12; cut as directed on pieces.

**2.** To make one violet butterfly, mark a diagonal line on the wrong side of each B and D square. Align corners of a cream B square right sides together on a violet A square referring to Figure 7; stitch on the marked line. Trim seam to ¼"; press B to the right side. Repeat on the opposite corner of A to complete an A-B unit referring to Figure 8. Repeat to make two units.

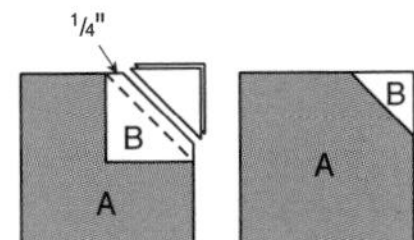


**Figure 7**

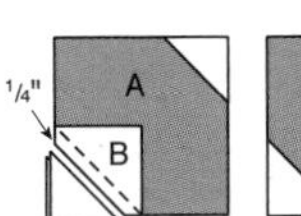


**Figure 8**

**3.** Join one each blue solid and green print C triangles to make a C unit as shown in Figure 9; press. Repeat to make two units.

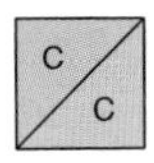


**Figure 9**

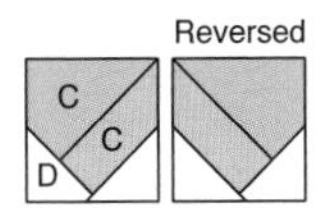


**Figure 10**

**4.** Repeat step 2 with a cream D on two adjacent corners of one C unit to make a C-D unit referring to Figure 10 for positioning. Repeat to make a reversed C-D unit, again referring to Figure 10.

**5.** Referring to Figure 11, join the two A-B units to make a row and the C-D and reversed C-D units to make a second row; press seams in opposite directions. Join the rows to complete the violet butterfly block.

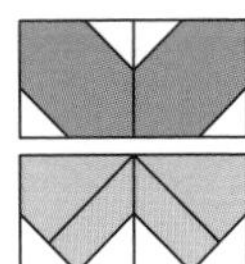

**Figure 11**

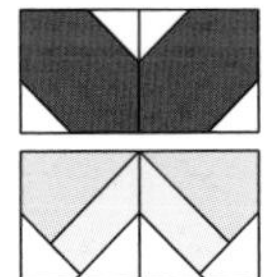

**Figure 12**

**6.** Repeat steps 2–5 to make two magenta butterfly blocks referring to Figure 12 for positioning of colors in blocks.

**7.** Sew the violet butterfly block between the two magenta butterfly blocks to make a strip as shown in Figure 13; press.

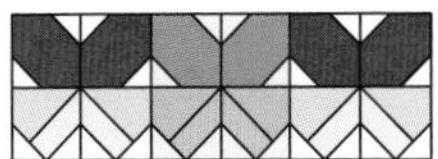

**Figure 13**

**8.** Appliqué body shapes over the center seam of each butterfly block.

**9.** Cut two 4" x 4¾" E pieces white solid. Sew E to each end of the pieced strip; press. Sew the F strip to the bottom edge; press.

**10.** Measure up 4" from the bottom edge of the tea towel; draw a line from side to side. Center and place the pieced strip right sides together with the towel with the butterfly edge aligned with the drawn line and stitch as shown in Figure 14.

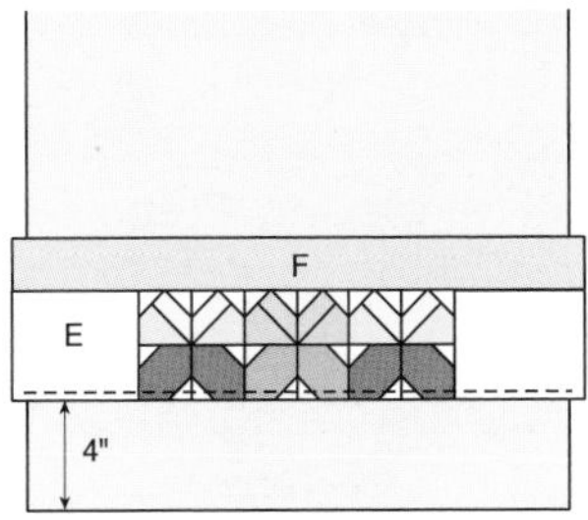


**Figure 14**

**11.** Press the strip to the right side. The F strip will extend beyond the bottom edge of the towel. Finish edge. Add antennae stitching referring to pattern.

**Butterfly**
Placement Diagram 18" x 25"

## Yellow Posy

### Materials

- 1 purchased or self-made towel in desired color
- 1 fat quarter each green, lavender, yellow and pink solids
- Scrap of print fabric with geometric motif for centering in center piece A
- Yellow 6-strand embroidery floss

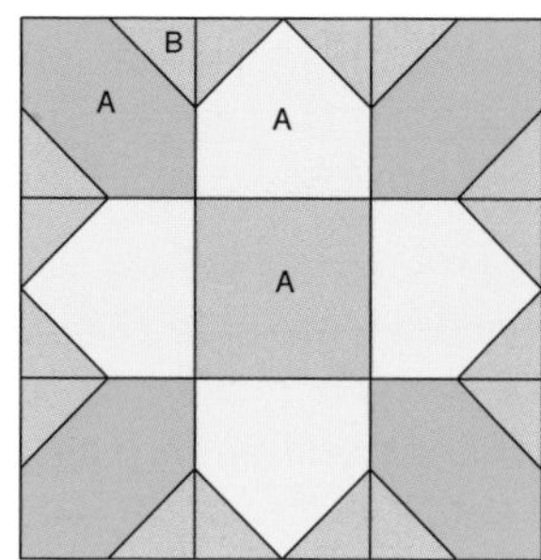


**Yellow Posy Block**
Make 4

### Instructions

**1.** Prepare towel for piecing. Prepare templates using patterns given on page 12; cut as directed on each piece.

**2.** Mark a diagonal line on the wrong side of each B square.

**3.** To make one Posy block, align corners of a B square on a green A square referring to Figure 15; stitch on the marked line. Trim seam to ¼"; press B to the right side. Repeat on the opposite corner of A to complete an A-B unit as shown in Figure 15. Repeat to make four green A-B units.

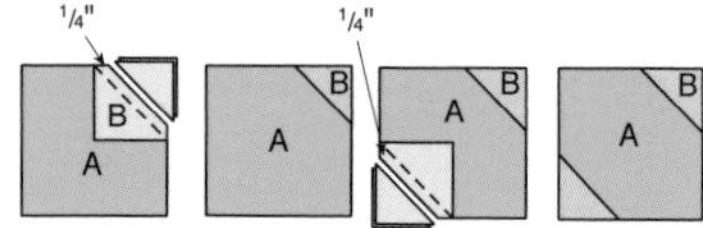


**Figure 15**

**4.** Repeat step 3 with two B squares on two adjacent corners of a yellow A to make four yellow A-B units referring to Figure 16.

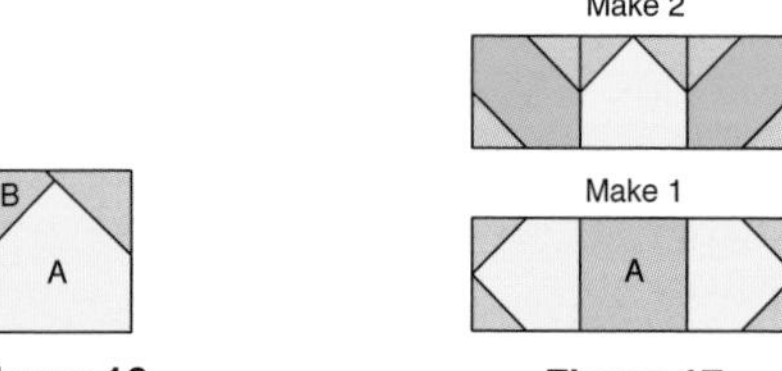


**Figure 16** **Figure 17**

**5.** Sew a yellow A-B unit between two green A-B units to make a row referring to Figure 17; repeat to make two rows; press.

**6.** Sew the geometric print A square between two yellow A-B units to make a row, again referring to Figure 17; press.

**7.** Join the rows to complete one Yellow Posy block referring to Figure 18.

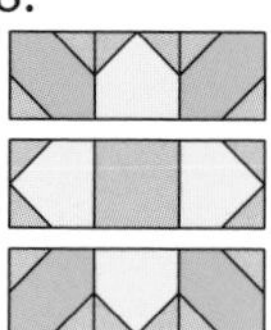

**Figure 18**

**8.** Repeat steps 3–7 to complete four Yellow Posy blocks.

**9.** Cut four 1½" x 4" C strips and two 2" x 4" D strips pink solid.

**10.** Join three blocks with two C strips and add a D strip to each end; press seams toward C and D.

**11.** Cut one 1½" x 19" E strip and one 2¼" x 19" F strip pink solid.

**12.** Sew the E strip to the top edge and the F strip to the bottom edge of the pieced strip; press seams toward E and F.

**13.** Cut one 1½" x 6" G strip pink solid.

**14.** Sew a C strip to opposites sides and the G strip to the top of the remaining block. Turn under the edges of the C and G strips ¼" and press.

**15.** Measure up 5" from the bottom edge of the tea towel; draw a line from side to side.

**16.** Center the bottom edge of the single block right side up on the marked line as shown in Figure 19; pin in place.

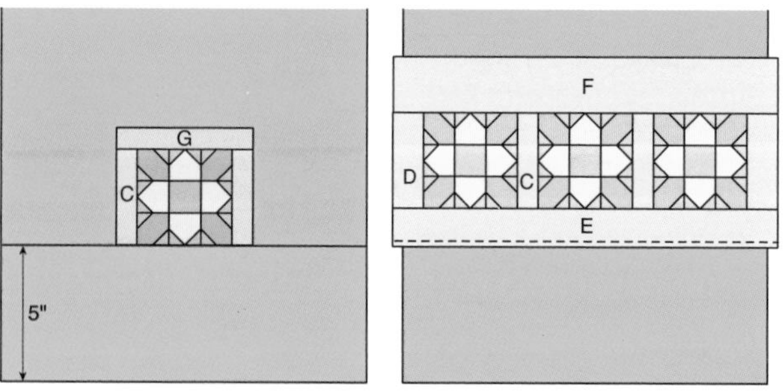


**Figure 19**

**17.** Appliqué the C and G edges in place by hand or machine.

**18.** Center and place the bordered block strip right sides together on the towel with the E edge aligned with the marked line; the bordered strip will cover the single unit. Stitch, again referring to Figure 19.

**19.** Press the bordered strip down to the right side. The F strip will extend beyond the bottom edge of the towel.

**20.** Add blanket stitch around edges of yellow petal pieces using 2 strands of yellow embroidery floss. Finish edge.

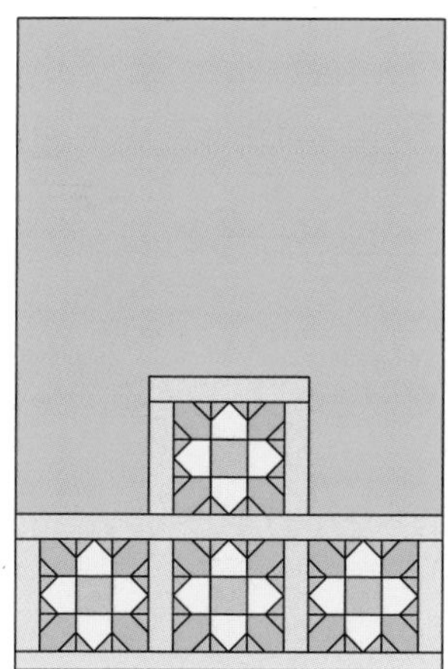

**Yellow Posy**
Placement Diagram 18" x 25"

## Flower Garden

### Materials

- 1 purchased or self-made towel in desired color
- 1 fat eighth turquoise solid, and pink and yellow prints
- 1 fat quarter pink solid
- 2¼" x 19" F strip yellow tonal fabric

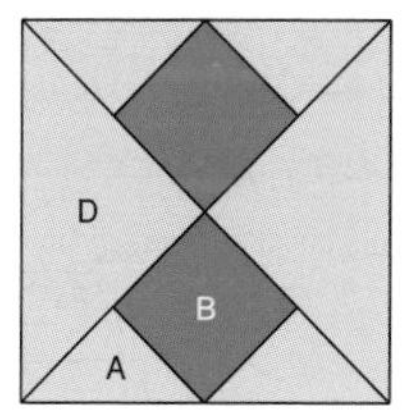


**Garden Square Block**
Make 1

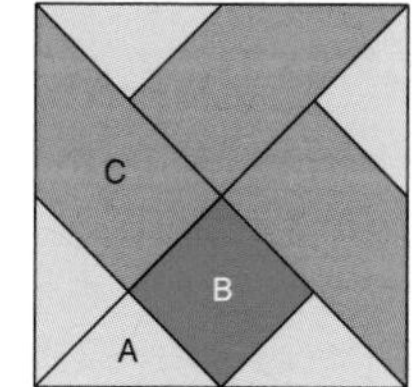


**Twirling Flowers Block**
Make 3

### Instructions

**1.** Prepare towel for piecing. Prepare templates using patterns given on page 13; cut as directed on each piece.

**2.** Sew A to C as shown in Figure 20; press. Repeat to make 9 A-C units.

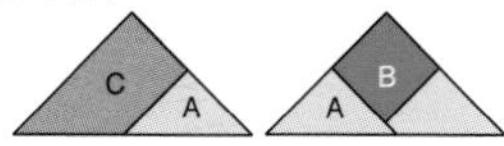


**Figure 20**

**3.** Sew A to two adjacent short sides of B, again referring to Figure 20; press. Repeat to make five A-B units.

**4.** To complete one Twirling Flower block, join two A-C units as shown in Figure 21; press.

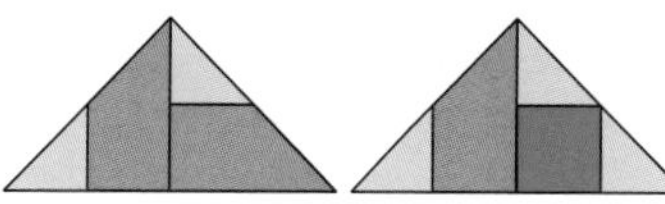

**Figure 21**

**5.** Join one A-C unit and one A-B unit, again referring to Figure 21; press.

**6.** Join the two pieced units to complete one Twirling Flower block referring to the block drawing; press. Repeat to make three blocks.

**7.** Join one D with one A-B unit as shown in Figure 22; press. Repeat. Join the two pieced units to complete the Garden Square block, again referring to Figure 22.

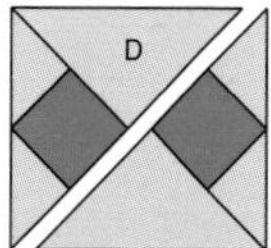


**Figure 22**

**8.** Sew the Garden Square block between two Twirling Flower blocks and add D to each end as shown in Figure 23; press.

**Figure 23**

**9.** Sew E to two sides and D to one side of the remaining Twirling Flower block as shown in Figure 24; press.

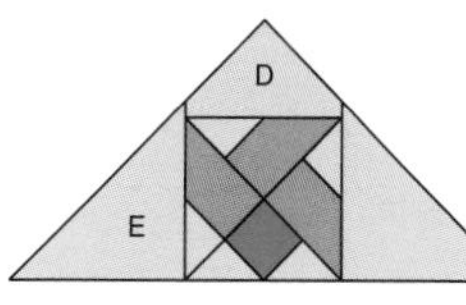


**Figure 24**

**Figure 25**

**10.** Join the two pieced units as shown in Figure 25.

**11.** Cut 1" strips yellow print and join to make a 26"-long binding strip.

**12.** Press under one long edge of the strip ¼". Bind all sides of pieced unit except the Garden-Square side as shown in Figure 26. Turn the binding to the back side and press.

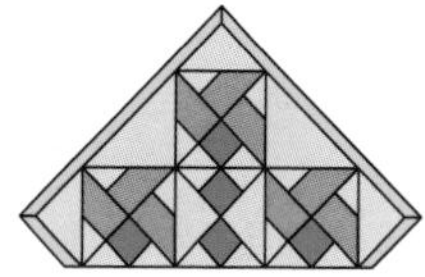

**Figure 26**

**13.** Measure up ½" from the bottom edge of the towel; draw a line from side to side.

**14.** Center the raw edge of the pieced unit on the marked line and pin; appliqué the bound edges of the pieced unit to the towel.

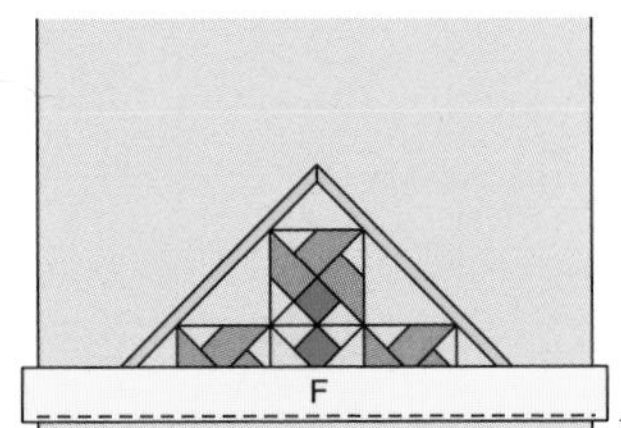


**Figure 27**

**15.** Place the F strip right sides together with the towel with the strip edge aligned with the drawn line and stitch as shown in Figure 27. Press the F strip to the right side; it will extend below the bottom of the towel. Finish edge.

**Flower Garden**
Placement Diagram 18" x 25"

## Prairie Points

### Materials

- 1 purchased or self-made towel in desired color
- 1 fat quarter each light green, blue and coral solids
- 1 fat quarter blue and coral prints

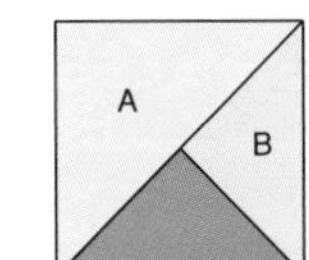


**Prairie Points Block**
Make 9

### Instructions

**1.** Prepare towel for piecing. Prepare templates using patterns given on page 13; cut as directed on each piece.

**2.** Sew a coral solid B to a blue print B and add A as shown in Figure 28; press. Repeat to make nine Prairie Points blocks.

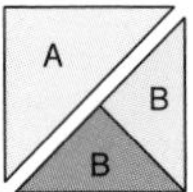


**Figure 28**

**3.** Join the blocks to make a strip as shown in Figure 29; press.

**Figure 29**

**4.** Cut one ¾" x 2½" strip each blue and coral prints. Sew the blue strip to the blue end and the coral strip to the coral end of the pieced strip; press.

**5.** Cut (17) 1½" x 4" strips and one 2¼" x 19" strip light green solid.

**6.** Sew the longer green strip to the bottom of the pieced block strip; press.

**7.** Press ¼" to the wrong side on one long edge of each 1¼" x 4" green strip.

**8.** Fold the ends of one pressed strip as shown in Figure 30 to make a prairie point; press. Trim ends even with bottom edge of prairie point. Repeat to make 17 prairie points.

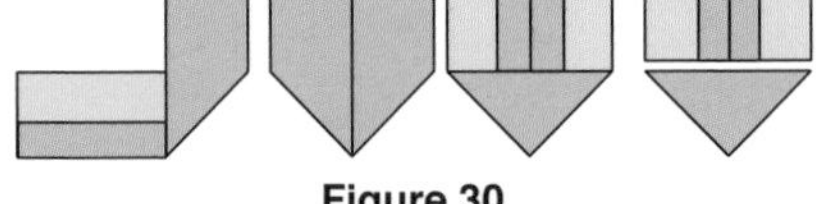

**Figure 30**

**9.** Cut one 1¾" x 19" strip blue solid.

**10.** Starting ½" in from each short raw end of the strip, arrange and evenly space the prairie points on the right side of one long side of the blue strip as shown in Figure 31. When satisfied with positioning, stitch to hold in place. Press the blue solid strip away from the prairie points.

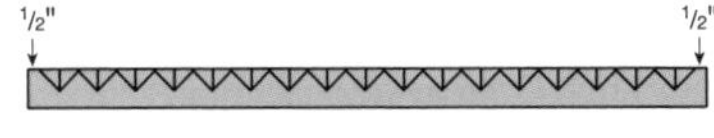


**Figure 31**

**11.** Measure up 3" and 4¾" on the towel and draw lines from side to side on the right side of the towel.

**12.** Center and place the pieced block strip right sides together on the towel with the pieced edge of the strip aligned with the lower marked line as shown in Figure 32; stitch and press the strip to the right side. The green strip will extend below the bottom of the towel.

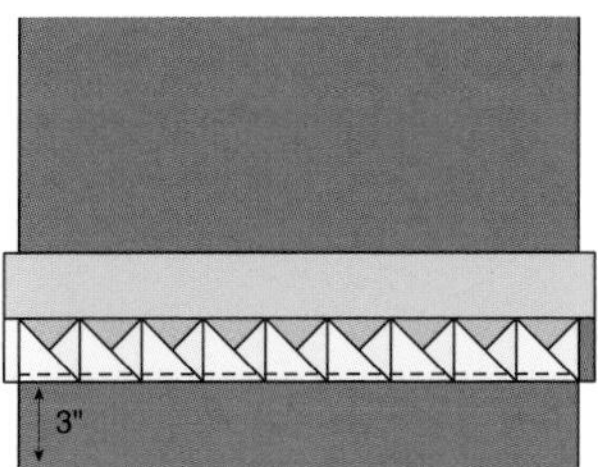


Figure 32

**13.** Center and place the prairie-point strip right sides together on the upper marked line as shown in Figure 33; stitch and press the strip to the right side.

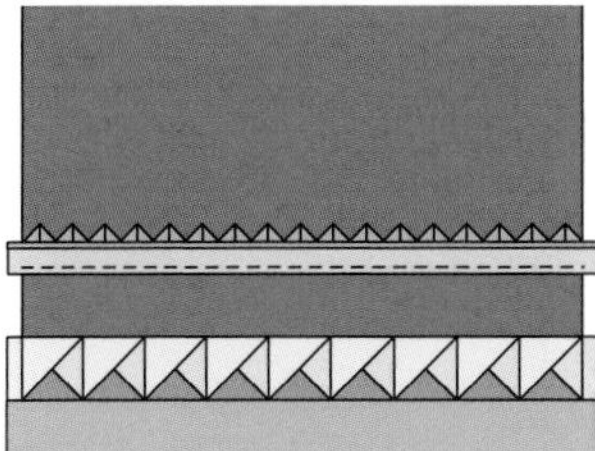

Figure 33

**14.** Topstitch along the top edge of the prairie points in the ditch of the seam of the blue strip. Finish edges. ❖

**Prairie Points**
Placement Diagram 18" x 25"

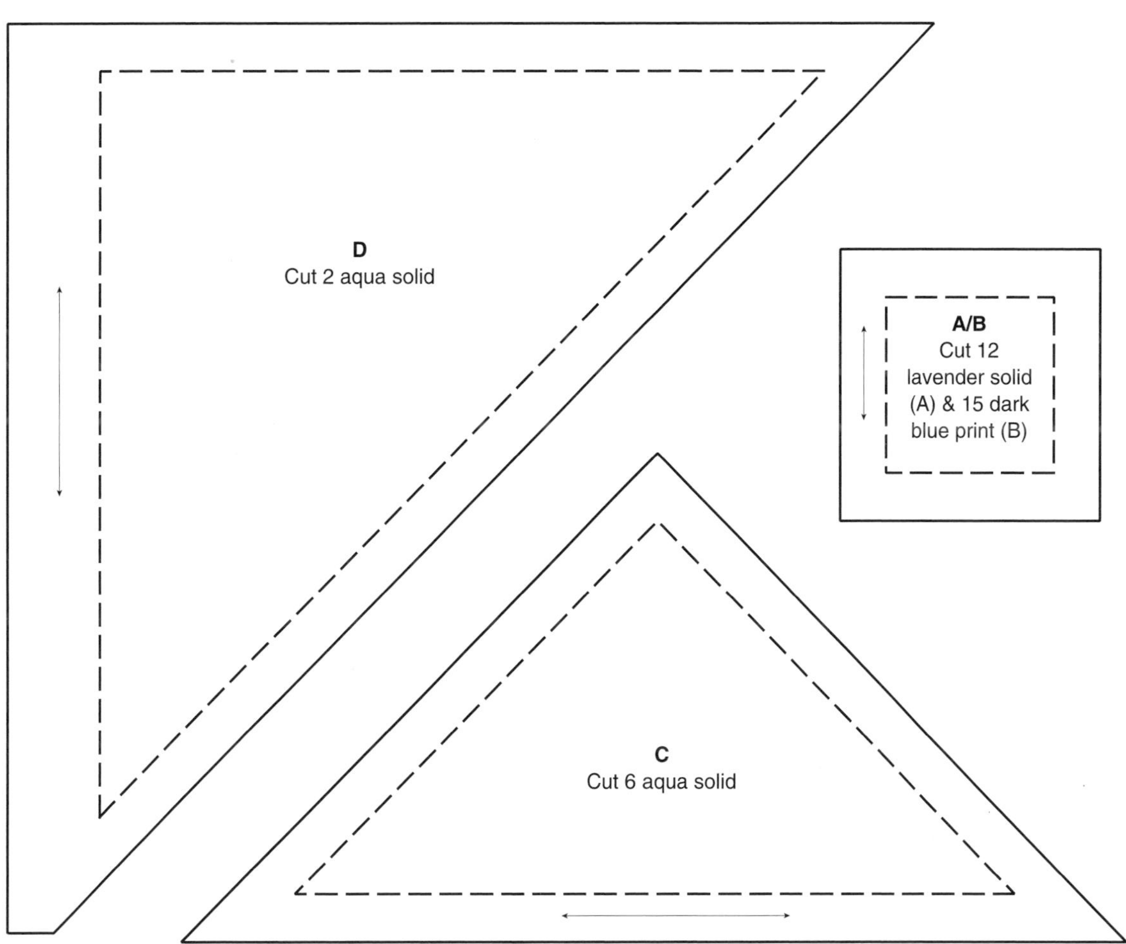


**Nine-Patch Templates**

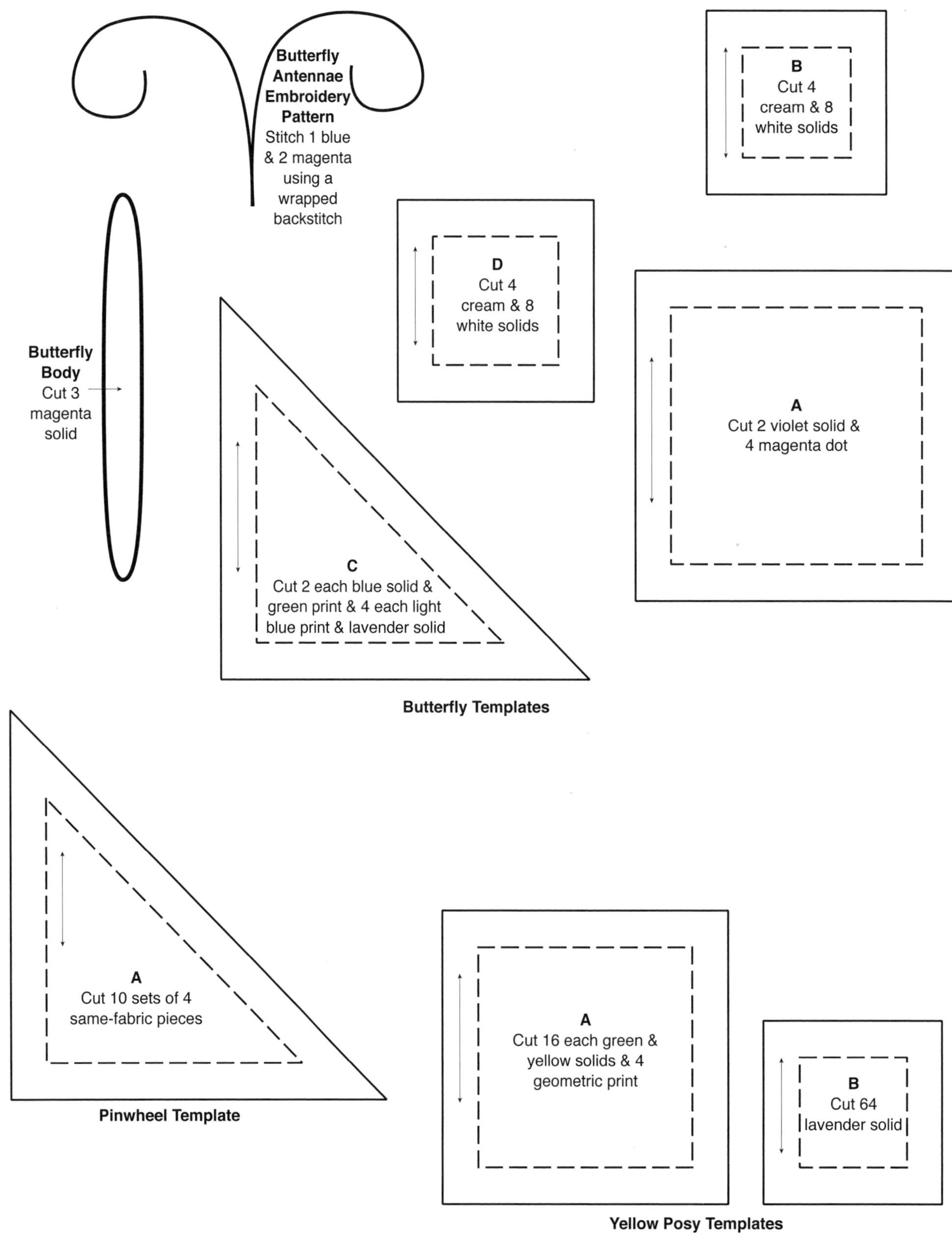
Butterfly
Antennae
Embroidery
Pattern
Stitch 1 blue
& 2 magenta
using a
wrapped
backstitch
B
Cut 4
cream & 8
white solids
D
Cut 4
cream & 8
white solids
Butterfly
Body
Cut 3
magenta
solid
A
Cut 2 violet solid &
4 magenta dot
C
Cut 2 each blue solid &
green print & 4 each light
blue print & lavender solid
Butterfly Templates
A
Cut 10 sets of 4
same-fabric pieces
Pinwheel Template
A
Cut 16 each green &
yellow solids & 4
geometric print
B
Cut 64
lavender solid
Yellow Posy Templates

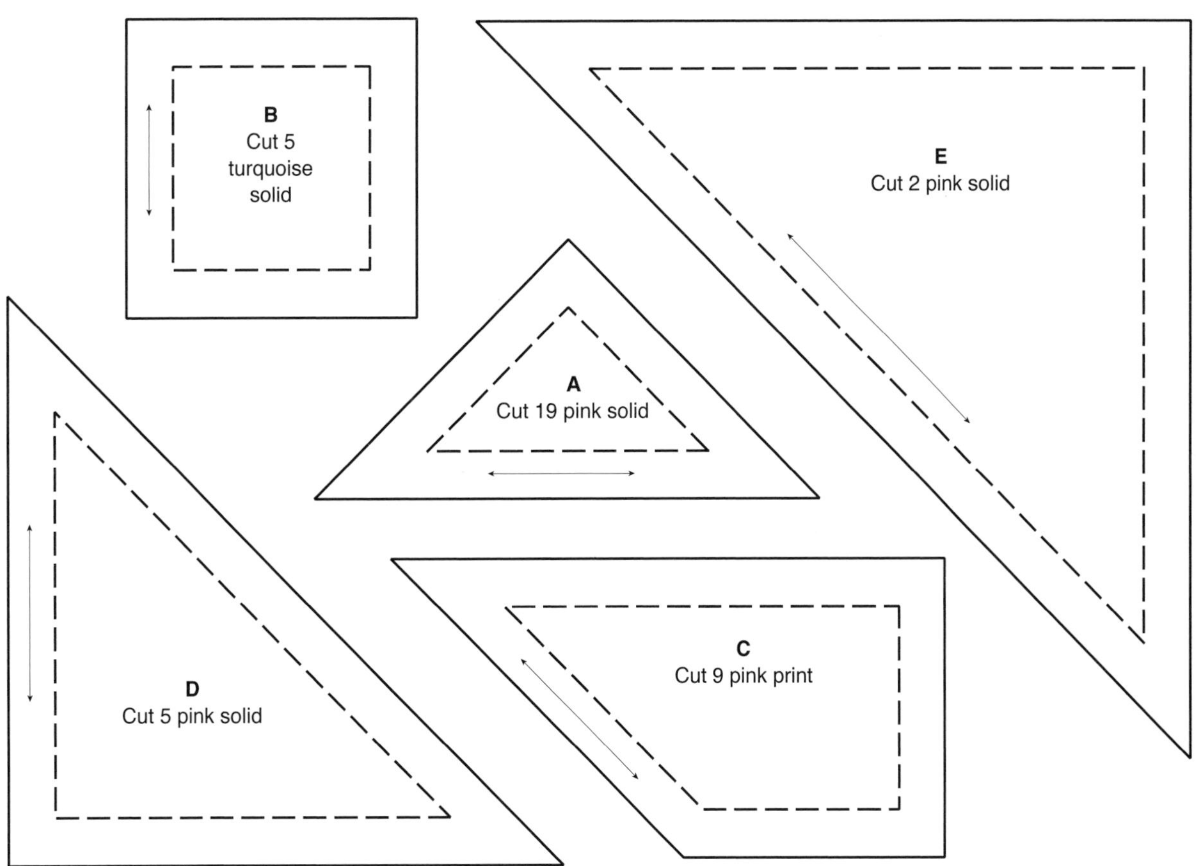


**Flower Garden Templates**

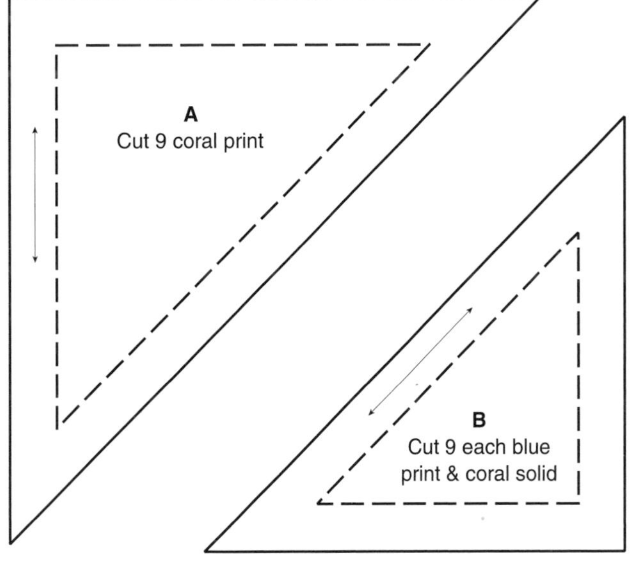


**Prairie Points Templates**

# Quilted Kaleidoscopes

### Project Note

Refer to Piecing General Instructions (page 4) to prepare tea towel for piecing and to finish edges.

## Turquoise Turns

### Materials

- 1 purchased or self-made towel in desired color
- Fabric scraps: gray check, deep aqua solid and yellow print
- Red embroidery floss
- 19" length white baby rickrack
- 1¼" x 19" E strip aqua solid fabric
- 2½" x 19" F strip green print fabric
- 1" x 25" strip black solid for binding

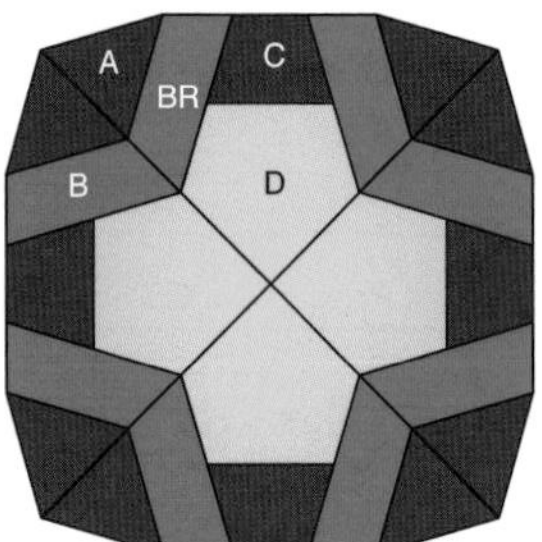


**Turquoise Turns Block**
Make 1

### Instructions

**1.** Prepare towel for piecing. Prepare templates using patterns given on page 16; cut as directed on each piece.

**2.** Sew A to B, A to BR and C to D as shown in Figure 34; press. Repeat to make four each A-B, C-D and reversed A-B units, again referring to Figure 34.

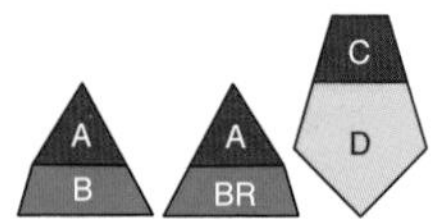


**Figure 34**

**3.** Sew an A-B and reversed A-B unit to two sides of a C-D unit as shown in Figure 35; press. Repeat to make four units.

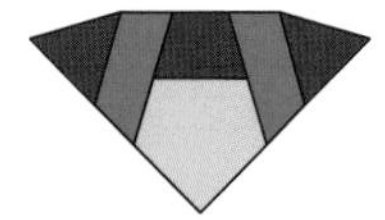

**Figure 35**

**4.** Join two units to make half the block; press. Repeat. Join the halves to complete the block; press.

**5.** Bind edges of the block with the 1"-wide black binding strip.

**6.** Using two strands red floss and a satin stitch, fill in the tips of the D pieces where they are joined in the center as shown in Figure 36.

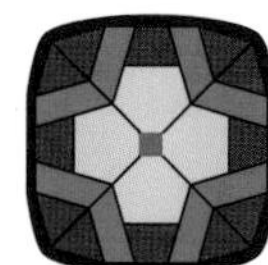

**Figure 36**

**7.** Measure up 2½" from the bottom edge of the towel and center the bound block on the towel. Hand-stitch in place.

**8.** Sew the E solid strip to the F strip; press.

**9.** Sew the white baby rickrack to the E strip ½" from the top raw edge.

**10.** Measure up 1½" from the bottom of the towel and mark a line from side to side on the right side of the towel.

**11.** Align the top raw edge of the pieced strip along the drawn line with right sides together; stitch. Press the strip down to the right side. The F strip will extend below the bottom of the towel. Finish edges.

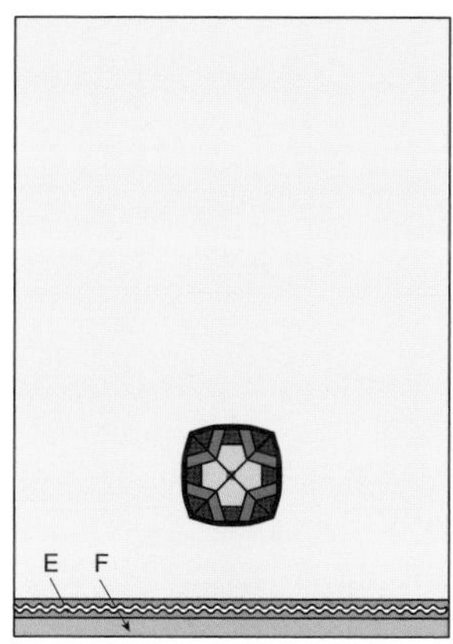


**Turquoise Turns**
Placement Diagram 18" x 25"

## Spring Green

### Materials

- 1 purchased or self-made towel in desired color
- Fabric scraps: black floral, cream solid, light green solid and green print
- 2¼" x 19" D strip white/red print fabric
- 1" x 25" strip black solid for binding

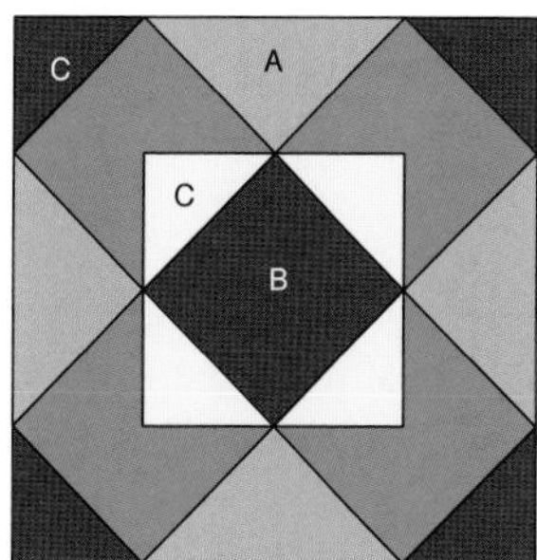


**Spring Green Block**
Make 1

### Instructions

**1.** Prepare towel for piecing. Prepare templates using patterns given on page 16; cut as directed on each piece.

**2.** Turn under the short edges of each cream C triangle; press.

**3.** Place a folded C triangle right side up on the right side of a green B square; hand-stitch the folded edges of each C to B. Repeat to make four B-C units.

**4.** Join two B-C units with the black B square; add a black C to each end of the strip to make the center strip as shown in Figure 37; press.

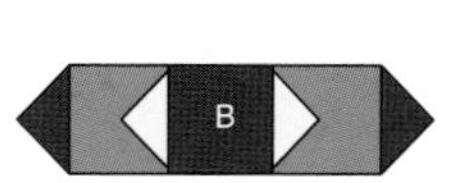


**Figure 37**

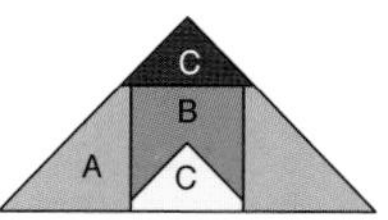


**Figure 38**

**5.** Sew an A triangle to two opposite sides of the remaining green B-C units and add a black C to make two corner units as shown in Figure 38; press.

**6.** Sew a corner unit to opposite sides of the center strip to complete the block; press.

**7.** Bind edges of block all around using the black binding.

**8.** Center and stitch the bound block 3½" from bottom edge of the towel.

**9.** Measure up 2¼" from the bottom of the towel and mark a line from side to side on the right side of the towel.

**10.** Align one edge of the D strip along the line with right sides together; stitch. Press the strip down to the right side. The D strip will extend below the bottom of the towel. Finish bottom edge. ❖

**Spring Green**
Placement Diagram 18" x 25"

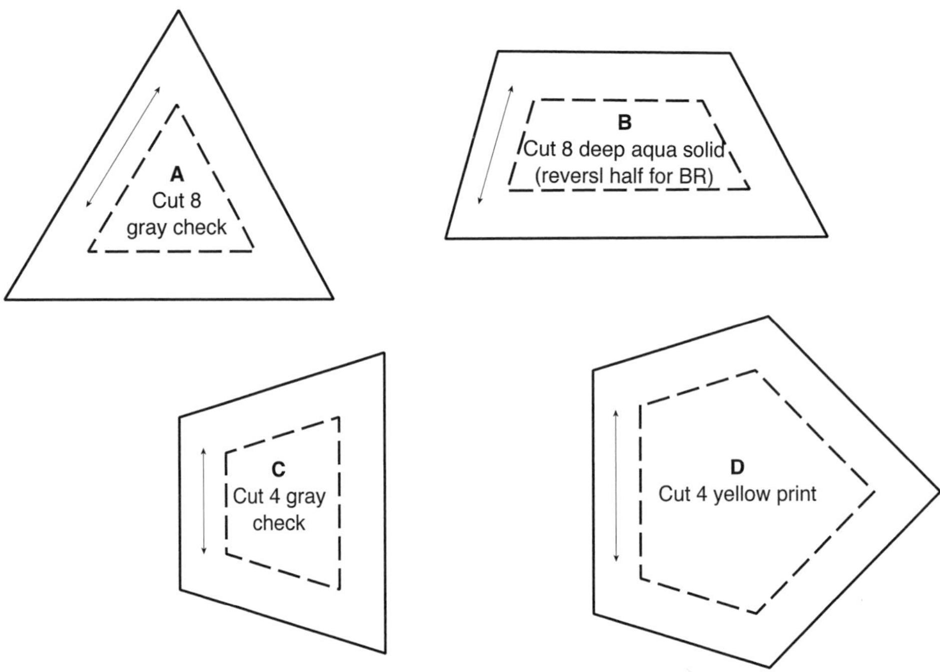


**Turquoise Turns Templates**

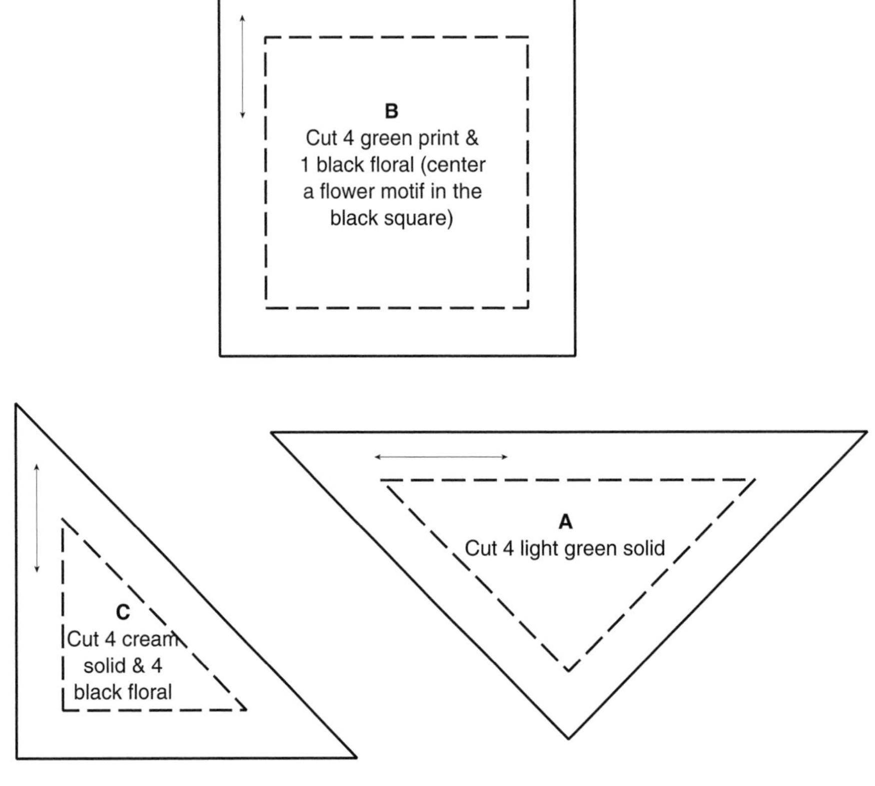


**Spring Green Templates**

# Piecing Pictures

## Project Note

Refer to Piecing General Instructions (page 4) to prepare tea towel for piecing and to finish edges.

## Flying Ace

### Materials

- 1 purchased or self-made towel in desired color
- Fabric scraps: medium blue solid, orange dot, bright pink tonal and yellow tonal
- 6-strand embroidery floss: gold, green and white
- 19" length yarn (optional)
- Scrap fusible web

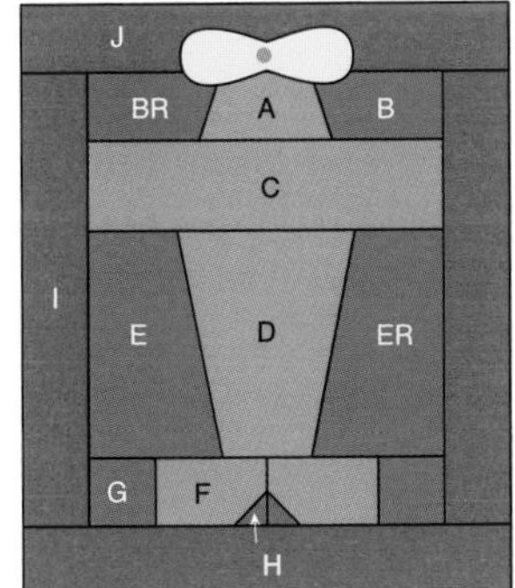


**Flying Ace Block**
Make 1

### Instructions

**1.** Prepare templates using patterns given on page 21; cut as directed on each piece.

**2.** Sew B and BR to A referring to Figure 39; press.

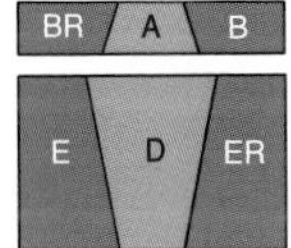


**Figure 39**

**3.** Sew E and ER to D, again referring to Figure 39; press.

**4.** Mark a diagonal line on the wrong side of each H square. Align corners of H and F with right sides together and sew on the marked line referring to Figure 40. Trim seam and press H to the right side to complete an F-H unit, again referring to Figure 40. Repeat to make a reversed F-H unit, again referring to Figure 40.

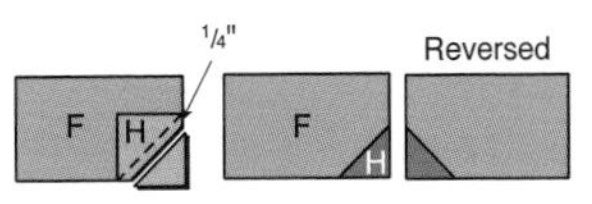


**Figure 40**

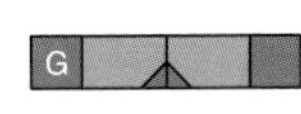


**Figure 41**

**5.** Join the F-H and reversed F-H units and add G to each end referring to Figure 41; press.

**6.** Join the pieced units with C referring to the block drawing to complete the airplane unit; press.

**7.** Cut two 1¼" x 5½" I strips and two 1¼" x 5¾" J strips bright pink tonal.

**8.** Sew the I strips to opposite long sides and J strips to the top and bottom of the airplane unit to complete the Flying Ace block; press.

**9.** Trace the propeller piece onto the paper side of the scrap of fusible web; cut out, leaving a margin all around. Fuse shape to the wrong side of the yellow tonal scrap; cut out on traced line. Remove paper backing.

**10.** Center and fuse the propeller on the A/J pieces; machine-appliqué in place referring to Machine Appliqué (page 69).

**11.** Using 2 strands gold embroidery floss, stem-stitch a ¼" circle in the center of the propeller referring to the Embroidery Stitch Guide (page 25).

**12.** Using 1 strand white embroidery floss, add meandering straight stitches to the E and ER pieces referring to the sample photo for suggestions.

**13.** Turn under the edges of the block ¼"; press.

**14.** Center and appliqué the block 2" from the finished bottom edge of the tea towel.

**15.** Using 2 strands green embroidery floss, straight-stitch ⅛" from edge all around to simulate quilting stitches.

**16.** If desired, machine zigzag stitch the piece of yarn 1" from bottom edge of the finished tea towel.

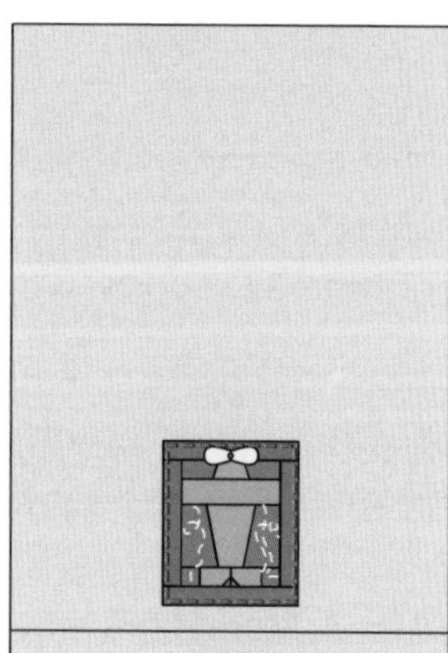

**Flying Ace**
Placement Diagram 18" x 25"

# Dressy Dolly

## Materials

- 1 purchased or self-made towel in desired color
- Fabric scraps: medium blue, brown/rust and peach solids; green tonal and yellow dots
- Red 6-strand embroidery floss
- 19" length brown ⅜"-wide grosgrain ribbon
- 19" length white baby rickrack

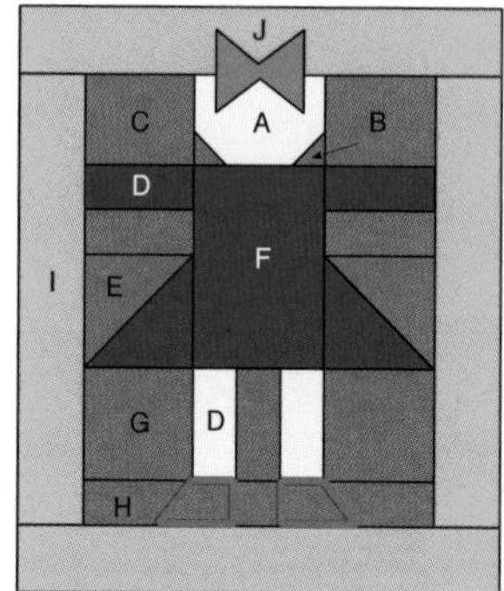


**Dressy Dolly Block**
Make 1

## Instructions

**1.** Prepare templates using patterns given on page 22; cut as directed on each piece.

**2.** Mark a diagonal line on the wrong side of each B square. Align corners of B and A with right sides together and sew on the marked line referring to Figure 42. Trim seam and press B to the right side. Repeat on the opposite end of A to complete an A-B unit, again referring to Figure 42.

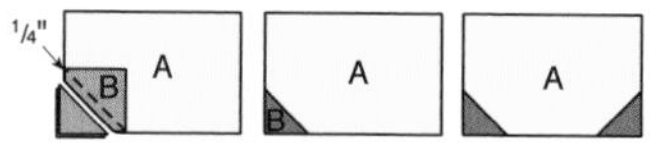


**Figure 42**

**3.** Sew C to each short side of the A-B unit to complete the head unit as shown in Figure 43; press.

**Figure 43**

**4.** Join one each brown/rust and medium blue D piece along length to make a D unit; press. Repeat to make two D units.

**5.** Sew a brown/rust E to a medium blue E along the diagonal to make an E unit; press. Repeat to make two E units.

**6.** Join one D and one E unit to make a D-E unit as shown in Figure 44; press. Repeat to make a reversed D-E unit, again referring to Figure 44.

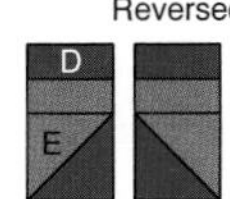


**Figure 44**

**7.** Sew the D-E and reversed D-E units to opposite sides of F to complete the body unit as shown in Figure 45; press.

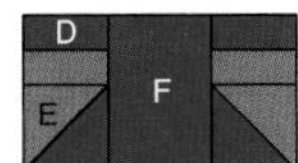


**Figure 45**

**8.** Sew a peach solid D to each long side of a brown/rust D and add G to each side to complete the leg unit as shown in Figure 46; press.

**Figure 46**

**9.** Join the head, body and leg units with H referring to Figure 47 to complete the dolly unit; press.

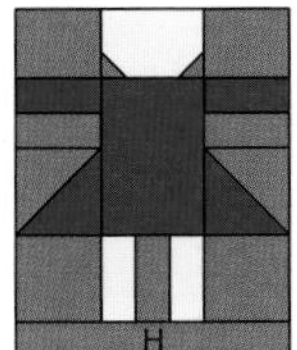


**Figure 47**

**10.** Cut two 1¼" x 5" I and two 1¼" x 5½" J strips yellow dots.

**11.** Sew an I strip to opposite sides and J strips to the top and bottom of the dolly unit to complete the Dressy Dolly block; press.

**12.** Cut the bow shape as directed; turn under edges ¼" all around.

**13.** Center and hand-stitch the bow on the A piece and J strip referring to the block drawing.

**14.** Transfer the shoe shapes from the H pattern to the H piece below the peach solid D pieces.

**15.** Using 2 strands of red embroidery floss, chain-stitch along marked lines for shoes.

**16.** Turn under edges of the block ¼" all around. Center and hand-stitch the block 2¼" from the bottom finished edge of the tea towel.

**17.** Sew the length of brown grosgrain ribbon 1½" from bottom edge turning each end to the back side.

**18.** Sew the baby rickrack in place ⅝" from bottom edge, turning each end to the back side to finish.

**Dressy Dolly**
Placement Diagram 18" x 25"

## Home Again

### Materials

- 1 purchased or self-made towel in desired color
- Fabric scraps: white, brown/rust and medium blue solids; black/gray print and bright pink dots
- Fat quarter light blue solid
- Black 6-strand embroidery floss
- 2¼" x 19" G strip dark blue print fabric

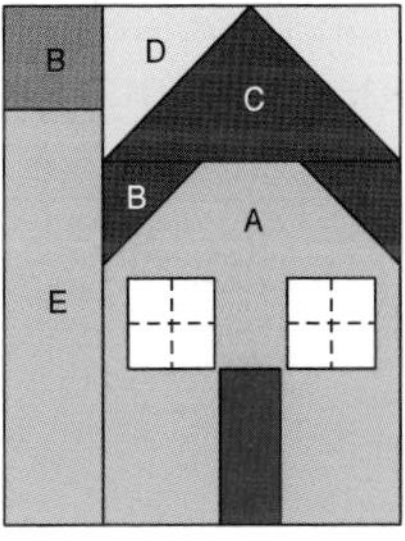


**Home Again Block**
Make 1

### Instructions

**1.** Prepare towel for piecing. Prepare templates using patterns given on page 23; cut as directed on each piece.

**2.** Sew D to each short side of C to complete the roof unit referring to Figure 48; press.

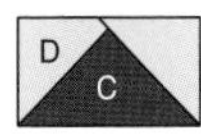


**Figure 48**

**3.** Mark a diagonal line on the wrong side of the black/gray B squares. Align corners of B and A with right sides together and sew on the marked line referring to Figure 49. Trim seam and press B to the right side, again referring to Figure 49. Repeat on the opposite corner of A, again referring to Figure 49, to complete the house unit.

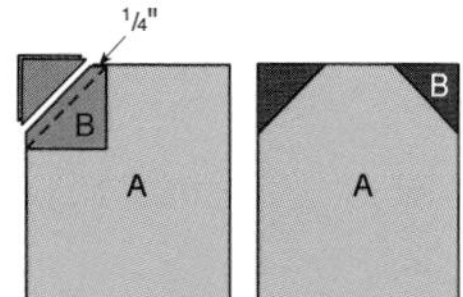

**Figure 49**

**4.** Sew the brown/rust B to E to complete the chimney unit; press.

**5.** Sew the roof unit to the house unit and add the chimney unit referring to Figure 50 to complete the Home Again block; press.

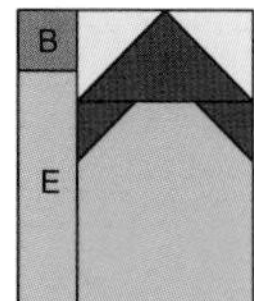

**Figure 50**

**6.** Cut two 7¾" x 5¼" F pieces light blue solid.

**7.** Sew an F piece to opposite sides of the finished Home Again block; press.

**8.** Cut cloud pieces as directed, adding ¼" all around. Turn under ¼" all around; baste to hold.

**9.** Arrange and baste clouds on the F pieces referring to the Placement Diagram for positioning. Hand-stitch in place.

**10.** Repeat with door and window pieces.

**11.** Using 2 strands black embroidery floss and a small stem stitch, divide window pieces in quarters referring to the block drawing.

**12.** Sew the dark blue print G strip to the bottom of the house strip.

**13.** Measure up 5¼" from bottom edge and mark a line from side to side on the right side of the tea towel.

**14.** Align the pieced strip right sides together on the towel with house edge along marked line; stitch. Press the pieced strip down to the right side. The G strip will extend below the bottom of the towel. Finish edge. ❖

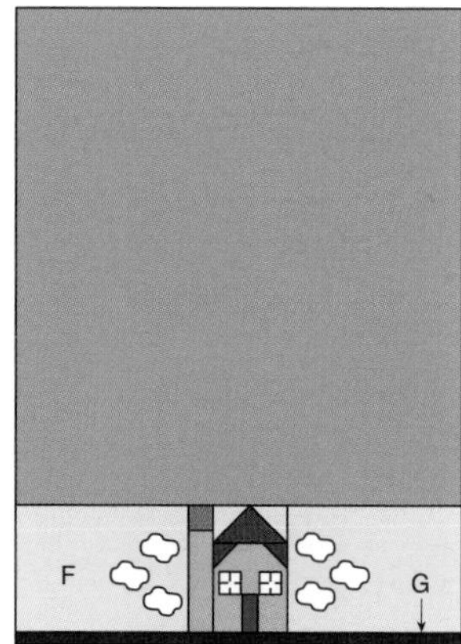

**Home Again**
Placement Diagram 18" x 25"

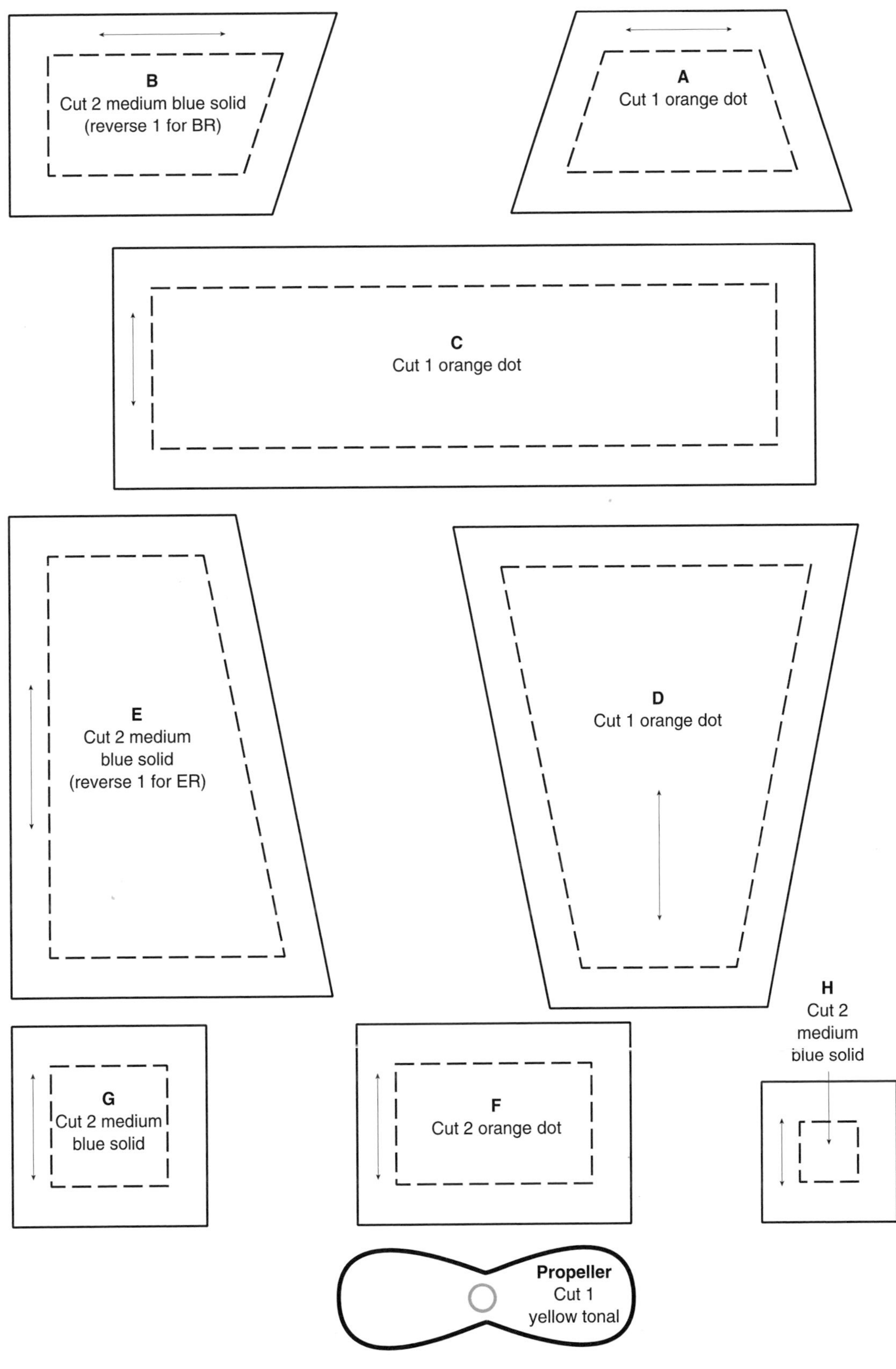


**Flying Ace Templates**

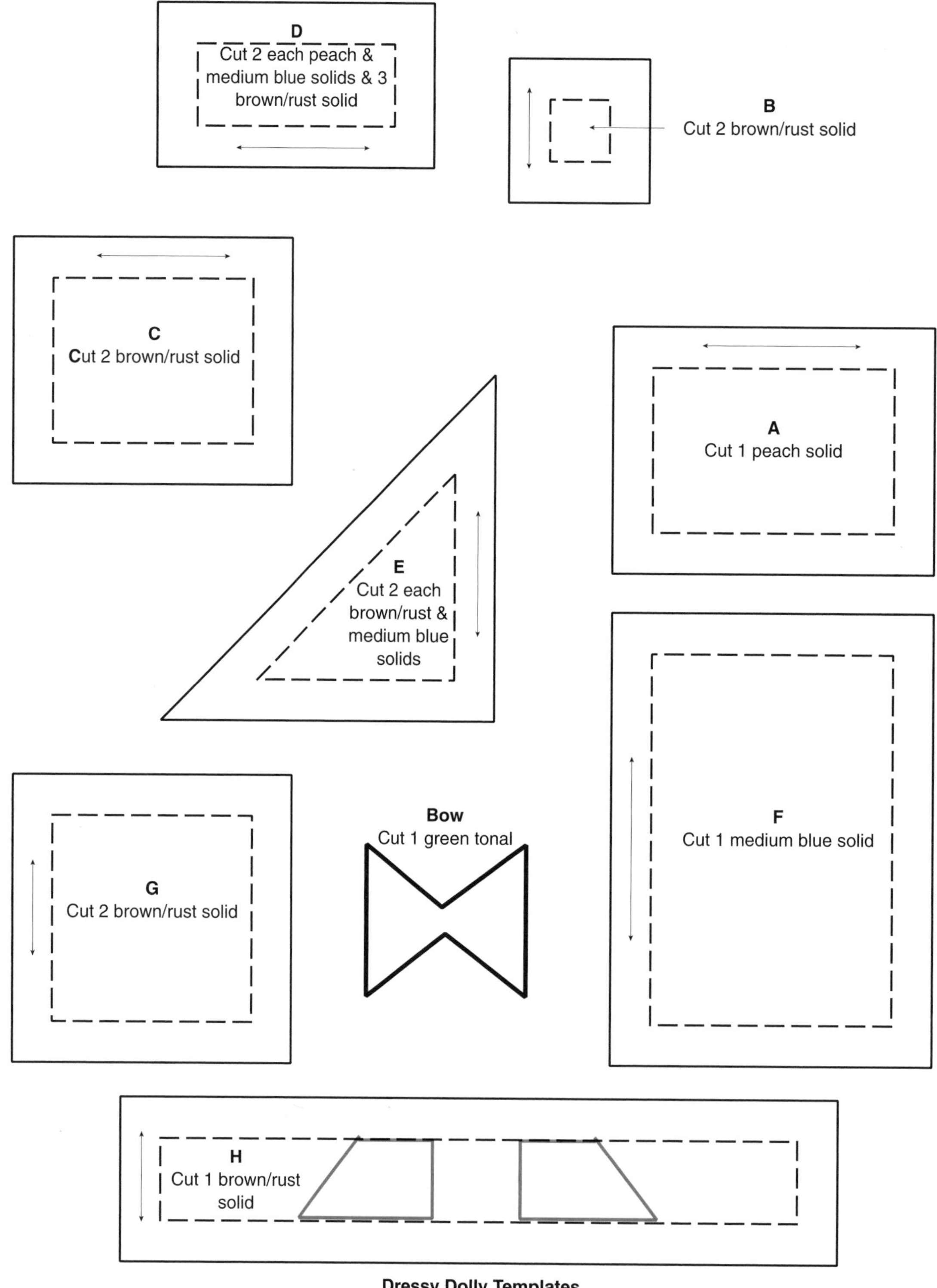


Dressy Dolly Templates

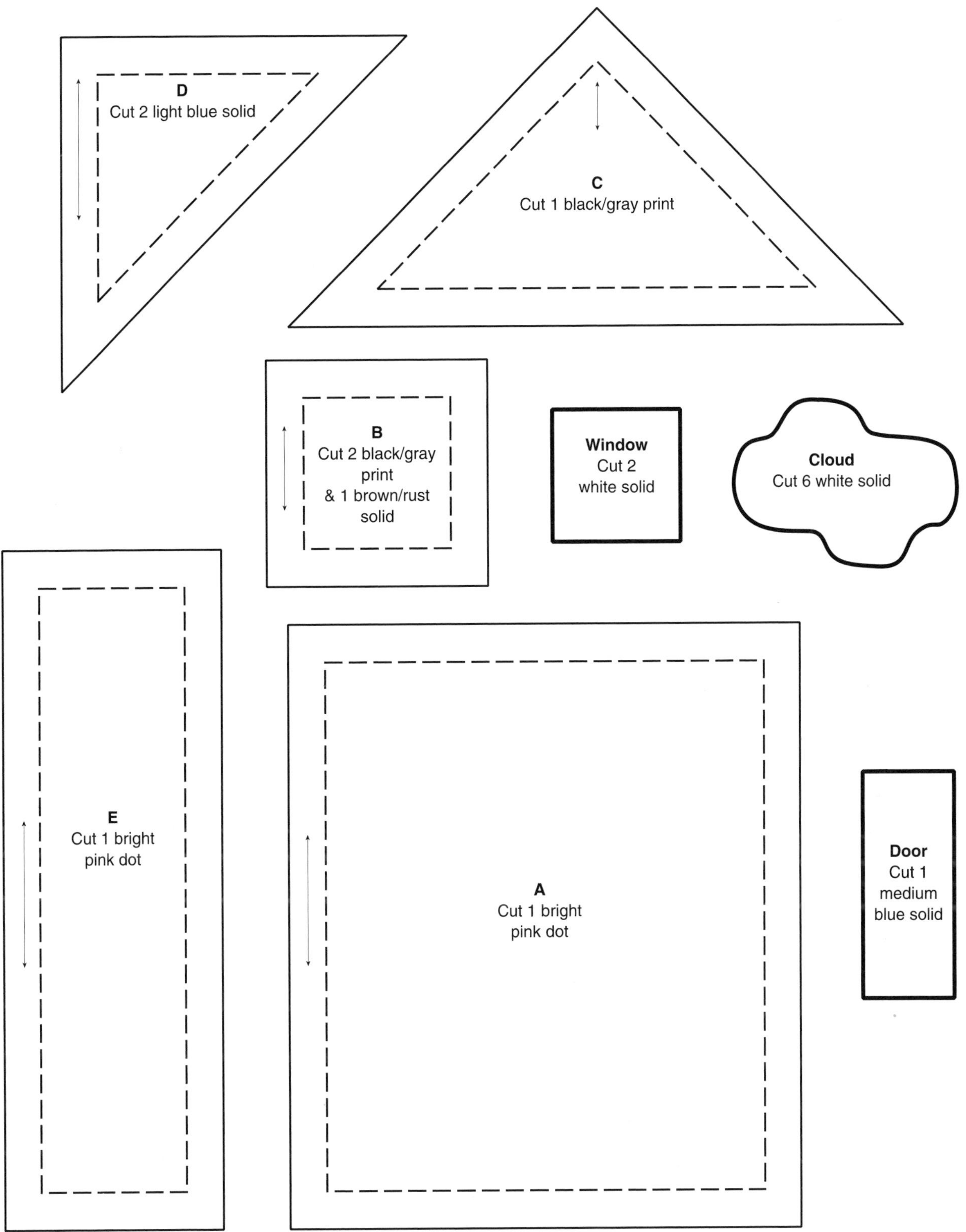


**Home Again Templates**

# Embroidery

## General Instructions

A needle and floss can be used much like paint and a brush to add decoration to your favorite tea towels. Stitching may take longer than painting, but it is permanent, washable and tactile. Use the stitches suggested with the patterns given in this section or experiment with additional stitches to enhance your needlework.

Use 100 percent cotton fabrics that are preshrunk, soft to the touch and colorfast.

### Supplies & Tools

- Scissors—small, very sharp point
- Marking tools—An air-soluble pen, water-soluble pen, pencil or carbon paper are the most common choices. The ink from an air-soluble pen will disappear after several days. The ink from a water-soluble pen will disappear by spritzing or blotting the fabric with water. Pencil marks are more permanent and any visible marks should be erased with a clean eraser when finished. Marks from carbon paper can be washed out after stitching is complete. If you will be finishing the embroidery quickly, using an air-soluble pen will suffice. If you think the embroidery will take longer, use a pencil or carbon paper or a water-soluble pen. Remember, no trace of the marks should be visible on the finished tea towel.
- Embroidery needle—Choose a needle with an eye large enough to hold the thread you are using and that will not leave too large a hole in your background fabric. The larger the needle-size number, the thinner the needle. For embroidery you need a pointed, sharp needle. Longer needles allow for wrapping thread, which is used for some stitches. In general, an embroidery needle is medium-sized, has a long eye and a sharp point. The long eye allows for more than 1 strand of embroidery floss to be threaded at the same time.
- Embroidery hoop—An 8" wooden or plastic hoop will work with all of the designs in this book. The traditional embroidery hoop is made with two wooden rings—one smaller than the other. There is a tension screw on the side of the top hoop that is loosened when placing the fabric in the hoop and then tightened after the fabric has been laid on the smaller hoop and the larger hoop has been placed on top. Hoops come in a variety of sizes from 4"–8" for hand embroidery and larger for quilting.
- Light source for tracing—You may use a light box or a window as a light source. There are manufactured light boxes and homemade light boxes, but windows are available everywhere.
- Fabrics—Preshrink fabrics if making your own tea towels. Fabrics should have a close weave, and should be absorbent if tea towels will actually be used. Osnaburg and muslin are two fabrics that work well.

### Marking the Design on Fabric

Trace the chosen design onto tracing paper using a black medium-point marker.

Tape the traced design on a window at eye level or on a light box.

To mark the chosen design on the fabric, determine the position of the embroidery design on the fabric and tape the fabric over the traced design.

Use a marking tool to trace the design onto the fabric. If using a pencil, use a light hand when tracing to reduce the lines showing through the stitches when stitching is complete.

If using carbon paper, place the fabric under the pattern and trace over it with a blunt pencil or pen.

Whatever method or tool you use to transfer the design, the important thing to remember is that the marks should not show when the project is complete.

### Stitching the Design

Stretch the fabric in an embroidery hoop to keep taut.

Cut a 15"–18" length of embroidery floss—longer lengths tend to tangle. Separate the cut piece into individual strands. For fine lines, choose 2 strands of floss, for medium weight lines, satin stitching and French knots, use 3 strands of floss.

Knot the end of the floss. To begin stitching, bring the needle from the back to the front of the fabric at the beginning stitch location. When the thread runs out, secure the end with a knot in the floss on the back of the fabric, as shown in Figure 1, and trim the excess floss beyond the knot.

Figure 1

## Removing Transfer Marks

When the embroidery is complete, remove the design transfer marks as directed according to your choice of marking tool. ❖

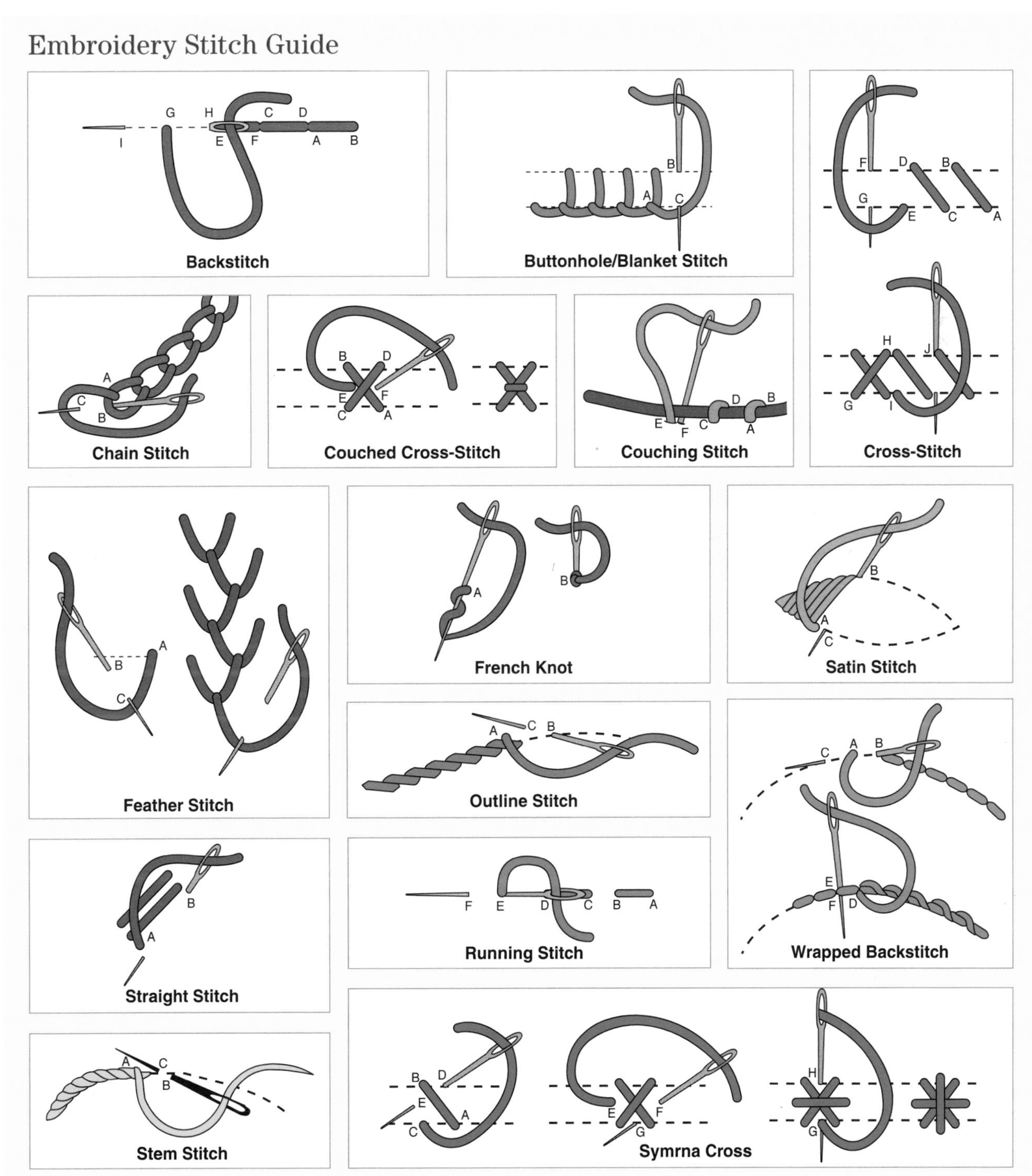

# Fruit Salad Set

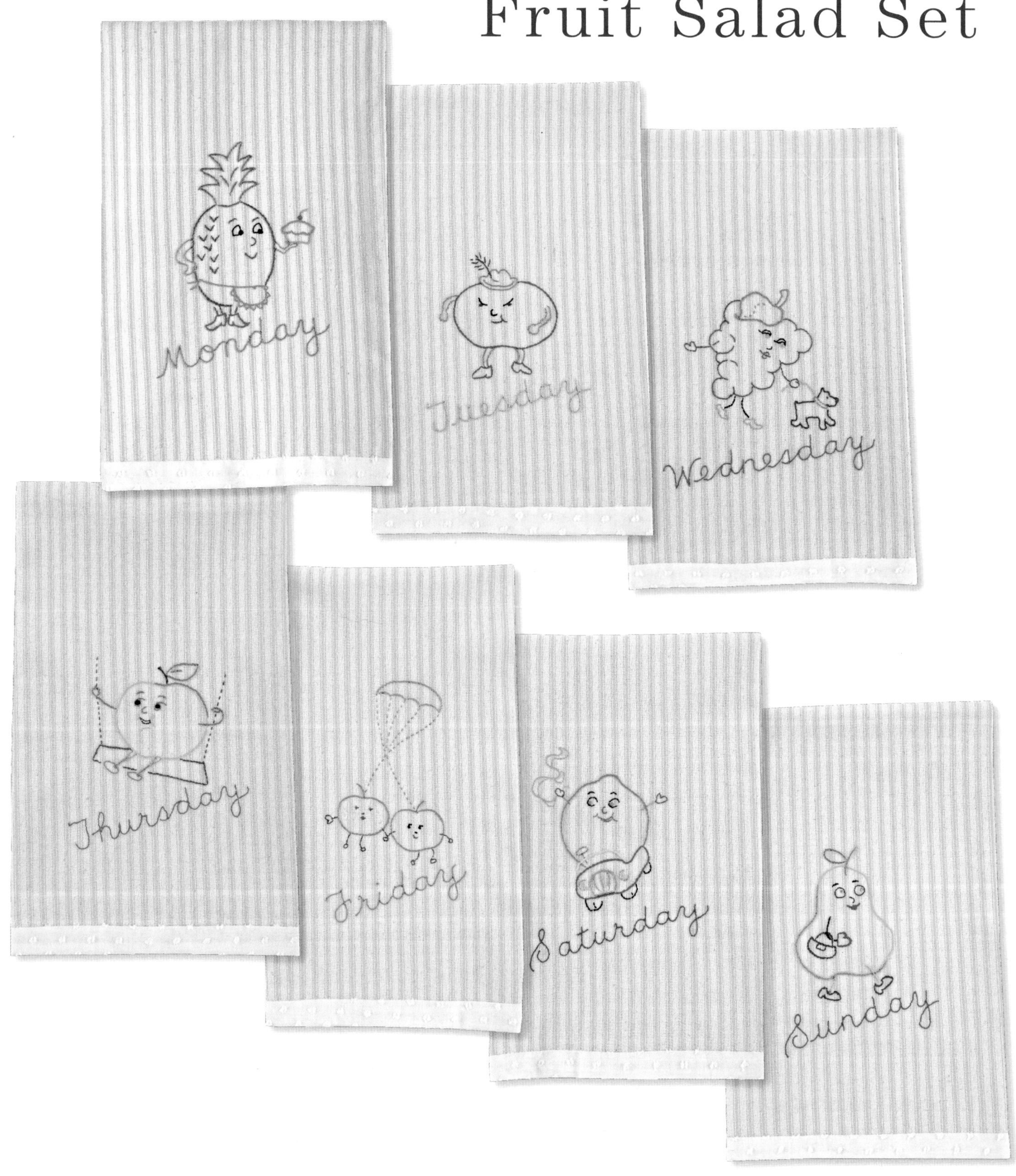

### Project Note
Refer to Marking the Design on Fabric (page 24) for transferring and removing designs. Refer to Stitching the Design (page 24) when working embroidery.

## Miss Pineapple Monday

### Materials
- 1 purchased or self-made tea towel in desired color
- 6-strand embroidery floss: black, red, orange, blue, turquoise, brown, purple, dark pink, tan and green

### Instructions
**1.** Center and transfer the Miss Pineapple Monday design to the tea towel 2½" from the bottom hemmed edge.

**2.** Stitch the design on the tea towel along marked lines referring to the pattern for color and stitch choices.

**3.** Remove transfer lines according to type of marking tool used, or as directed by the manufacturer.

**Miss Pineapple Monday**
Placement Diagram 18" x 25"

## Mr. Tomato Tuesday

### Materials
- 1 purchased or self-made tea towel in desired color
- 6-strand embroidery floss: black, tan, dark mauve, red, green, blue and turquoise

### Instructions
**1.** Complete the towel using Mr. Tomato Tuesday design referring to the instructions for Miss Pineapple Monday.

**Mr. Tomato Tuesday**
Placement Diagram 18" x 25"

## Miss Grape Wednesday

### Materials
- 1 purchased or self-made tea towel in desired color
- 6-strand embroidery floss: medium gray, red, coral, blue, turquoise, purple, green, brown and black

### Instructions
**1.** Complete the towel using Miss Grape Wednesday design referring to the instructions for Miss Pineapple Monday.

**Miss Grape Wednesday**
Placement Diagram 18" x 25"

## Miss Peach Thursday

### Materials
- 1 purchased or self-made tea towel in desired color
- 6-strand embroidery floss: turquoise, dark peach, pink, bright pink, green, brown, black, purple and rust

### Instructions

**1.** Complete the towel using Miss Peach Thursday design referring to the instructions for Miss Pineapple Monday.

**Miss Peach Thursday**
Placement Diagram 18" x 25"

## Cherry Twins Friday

### Materials

- 1 purchased or self-made tea towel in desired color
- 6-strand embroidery floss: black, dark pink, light pink, red, purple, green, blue and turquoise

### Instructions

**1.** Complete the towel using the Cherry Twins Friday design referring to the instructions for Miss Pineapple Monday.

**Cherry Twins Friday**
Placement Diagram 18" x 25"

## Mr. Lime Saturday

### Materials

- 1 purchased or self-made tea towel in desired color
- 6-strand embroidery floss: black, red, dark rust, light blue, medium blue, green, brown, yellow, turquoise, pink and purple

### Instructions

**1.** Complete the towel using Mr. Lime Saturday design referring to the instructions for Miss Pineapple Monday.

**Mr. Lime Saturday**
Placement Diagram 18" x 25"

## Miss Pear Sunday

### Materials

- 1 purchased or self-made tea towel in desired color
- 6-strand embroidery floss: gold, butterscotch, dark blue, turquoise, red, purple, green and brown

### Instructions

**1.** Complete the towel using Miss Pear Sunday design referring to the instructions for Miss Pineapple Monday. ❖

**Miss Pear Sunday**
Placement Diagram 18" x 25"

**Miss Pineapple Monday Pattern**
All unmarked stitches are wrapped backstitch.

**Mr. Tomato Tuesday Pattern**
All unmarked stitches are wrapped backstitch.

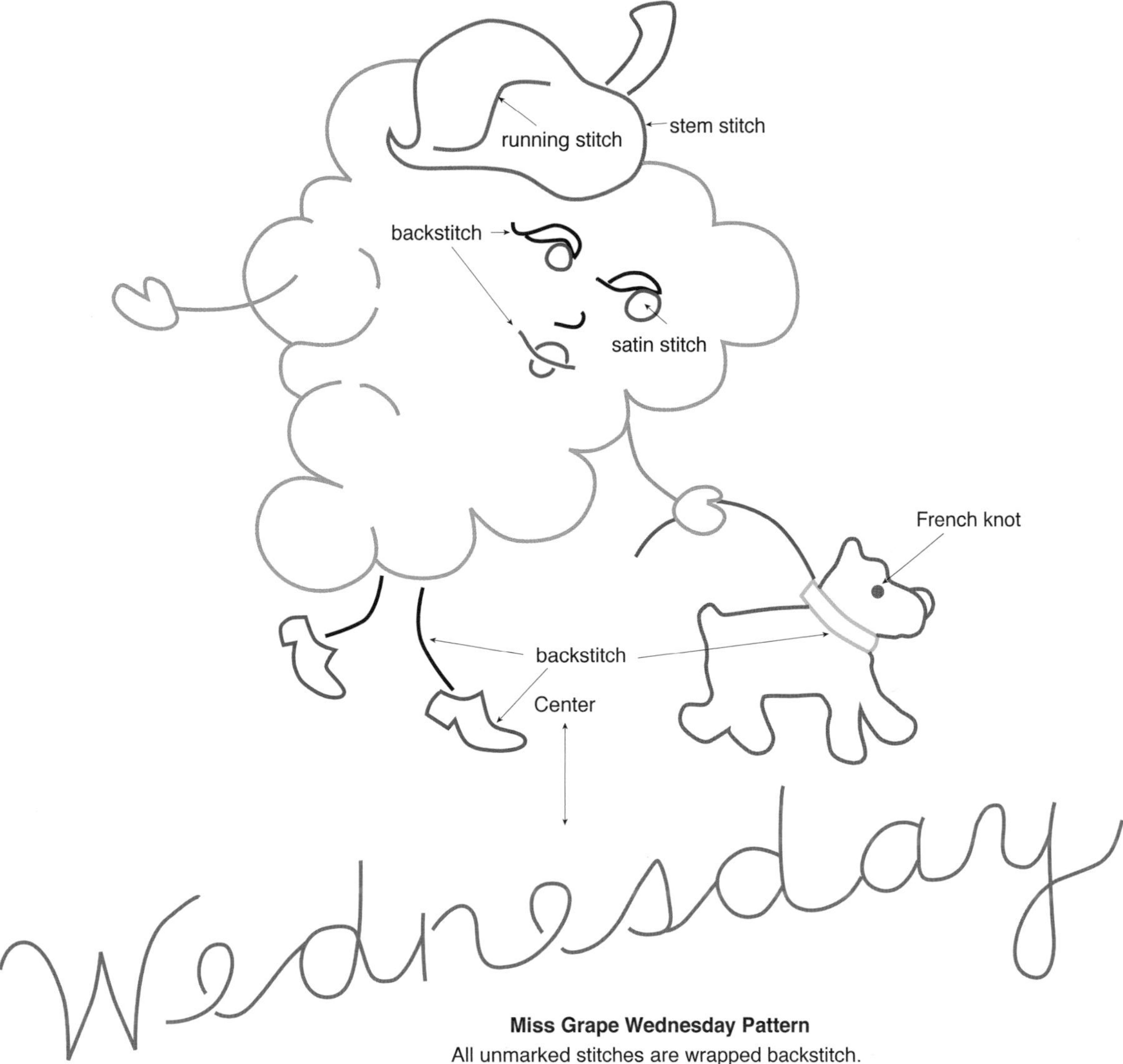


**Miss Grape Wednesday Pattern**

All unmarked stitches are wrapped backstitch.

**Miss Peach Thursday Pattern**
All unmarked stitches are wrapped backstitch.

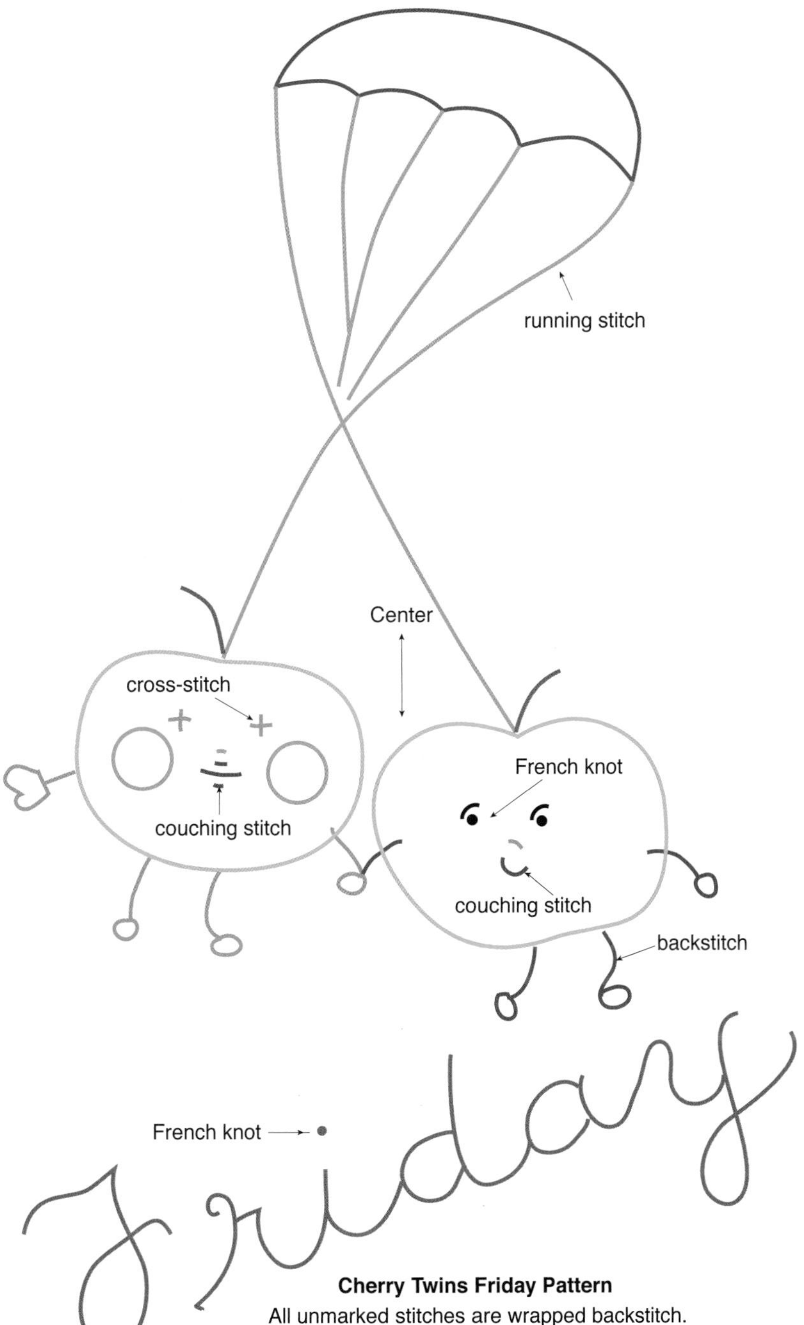


**Cherry Twins Friday Pattern**
All unmarked stitches are wrapped backstitch.

**Mr. Lime Saturday Pattern**
All unmarked stitches are wrapped backstitch.

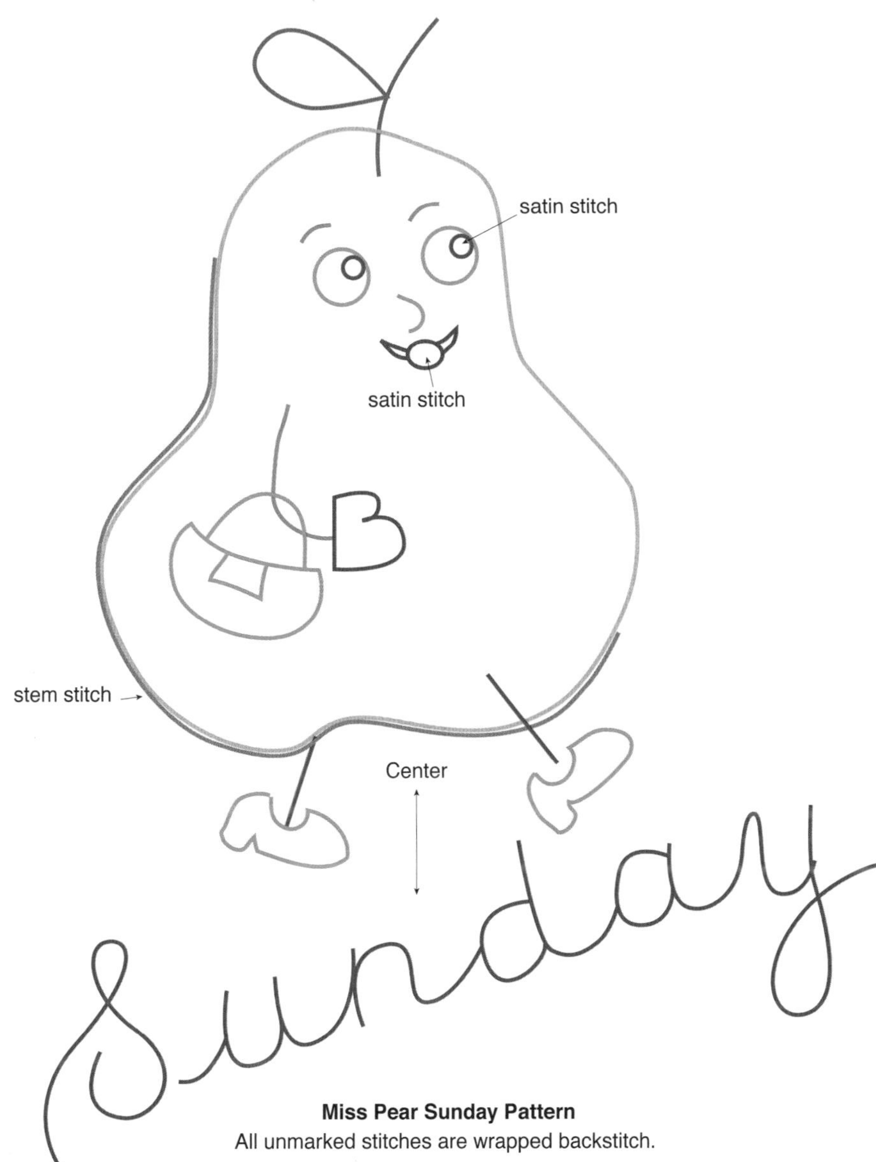


**Miss Pear Sunday Pattern**
All unmarked stitches are wrapped backstitch.

# Mealtime Set

### Project Note

Refer to Marking the Design on Fabric (page 24) for transferring and removing designs. Refer to Stitching the Design (page 24) when working embroidery.

## Let's Eat

### Materials

- 1 purchased or self-made tea towel in desired color
- 6-strand embroidery floss: rust, gold and brown

### Instructions

**1.** Center and transfer the Let's Eat embroidery design to the tea towel 2¼" from the bottom hemmed edge.

**2.** Stitch the design on the tea towel along marked lines referring to the pattern for color and stitch choices.

**3.** Remove transfer lines according to type of marking tool used, or as directed by the manufacturer.

**Let's Eat**
Placement Diagram 18" x 25"

## Time for Dinner

### Materials

- 1 purchased or self-made tea towel in desired color
- 6-strand embroidery floss: green, burgundy variegated and blue

## Instructions

**1.** Complete the towel using the Time for Dinner design 2½" from the bottom hemmed edge, referring to the instructions for Let's Eat.

**Time for Dinner**
Placement Diagram 18" x 25"

# Blue-Plate Special

## Materials

- 1 purchased or self-made tea towel in desired color
- 6-strand embroidery floss: black, burgundy, blue, orange and turquoise

## Instructions

**1.** Complete the towel using the Blue Place Special design 2½" from the bottom hemmed edge, referring to the instructions for Let's Eat. ❖

**Blue-Plate Special**
Placement Diagram 18" x 25"

**Let's Eat Pattern**
All unmarked stitches are backstitch.

**Time for Dinner Pattern**
All unmarked stitches are backstitch.

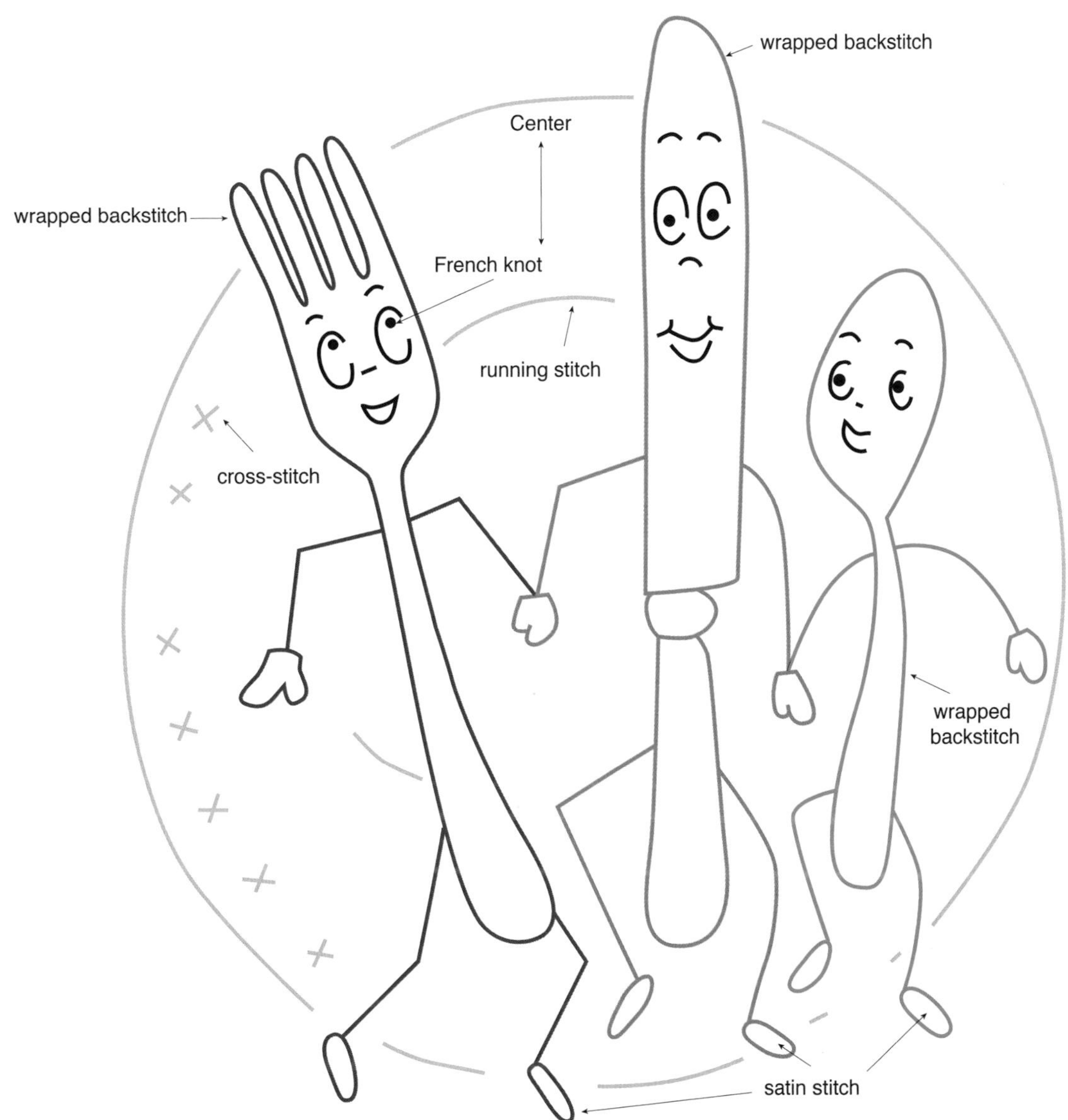


**Blue-Plate Special Pattern**
All unmarked stitches are backstitch.

# Fifties Favorites

## Project Note

Refer to Marking the Design on Fabric (page 24) for transferring and removing designs. Refer to Stitching the Design (page 24) when working embroidery.

## His

### Materials

- 1 purchased or self-made tea towel in desired color
- 6-strand embroidery floss: dark gray, cream, orange, brown, burgundy variegated and olive
- 19" length ⅝"-wide crocheted lace
- 19" length white baby rickrack

### Instructions

**1.** Center and transfer the His embroidery design to the tea towel 3" from the bottom hemmed edge.

**2.** Stitch the design on the tea towel along marked lines referring to the pattern for color and stitch choices.

**3.** Remove transfer lines according to type of marking tool used, or as directed by the manufacturer.

**4.** Sew the crocheted lace 2" up from bottom edge and the baby rickrack 1¼" from bottom edge to finish.

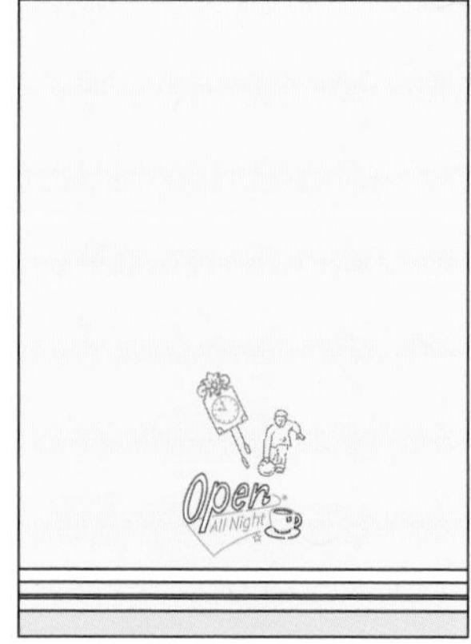

**His**
Placement Diagram 18" x 25"

## Hers

### Materials

- 1 purchased or self-made tea towel in desired color
- 6-strand embroidery floss: turquoise, green, gold, peach, dark pink and blue
- 19" length ⅝"-wide crocheted lace
- 19" length white baby rickrack

### Instructions

**1.** Complete the towel using the Hers embroidery design referring to the instructions for His towel. ❖

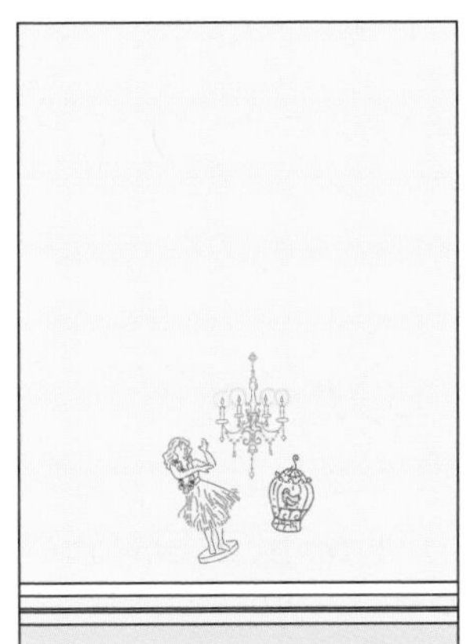

**Hers**
Placement Diagram 18" x 25"

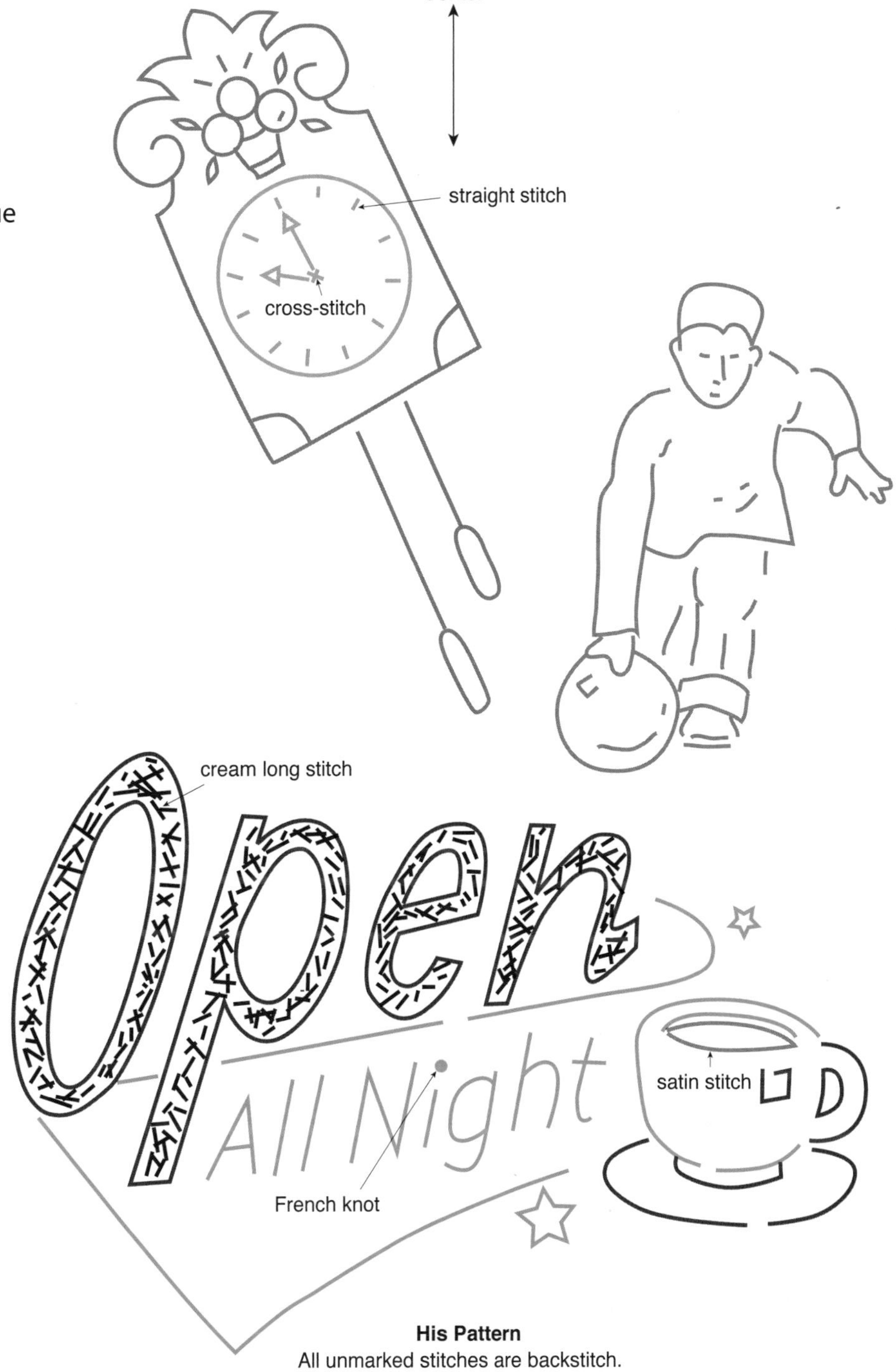
Center
straight stitch
cross-stitch
cream long stitch
Open
All Night
satin stitch
French knot

**His Pattern**
All unmarked stitches are backstitch.

**Hers Pattern**
All unmarked stitches are backstitch.

# Chore Time

### Project Note

Refer to Marking the Design on Fabric (page 24) for transferring and removing designs. Refer to Stitching the Design (page 24) when working embroidery.

## Sunday Resting

### Materials

- 1 purchased or self-made tea towel in desired color
- 6-strand embroidery floss: green and pink

### Instructions

**1.** Center and transfer the Sunday Resting embroidery design to the tea towel 1¾" from the bottom hemmed edge.

**2.** Stitch the design on the tea towel along marked lines referring to the pattern for color and stitch choices.

**3.** Remove transfer lines according to type of marking tool used, or as directed by the manufacturer.

**Sunday Resting**
Placement Diagram 18" x 25"

**Monday Washing**
Placement Diagram 18" x 25"

## Monday Washing

### Materials

- 1 purchased or self-made tea towel in desired color
- 6-strand embroidery floss: red and blue

### Instructions

**1.** Complete the towel using the Monday Washing embroidery design referring to the instructions for Sunday Resting.

## Tuesday Ironing

### Materials

- 1 purchased or self-made tea towel in desired color
- 6-strand embroidery floss: red and blue

### Instructions

**1.** Complete the towel using the Tuesday Ironing embroidery design referring to the instructions for Sunday Resting.

**Tuesday Ironing**
Placement Diagram 18" x 25"

## Wednesday Sewing

### Materials

- 1 purchased or self-made tea towel in desired color
- 6-strand embroidery floss: green and pink

### Instructions

**1.** Complete the towel using the Wednesday Sewing embroidery design referring to the instructions for Sunday Resting.

**Wednesday Sewing**
Placement Diagram 18" x 25"

## Thursday Shopping

### Materials

- 1 purchased or self-made tea towel in desired color
- 6-strand embroidery floss: blue and burgundy

### Instructions

**1.** Complete the towel using the Thursday Shopping embroidery design referring to the instructions for Sunday Resting.

**Thursday Shopping**
Placement Diagram 18" x 25"

## Friday Cleaning

### Materials

- 1 purchased or self-made tea towel in desired color
- 6-strand embroidery floss: rust and blue

### Instructions

**1.** Complete the towel using the Friday Cleaning embroidery design referring to the instructions for Sunday Resting.

**Friday Cleaning**
Placement Diagram 18" x 25"

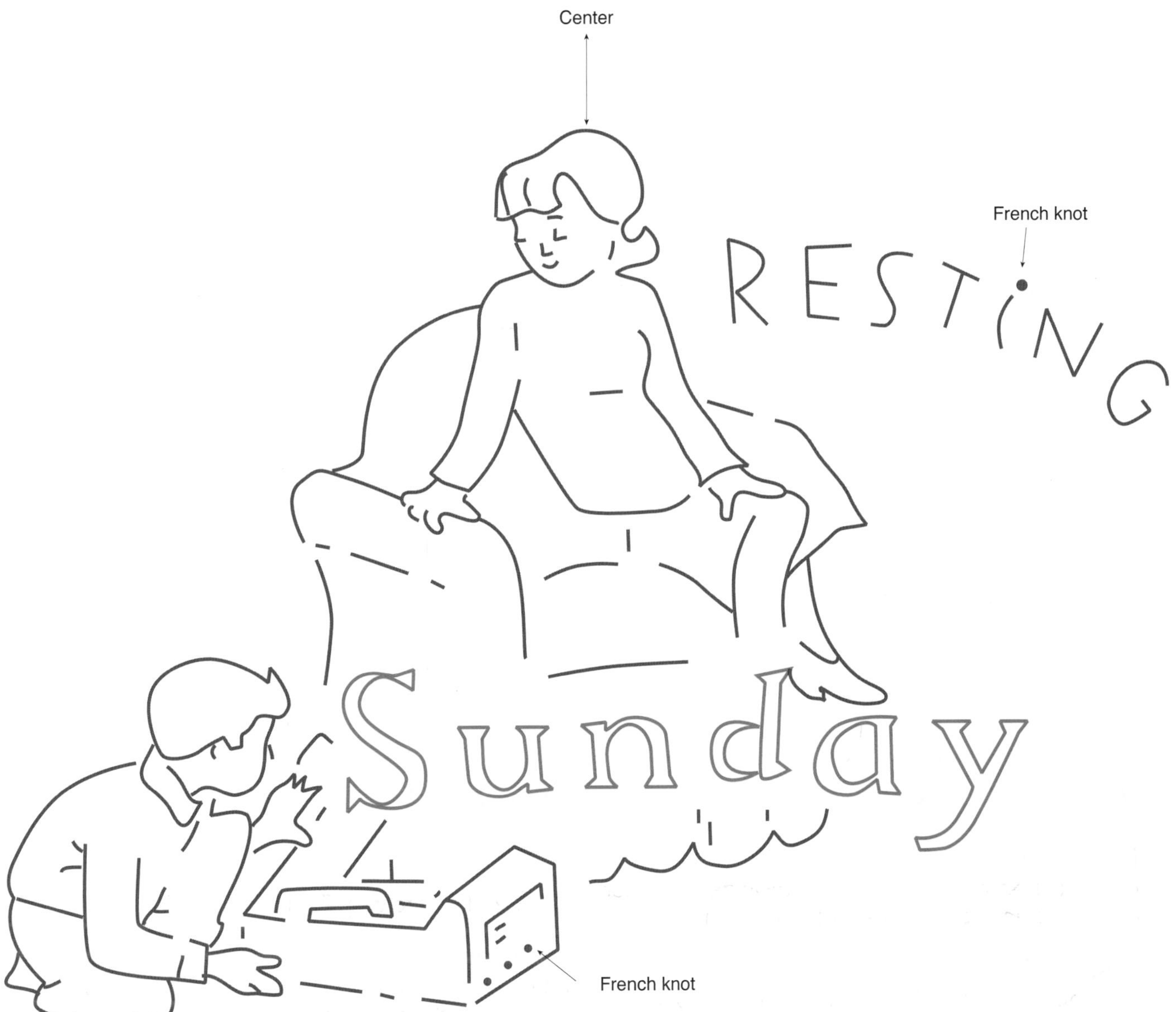

Center

French knot

RESTING

Sunday

French knot

**Sunday Resting Pattern**
All unmarked stitches are backstitch.

## Saturday Baking

### Materials

- 1 purchased or self-made tea towel in desired color
- 6-strand embroidery floss: green and orange

### Instructions

**1.** Complete the towel using the Saturday Baking embroidery design referring to the instructions for Sunday Resting. ❖

**Saturday Baking**
Placement Diagram 18" x 25"

**Monday Washing Pattern**
All unmarked stitches are backstitch.

**Tuesday Ironing Pattern**
All unmarked stitches are backstitch.

**Wednesday Sewing Pattern**
All unmarked stitches are backstitch.

**Thursday Shopping Pattern**
All unmarked stitches are backstitch.

**Friday Cleaning Pattern**
All unmarked stitches are backstitch.

**Saturday Baking Pattern**
All unmarked stitches are backstitch.

# Floral Stitchery

### Project Note

Refer to Marking the Design on Fabric (page 24) for transferring and removing designs. Refer to Stitching the Design (page 24) when working embroidery.

## Bluebird

### Materials

- 1 purchased or self-made tea towel in desired color
- 6-strand embroidery floss: dark blue, gold, brown, light green, dark green, light blue, yellow, orange and pink

### Instructions

**1.** Center and transfer the Bluebird embroidery design to the tea towel 1½" from the bottom hemmed edge.

**2.** Stitch the design on the tea towel along marked lines referring to the pattern for color and stitch choices.

**3.** Remove transfer lines according to type of marking tool used, or as directed by the manufacturer.

**Bluebird**
Placement Diagram 18" x 25"

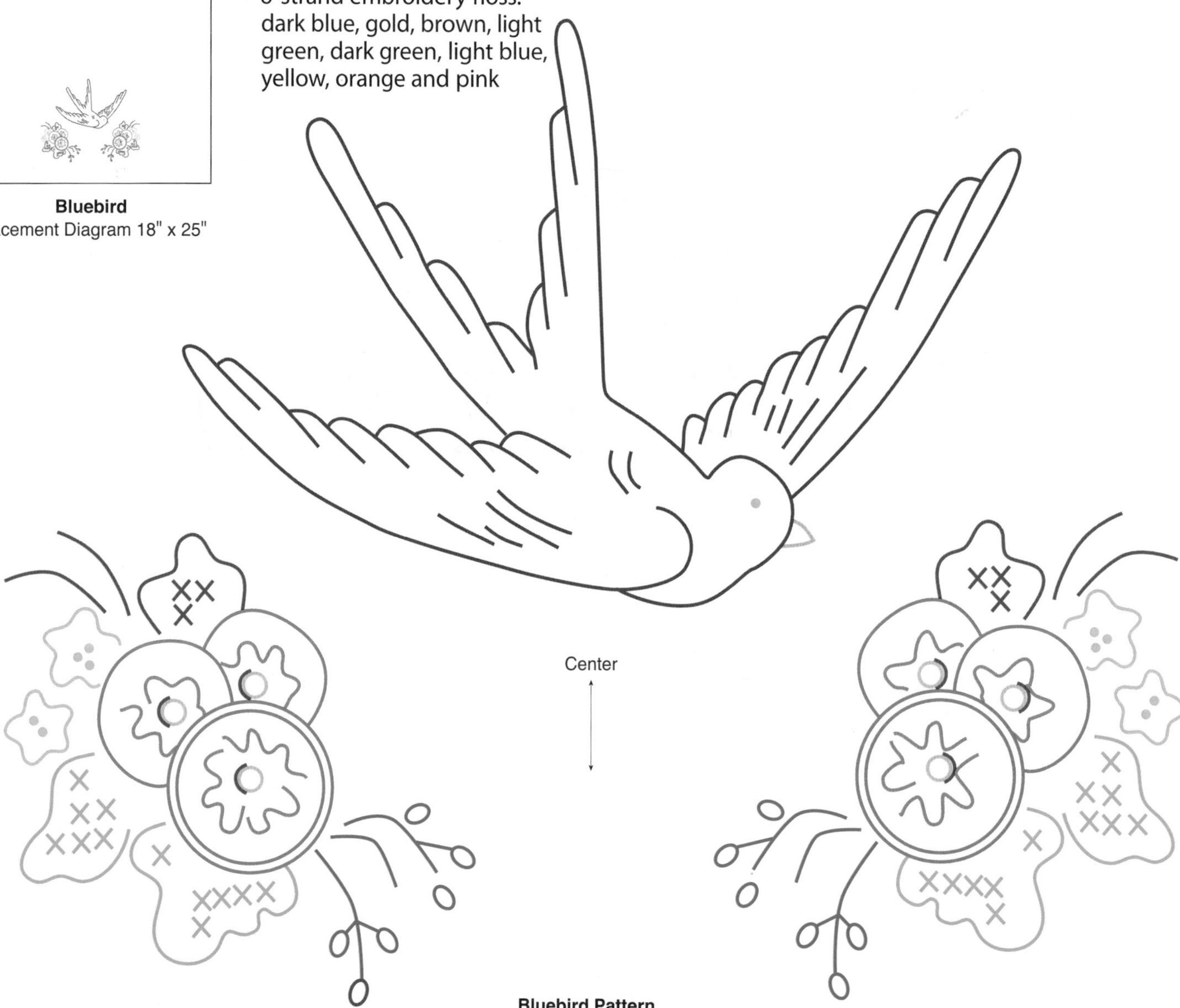


**Bluebird Pattern**
All unmarked stitches are wrapped backstitch.

## Cottage Teapot

### Materials

- 1 purchased or self-made tea towel in desired color
- 6-strand embroidery floss: orange, gold, light blue, dark blue, light green, turquoise and orchid

### Instructions

**1.** Complete the towel using the Cottage Teapot embroidery design referring to the instructions for Bluebird. ❖

**Cottage Teapot**
Placement Diagram 18" x 25"

Center

straight stitch

running stitch

straight stitch

French knot

running stitch

French knot

straight stitch

**Cottage Teapot Pattern**
All unmarked stitches are wrapped backstitch.

# Down on the Farm

## Project Note

Refer to Marking the Design on Fabric (page 24) for transferring and removing designs. Refer to Stitching the Design (page 24) when working embroidery.

## Little Lamb

### Materials

- 1 purchased or self-made tea towel in desired color
- 6-strand embroidery floss: gray, medium blue, dark blue, gold, light green, dark green, orchid, lavender and dark pink

### Instructions

**1.** Center and transfer the Little Lamb embroidery design to the tea towel 2" from the bottom hemmed edge.

**2.** Stitch the design on the tea towel along marked lines referring to the pattern for color and stitch choices.

**3.** Remove transfer lines according to type of marking tool used, or as directed by the manufacturer.

**Little Lamb**
Placement Diagram 18" x 25"

**Cow & Birds**
Placement Diagram 18" x 25"

## Cow & Birds

### Materials

- 1 purchased or self-made tea towel in desired color
- Scrap gold solid fabric
- 6-strand embroidery floss: taupe, pink, blue, rust, gold and orange

## Instructions

**1.** Complete the towel using the Cow & Birds embroidery design referring to the instructions for Little Lamb.

**2.** Referring to the Hand Appliqué section on page 86 and using the gold fabric, prepare the bird design for hand appliqué; stitch appliqués in place within the embroidery design area referring to the embroidery pattern for placement.

# Pink Pig

## Materials

- 1 purchased or hemmed self-made tea towel in desired color
- 6-strand embroidery floss: dark pink, dark brown, black, yellow-green, dark green, yellow and lavender

## Instructions

**1.** Complete the towel using the Pink Pig embroidery design referring to the instructions for Little Lamb.

**Pink Pig**
Placement Diagram 18" x 25"

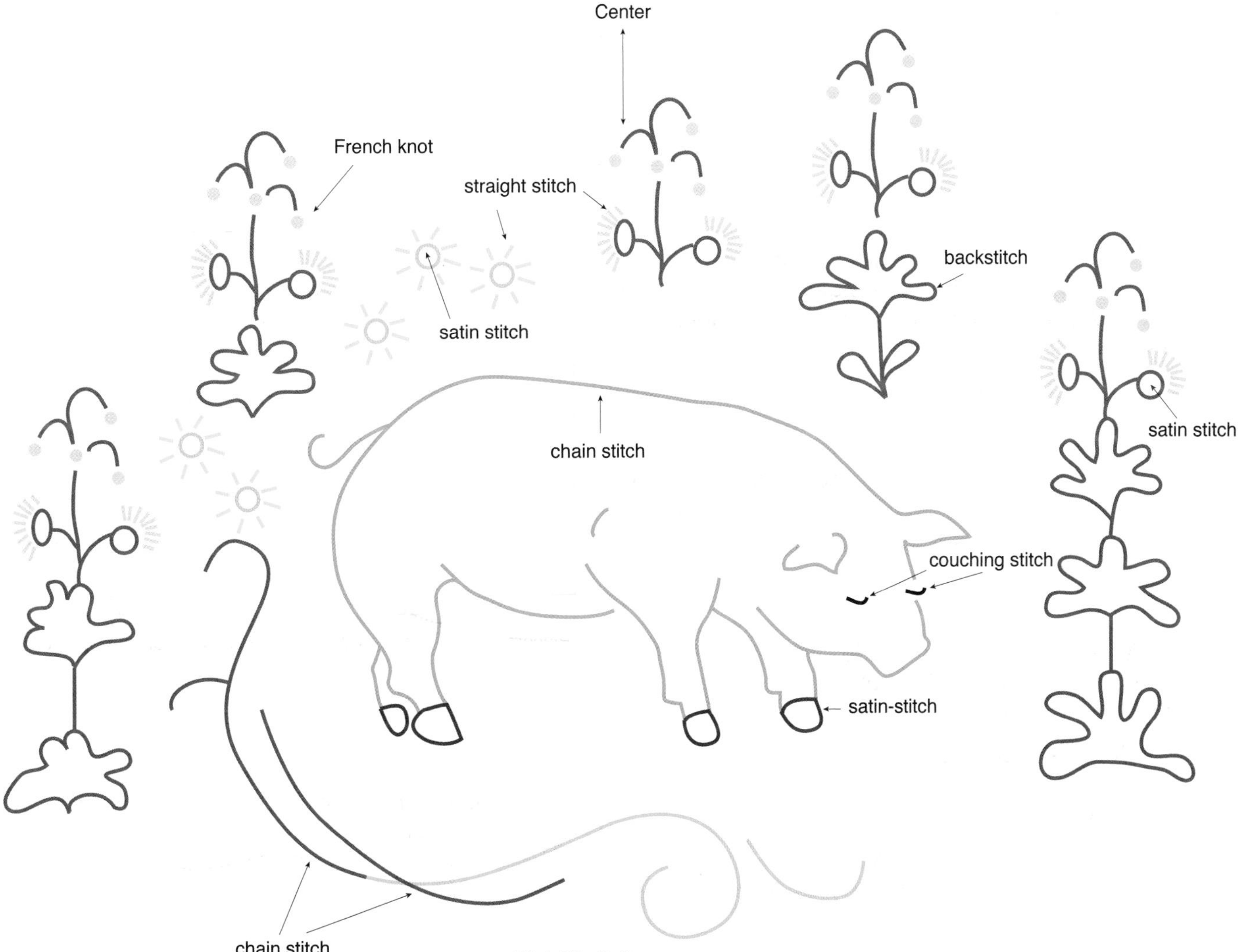

Center
French knot
straight stitch
backstitch
satin stitch
chain stitch
satin stitch
couching stitch
satin-stitch
chain stitch

**Pink Pig Pattern**

## Mother Hen

### Materials

- 1 purchased or self-made tea towel in desired color
- 6-strand embroidery floss: red, yellow variegated, mint green and pink

### Instructions

**1.** Complete the towel using the Mother Hen embroidery design referring to the instructions for Little Lamb. ❖

**Mother Hen**
Placement Diagram 18" x 25"

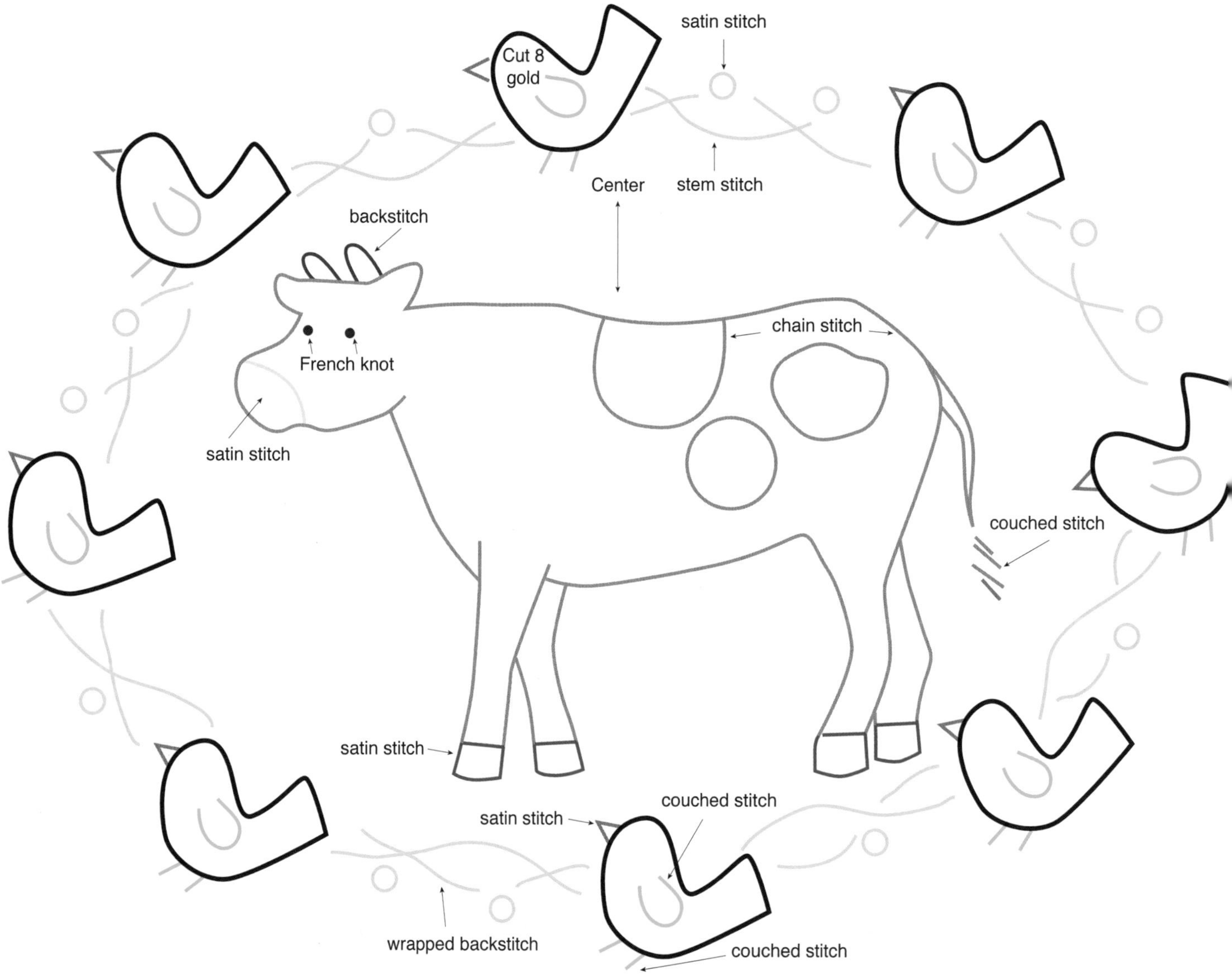

Cut 8 gold
satin stitch
stem stitch
Center
backstitch
chain stitch
French knot
satin stitch
couched stitch
satin stitch
satin stitch
couched stitch
wrapped backstitch
couched stitch

**Cow & Birds Pattern**

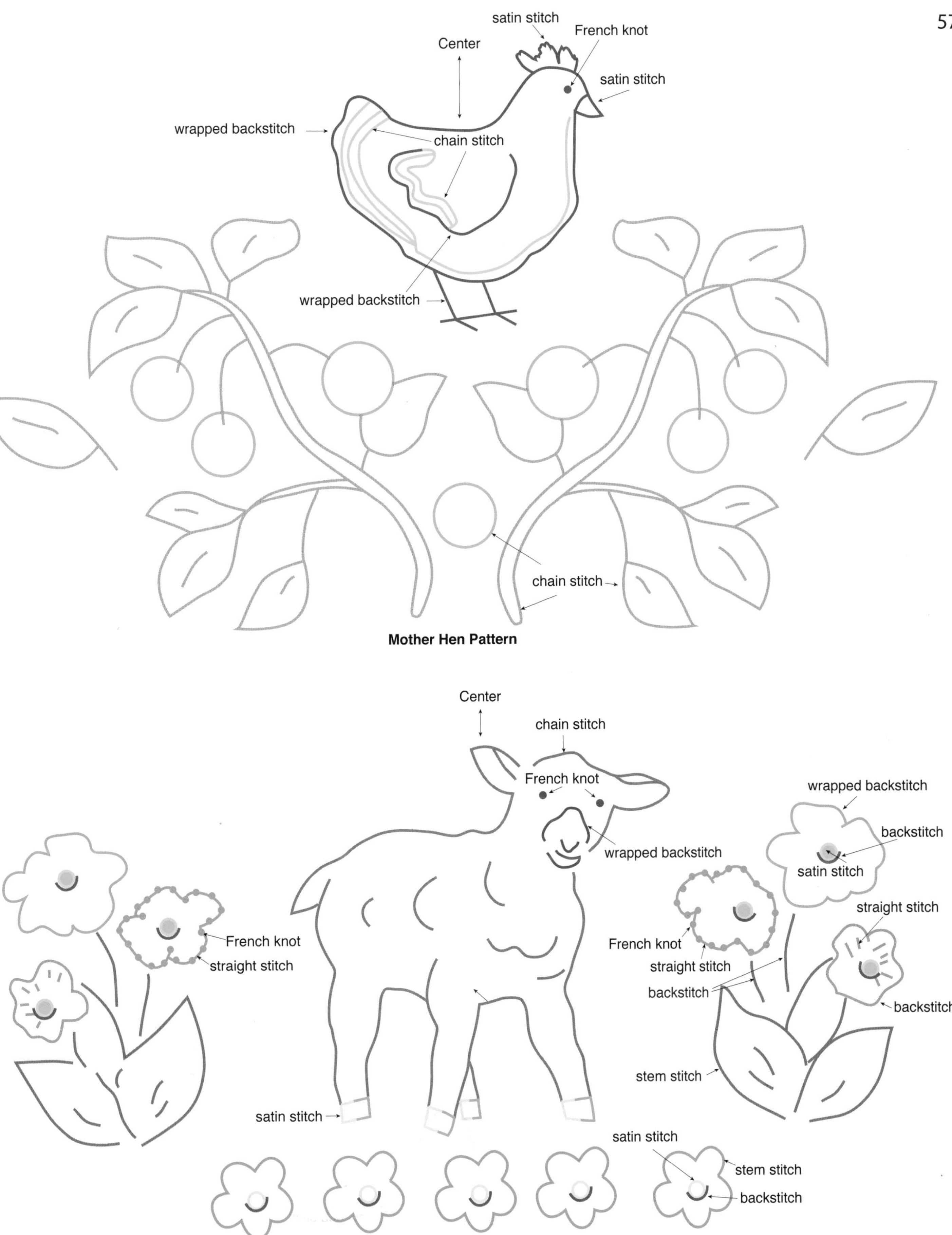


**Mother Hen Pattern**

**Little Lamb Pattern**

# Ticking Stitchery

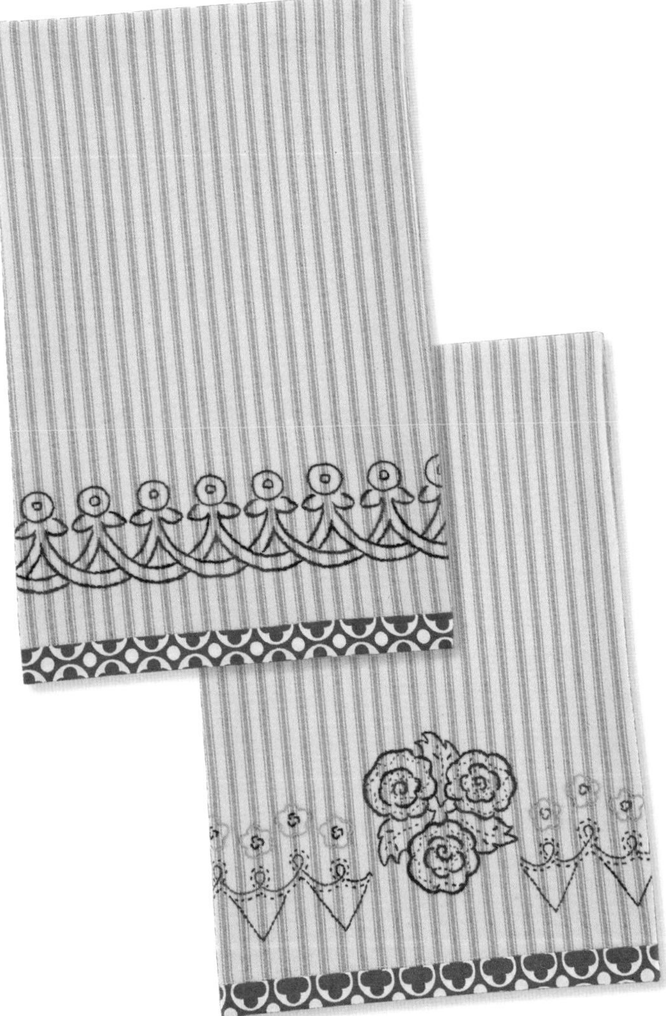

## Project Note

Refer to Marking the Design on Fabric (page 24) for transferring and removing designs. Refer to Stitching the Design (page 24) when working embroidery.

## Blue Swag

### Materials

- 1 purchased or self-made tea towel in desired color
- Blue variegated 6-strand embroidery floss

### Instructions

**1.** Center and transfer the Blue Swag embroidery design to the tea towel 1¼" from the bottom hemmed edge, repeating as needed and referring to the placement diagram.

**Blue Swag**
Placement Diagram 18" x 25"

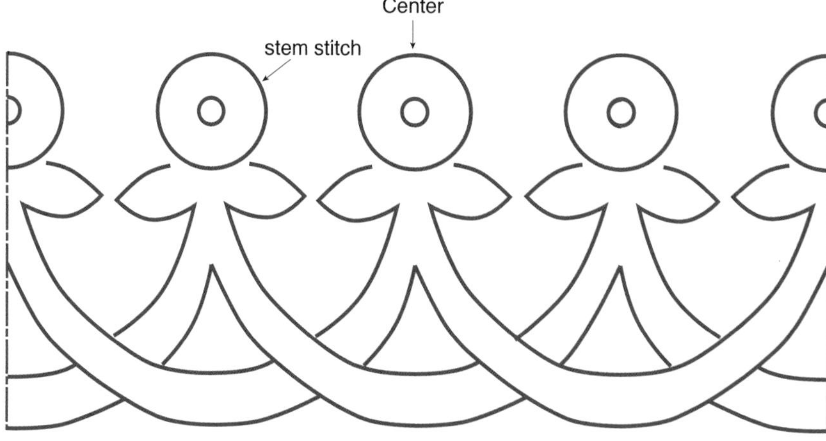


**Blue Swag Pattern**

**2.** Stitch the design on the tea towel along marked lines referring to the pattern for color and stitch choices.

**3.** Remove transfer lines according to type of marking tool used, or as directed by the manufacturer.

## Rosie Posy

### Materials

- 1 purchased or self-made tea towel in desired color
- 6-strand embroidery floss: burgundy variegated, green and pink

### Instructions

**1.** Place center mark on pattern at center point of towel width and transfer the Rosie Posy embroidery design to the tea towel 1¼" from the bottom hemmed edge referring the placement diagram. Flip design and transfer remaining side design to towel.

**2.** Stitch the design on the tea towel along marked lines referring to the pattern for color and stitch choices.

**3.** Remove transfer lines according to type of marking tool used, or as directed by the manufacturer. ❖

**Rosy Posy**
Placement Diagram 18" x 25"

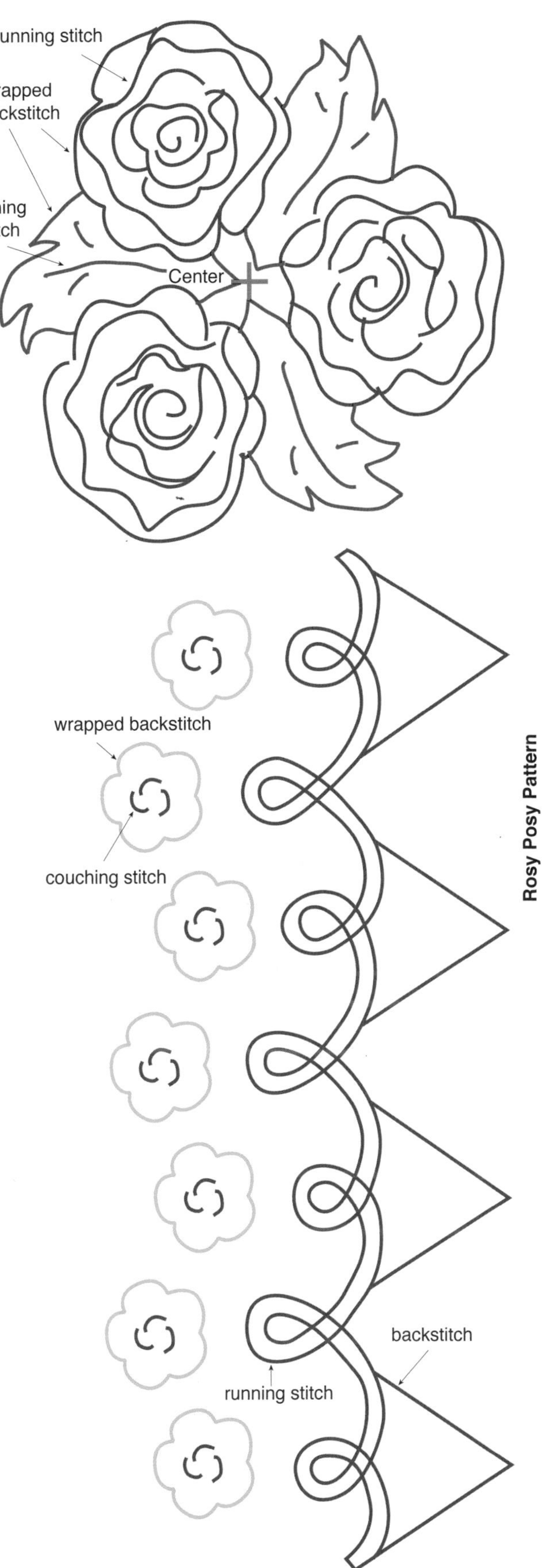

# Three Bears

## Project Note

Refer to Marking the Design on Fabric (page 24) for transferring and removing designs. Refer to Stitching the Design (page 24) when working embroidery.

## Too Hot

### Materials

- 1 purchased or self-made tea towel in desired color
- 6-strand embroidery floss: black, medium gray, dark brown, light green, dark green, red, blue, gold and tan

### Instructions

**1.** Center and transfer the Too Hot embroidery design to the tea towel 2" from the bottom hemmed edge.

**2.** Stitch the design on the tea towel along marked lines referring to the pattern for color and stitch choices.

**3.** Remove transfer lines as directed by the manufacturer.

**Too Hot**
Placement Diagram 18" x 25"

**Too Cold**
Placement Diagram 18" x 25"

## Too Cold

### Materials

- 1 purchased or self-made tea towel in desired color
- 6-strand embroidery floss: dark brown, light green, medium green, dark blue, medium blue, red, tan, lavender, pink, orchid and plum

### Instructions

**1.** Complete the towel using the Too Cold embroidery design referring to the instructions for Too Hot.

## Just Right

### Materials

- 1 purchased or self-made tea towel in desired color
- 6-strand embroidery floss: dark brown, black, medium gray, lavender, red, mint green, turquoise, gold, pink and tan

### Instructions

**1.** Complete the towel using the Just Right embroidery design referring to the instructions for Too Hot. ❖

**Just Right**
Placement Diagram 18" x 25"

Center
French knot
straight stitch
cross-stitch
satin stitch
running stitch
satin stitch
backstitch
too hot
lazy-daisyt stitch
French knot

**Too Hot Pattern**
All unmarked stitches are wrapped backstitch.

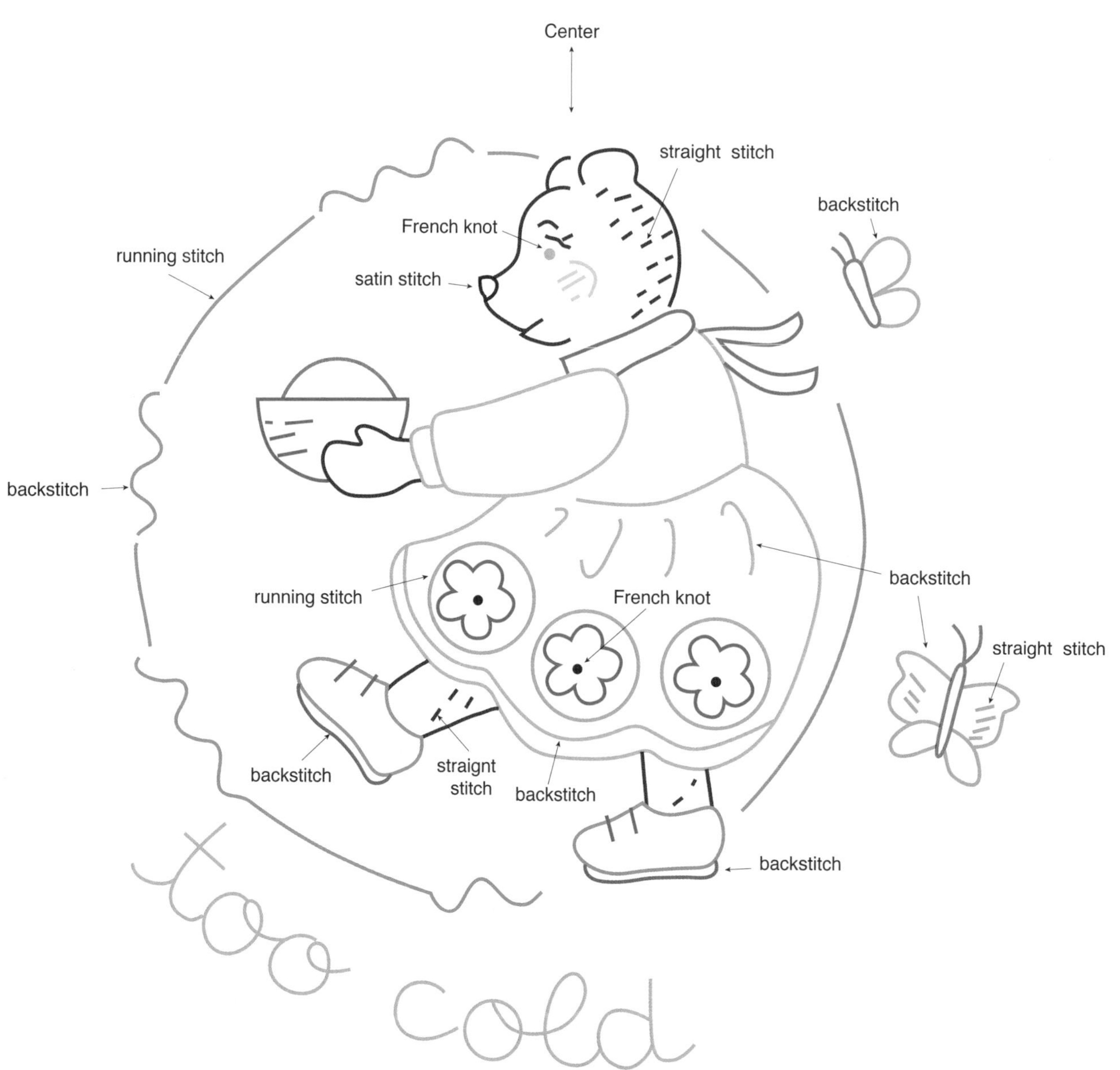


**Too Cold Pattern**
All unmarked stitches are wrapped backstitch.

**Just Right Pattern**
All unmarked stitches are wrapped backstitch.

# Vintage Charm

## Project Note

Refer to Marking the Design on Fabric (page 24) for transferring and removing designs. Refer to Stitching the Design (page 24) when working embroidery.

# Blooming Bulb

## Materials

- 12" x 12" square light blue solid fabric
- 4" x 6" rectangle muslin
- 18" x 17¾" rectangle Osnaburg
- 18" x 26¾" rectangle green solid fabric
- 2½ yards prepared coordinating binding
- 1 lace-edged handkerchief
- 2 (½") cream buttons
- 6-strand embroidery floss: dark green, olive, yellow, purple, lavender and pink

## Instructions

**1.** Hem one 18" edge of the green fabric rectangle referring to Making a Tea Towel on page 3.

**2.** Measure up 8" from the hemmed edge and mark a line from edge to edge across the 18" width with a water-erasable marker; fold and crease to mark the vertical center. Set aside.

**3.** Center and transfer the Blooming Bulb embroidery design on page 67 to the light blue fabric square.

**4.** Stitch the design on the square along marked lines referring to the pattern for color and stitch choices.

**5.** Remove transfer lines according to type of marking tool used, or as directed by the manufacturer.

**6.** Center design and trim stitched square to a 4" x 6" rectangle.

**7.** Place the embroidered rectangle right sides together with the muslin rectangle; stitch around three sides, leaving the top short edge open. Turn right side out; press edges flat.

**8.** Cut two corners from the lace handkerchief to make two triangles with 2½" short sides as shown in Figure 2.

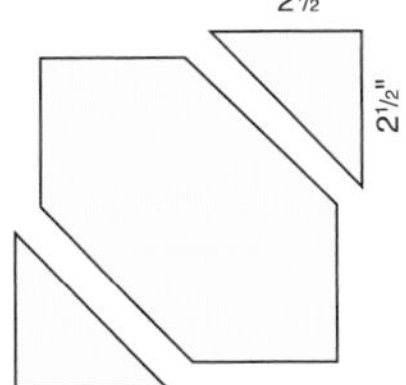

Figure 2

**9.** Baste a triangle to each side of the center along the marked line on the green fabric rectangle with triangle points 5" apart, as shown in Figure 3.

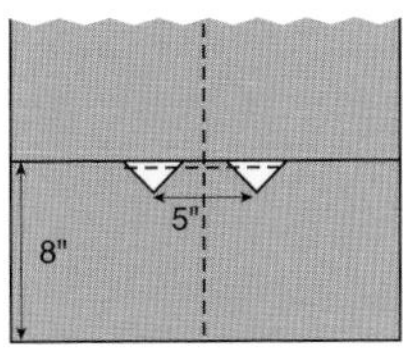

Figure 3

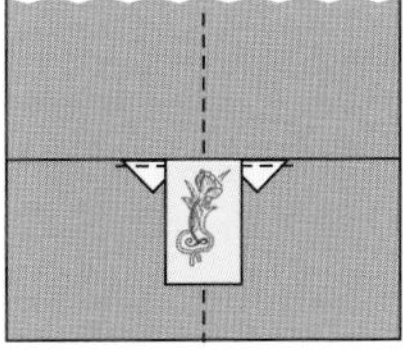
Figure 4

**10.** Center the embroidered panel on top of the triangles as shown in Figure 4; baste to hold in place.

**11.** Place the Osnaburg rectangle right sides together on top of the basted pieces, aligning one raw edge with the marked line as shown in Figure 5; pin in place.

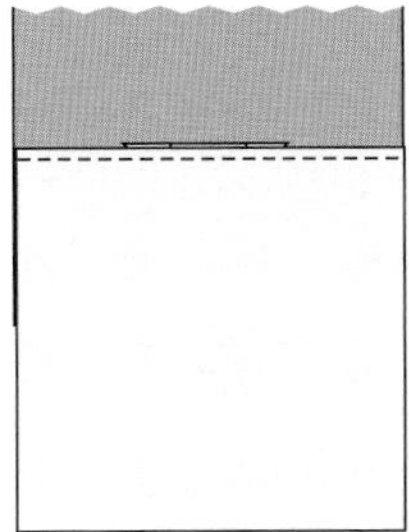
Figure 5

**12.** Stitch ¼" from the aligned raw edges, again referring to Figure 5. Press the Osnaburg rectangle to the right side.

**13.** Trim edges even with the green rectangle.

**14.** Bind the remaining end and both long edges referring to Finishing Towel Edges on page 2.

**15.** Sew a button to each bottom corner of the embroidered blue rectangle to finish the tea towel.

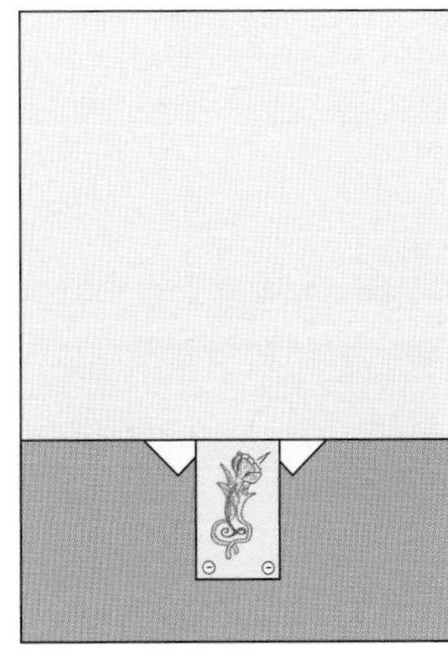
**Blooming Bulb**
Placement Diagram 18" x 25"

## Ribbit Rhythm

### Materials

- 12" x 12" square muslin
- 4" x 6" rectangle muslin
- 18" x 18¾" rectangle Osnaburg
- 18" x 26½" rectangle cream metallic fabric
- 2½ yards prepared coordinating binding
- 1 (8"-square) lace-edged handkerchief
- 6-strand embroidery floss: mint green, gold, brown, pink, lavender, tan and blue

### Instructions

**1.** Follow steps 1 and 2 of the Blooming Bulb tea towel using the cream metallic fabric rectangle except measure up 7" from the hemmed edge.

**2.** Center and transfer the Ribbit Rhythm embroidery design on page 68 to the muslin square.

**3.** Follow steps 4–7 for Blooming Bulb except leave the top long edge of the embroidered panel open.

**4.** Cut the handkerchief in half across one diagonal to make two large triangles. Center and baste the diagonal edge of one handkerchief triangle to the marked line on the cream-metallic rectangle as shown in Figure 6. Set aside remaining handkerchief triangle for another project.

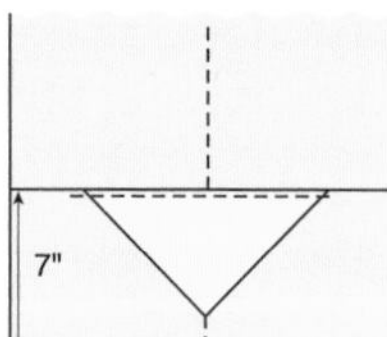


Figure 6

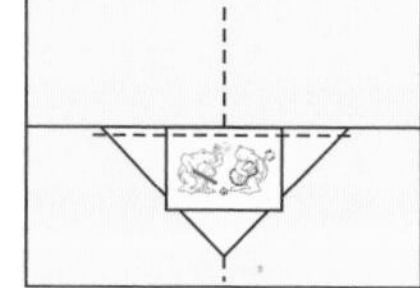

Figure 7

**5.** Center the embroidered panel on top of the triangle as shown in Figure 7; baste to hold in place.

**6.** Follow steps 11–14 for Blooming Bulb to complete the tea towel.

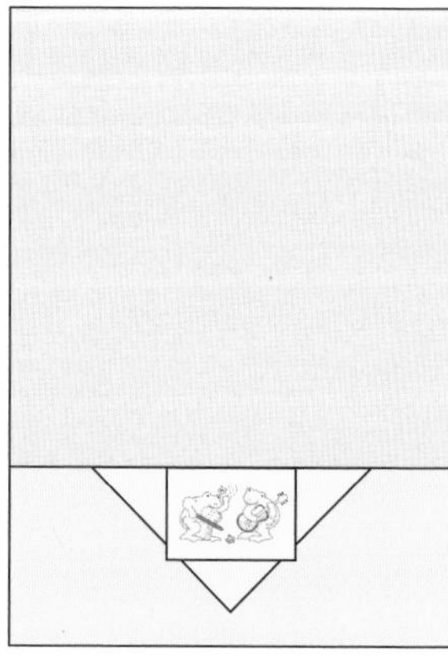

**Ribbit Rhythm**
Placement Diagram 18" x 25"

## Golden Posy

### Materials

- 12" x 12" square light blue solid fabric
- 5½" x 5" rectangle muslin
- 18" x 18¾" rectangle white solid fabric
- 18" x 26¾" rectangle gold print fabric
- 2½ yards prepared coordinating binding
- 2 (½") cream buttons
- 6-strand embroidery floss: gold, salmon, rust, blue, purple, lime green and olive green

### Instructions

**1.** Follow steps 1 and 2 of the Blooming Bulb tea towel using the gold print fabric rectangle except measure up 7" from the hemmed edge.

**2.** Center and transfer the Golden Posy embroidery design on page 68 to the light blue fabric square.

**3.** Follow steps 4–15 for Blooming Bulbs except trim the embroidered square to 5½" x 5", leave the top long edge open, use the white solid fabric rectangle in place of the Osnaburg rectangle, and eliminate use of handkerchief pieces to complete the tea towel.

**Golden Posy**
Placement Diagram 18" x 25"

## Half-Square Handkerchiefs

### Materials

- 18" x 18¾" rectangle white solid fabric
- 18" x 26¾" rectangle gold print fabric
- 2½ yards prepared coordinating binding
- 1 each 6"- and 10"-square lace-edge handkerchiefs

### Instructions

**1.** Follow steps 1 and 2 of the Blooming Bulb tea towel using the gold print fabric rectangle except measure up 7" from the hemmed edge.

**2.** Cut each handkerchief in half on one diagonal; center and baste one triangle each on the marked line with the smaller triangle on top. Set aside remaining triangles for use on another project.

**3.** Complete the tea towel referring to steps 11–14 for the Blooming Bulb except use the white solid fabric rectangle in place of the Osnaburg rectangle.

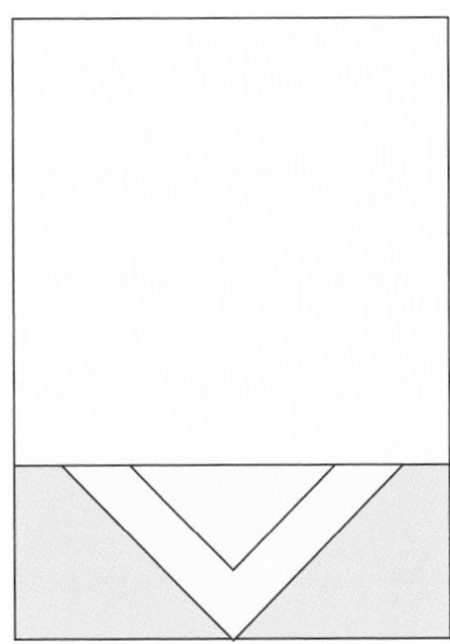

**Half-Square Handkerchiefs**
Placement Diagram 18" x 25"

**6.** Repeat steps 11–14 for the Blooming Bulb to complete the tea towel, using the muslin rectangle in place of the Osnaburg rectangle, and stitching the blue flower embellishment to the top center of the ribbon section. ❖

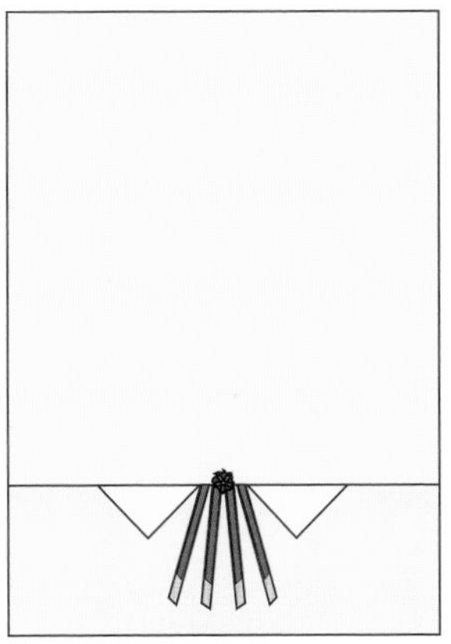

**Ribbon in Blue**
Placement Diagram 18" x 25"

## Ribbon in Blue

### Materials

- 18" x 19¾" rectangle muslin
- 18" x 26¾" rectangle cream metallic fabric
- 2½ yards prepared coordinating binding
- 1 lace-edged handkerchief
- 1 blue embroidered flower appliqué
- ½ yard ¼"-wide blue satin ribbon
- ½ yard ⅜"-wide cream satin ribbon

### Instructions

**1.** Follow steps 1 and 2 of the Blooming Bulb tea towel using the cream metallic fabric rectangle and measuring up 6" from the hemmed edge.

**2.** Cut the blue ribbon into four 2½" lengths and the cream ribbon into two 4" and two 5" lengths; trim one end of each length at an angle.

**3.** Cut two corners from the lace handkerchief to make two triangles with 3¼" short sides.

**4.** Baste a triangle to each side of the center on the marked line on the cream metallic fabric rectangle.

**5.** Place longer lengths of cream ribbon in the center and shorter ones on each side. Repeat with blue ribbon lengths on top of the cream; baste to hold in place.

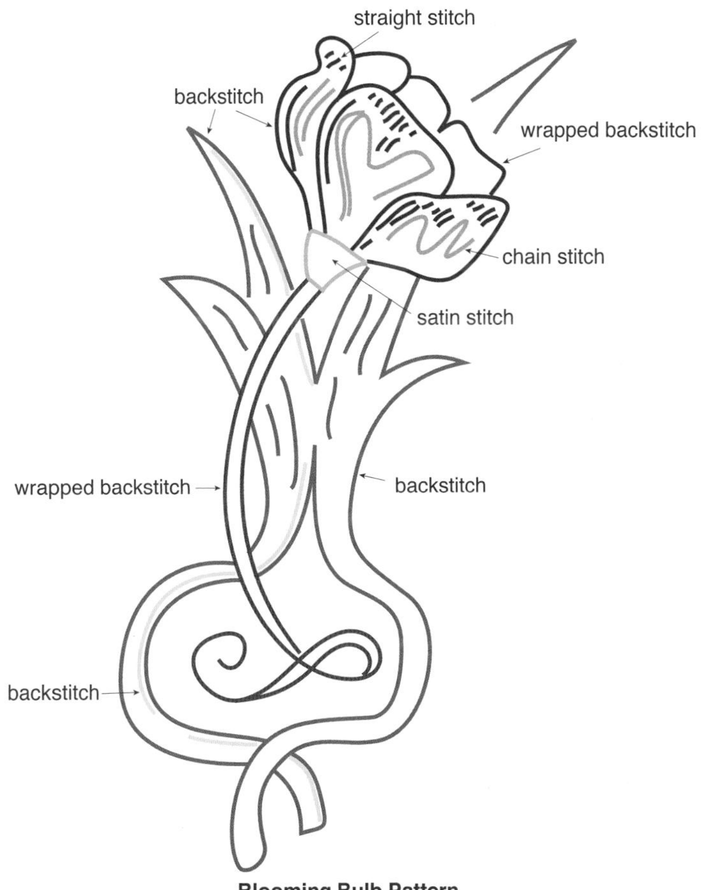


**Blooming Bulb Pattern**

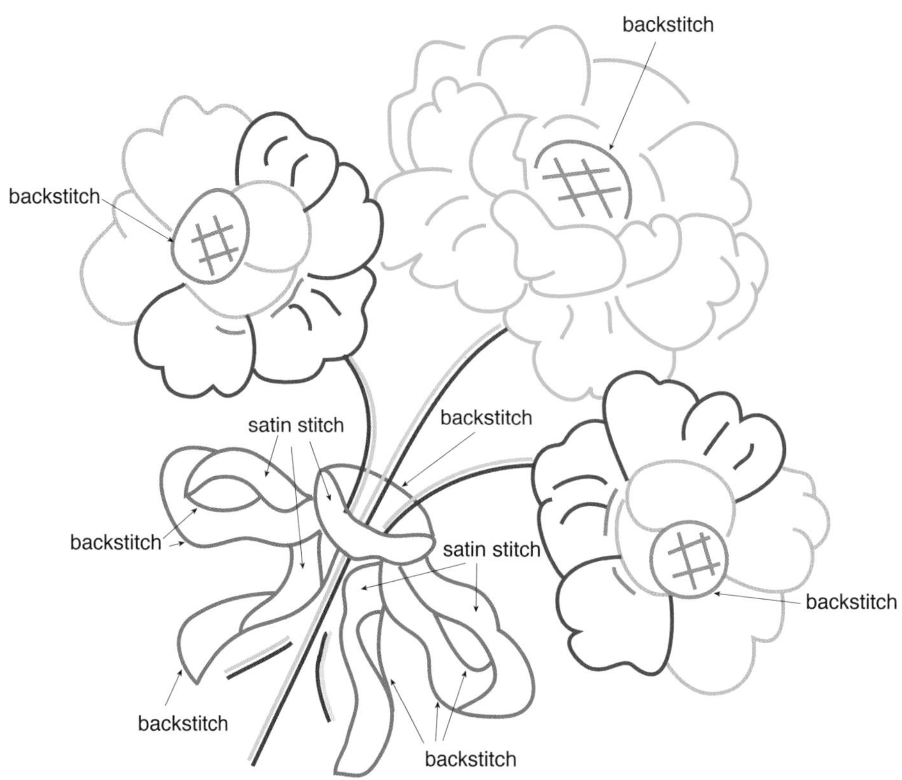


**Golden Posy Pattern**
All unmarked stitches are stem stitch.

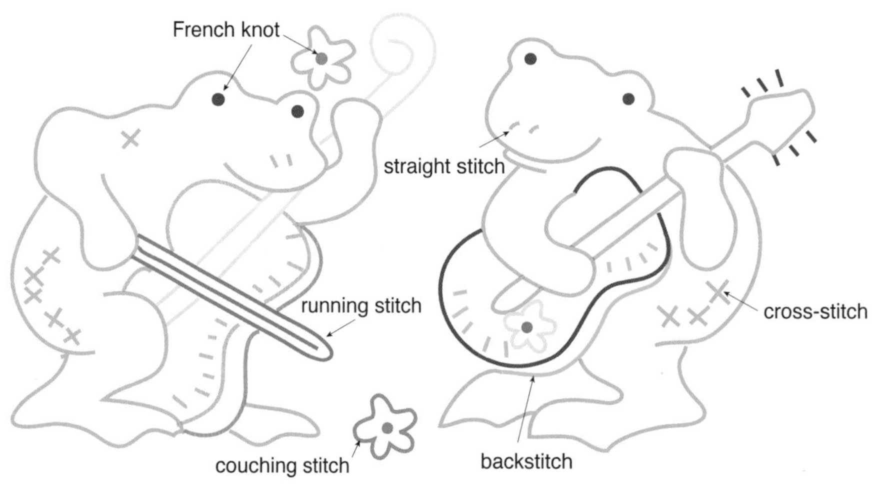


**Ribbit Rhythm Pattern**
All unmarked stitches are wrapped backstitch.

# Machine Appliqué

## General Instructions

Machine appliqué is the technique of layering colorful shapes on a background to create a graphic design similar to hand appliqué, which is covered in another chapter. The edge of each shape may be stitched in place either by hand or by machine.

Machine appliqué is easier and faster than hand appliqué and has a distinctly different appearance. Its satin-stitched or blanket-stitched outlines are a prominent design feature and give the composition the semblance of a crayon-colored picture in which the shapes were outlined before coloring.

Tightly woven, 100 percent cotton fabrics work best for machine appliqué. If the weave is too loose, the shapes may become distorted during handling.

When you are layering pieces, choose colors that contrast so that each shape will be distinct.

### Supplies & Tools

- Scissors—small, very sharp point
- Pencil or air-soluble marking pen
- Tracing paper or lightweight template plastic
- Fine-line permanent marker or pencil
- Fusible web, basting spray, fabric glue sticks or spray starch
- Fabric stabilizer—to help prevent stitching from puckering. There are many different types on the market. Follow manufacturer's instructions for use. For example, some stabilizers are simply torn off when stitching is complete while others may be water-soluble.
- Straight pins
- Appliqué pressing sheet
- All-purpose thread to match or contrast with fabrics

### Preparing the Appliqué Shapes

Shapes may be traced directly onto the fusible web from the pattern source, eliminating the need to prepare templates or patterns. If you prefer to keep patterns for future use, you might want to make templates from lightweight template plastic.

Tracing paper may be used to transfer a multilayered design. Tracing the design onto the paper allows you to use an appliqué pressing sheet to fuse the pieces together to make the motif before fusing to the background.

Fusible web is used to adhere pieces to the background and reduce fraying. Some fusible webs result in a stiff, rigid design. This would not be appropriate for a tea towel. An alternative option is to stiffen the fabric with spray starch and then baste it in place. Fabric glue sticks and basting spray may also be used to temporarily adhere shapes to a background before stitching the edges in place.

When using fusible web, the patterns need to be reversed. The appliqué patterns given in this section have already been reversed. Trace the selected shape from this book as directed for number to cut onto the paper side of the fusible web or by using a template; leave ½" between pieces when tracing.

Cut out traced shapes, adding a margin around each one. Fuse the paper shapes to the wrong side of fabrics as directed on patterns for color. Cut out shapes on the traced lines; remove paper backing.

If using the spray-starch method, apply a heavy layer of starch to the fabric and press to make fabric stiff. Prepare a template and trace around it on the wrong side of the fabric. Cut out on the marked lines.

Arrange and baste the shapes to the background, noting overlaps and numbers that indicate the order of placement.

### Machine Appliqué

If using fusible web when cutting pieces, arrange the first shape (No. 1) in place in the suggested location on the tea towel and press in place referring to the manufacturer's instructions.

Noting overlaps, place shapes on the background in numerical order and press in place.

An appliqué pressing sheet is helpful when layering pieces for fusing. To use, place the complete traced design under the sheet and arrange pieces on top of the sheet, fusing shapes together as you go. Be sure the traced design is reversed from that given in this book. When all pieces have been added, the entire shape may be picked up, and arranged and fused on the background as one piece.

Cut a piece of fabric stabilizer larger than the appliqué motif or area. Apply to the wrong side of the area to be appliquéd following manufacturer's instructions.

Using all-purpose sewing thread of a contrasting or coordinating color, adjust the machine to make a satin stitch (tight zigzag stitch). Practice on a scrap of fabric to achieve the desired width and coverage.

Carefully stitch all around the exposed edges of each shape.

When stitching is complete, remove fabric stabilizer. Pull thread ends to the back side, knot if desired and trim ends to finish.❖

---

# Appliqué Delight

## Sues Aplenty

### Materials

- 1 purchased or self-made tea towel in desired color with ¾" fabric band on the bottom edge
- Fabric scraps: light and dark in desired colors
- Thread to match or contrast with fabrics
- ½ yard 18"-wide fusible web

### Instructions

**1.** Fold and crease the tea towel along length to mark the center.

**2.** Leaving ½" between shapes, trace the individual appliqué shapes given on page 73 onto the paper side of the fusible web referring to pattern for number to cut.

**3.** Cut out shapes, leaving a margin around each one.

**4.** Fuse shapes to the wrong sides of the fabric scraps.

**5.** Cut out shapes on traced lines; remove paper backing.

**6.** Arrange, fuse and stitch the three motifs onto the tea towel referring to the Placement Diagram for positioning suggestions and referring to Preparing the Appliqué Shapes and Machine Appliqué sections on page 69.

**7.** Transfer the flower embroidery design to the tea towel, positioning as desired. Machine zigzag-stitch around design and to make flower centers using chosen thread colors as desired to finish.

**Sues Aplenty**
Placement Diagram 18" x 25"

**Puppy Love**
Placement Diagram 18" x 25"

## Puppy Love

### Materials

- 1 purchased or self-made tea towel in desired color with ¾" fabric band on the bottom edge
- 1 fat quarter dark brown tonal
- 8" length flower trim
- Dark brown and navy thread
- ½ yard 18"-wide fusible web

### Instructions

**1.** Complete the towel using puppy appliqué pattern and shoe embroidery design given on page 72 referring to the instructions for Sues Aplenty, adding a piece of flower trim to each puppy shape for collar to finish.

## Bushel of Berries

### Materials

- 1 purchased or self-made tea towel in desired color with ¾" fabric band on the bottom edge
- 1 fat quarter red check
- Lime green solid fabric scrap
- Red, green and white thread
- ½ yard 18"-wide fusible web

### Instructions

**1.** Complete the towel using the strawberry appliqué pattern and letter embroidery design given on page 72 referring to the instructions for Sues Aplenty, adding a white satin-stitched highlight on each berry.

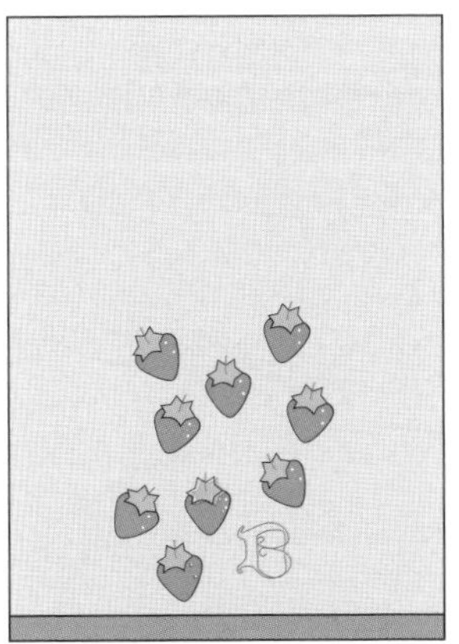

**Bushel of Berries**
Placement Diagram 18" x 25"

**Pink Parasols**
Placement Diagram 18" x 25"

## Pink Parasols

### Materials

- 1 purchased or self-made tea towel in desired color with ¾" fabric band on the bottom edge
- Fabric scraps: blue print, pink and blue solids
- Pink pearl cotton
- Thread to match fabrics
- ½ yard 18"-wide fusible web

### Instructions

**1.** Complete the towel using the parasol appliqué pattern and heart embroidery design given on page 72 referring to the instructions for Sues Aplenty.

**2.** Cut five 1½" lengths of pink pearl cotton. Clump four strands together and tie a knot around the center of the clump with the remaining length to make a bow shape. Repeat to make five bows.

**3.** Hand-stitch a bow in place at the top center of each parasol to finish.

## Blushing Bouquets

### Materials

- 1 purchased or self-made tea towel in desired color with ¾" fabric band on the bottom edge
- 1 fat quarter each pink dot and green print
- Pink, green and white thread
- ½ yard 18"-wide fusible web

### Instructions

**1.** Complete the towel using blushing bouquet appliqué pattern and clock embroidery designs given on page 73 referring to the instructions for Sues Aplenty, adding white satin-stitched highlights around center flowers. ❖

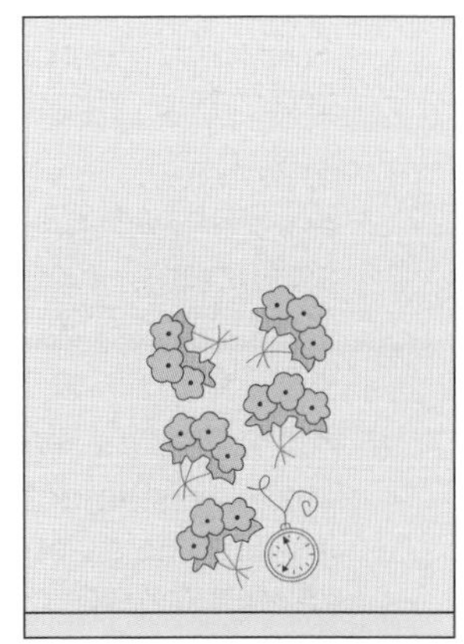

**Blushing Bouquets**
Placement Diagram 18" x 25"

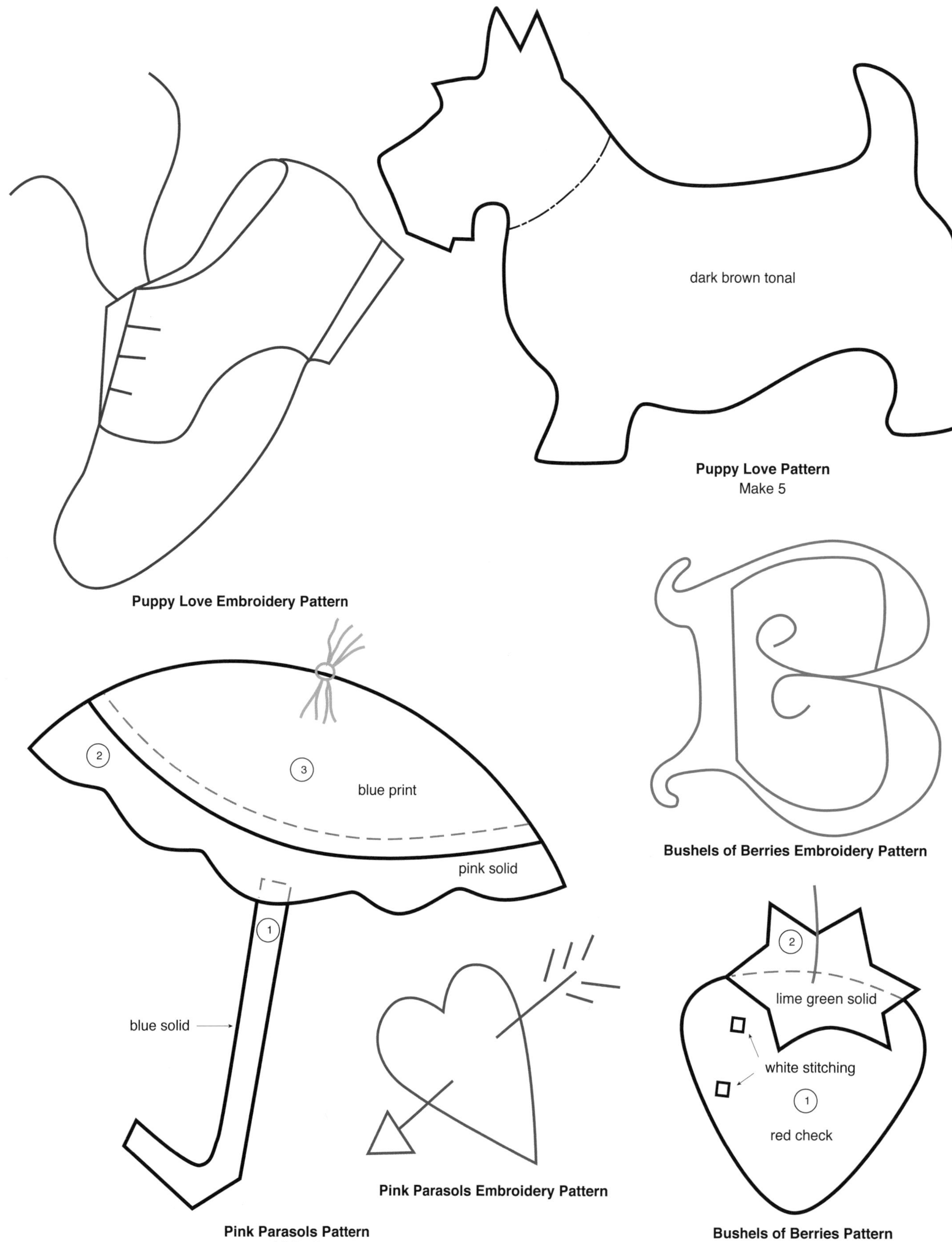


**Puppy Love Pattern**
Make 5

**Puppy Love Embroidery Pattern**

**Bushels of Berries Embroidery Pattern**

**Pink Parasols Embroidery Pattern**

**Pink Parasols Pattern**
Make 5

**Bushels of Berries Pattern**
Make 9

Blushing Bouquets Pattern
Make 5

Blushing Bouquets Embroidery Pattern

Sues Aplenty Embroidery Pattern

Sues Aplenty Pattern
Make 3

# Rickrack Latticework

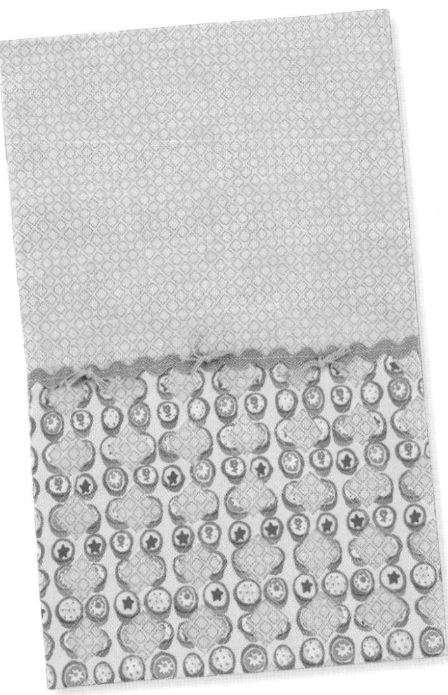

## Aqua Diamonds

### Materials

- 1 purchased or self-made tea towel in desired color
- 1 fat quarter light aqua print
- Thread to match fabric
- Gold pearl cotton
- 19" length blue rickrack
- Very sharp, small, pointed-tip scissors
- See-through ruler

### Instructions

**1.** If using a purchased tea towel, remove the finished edge from one short end.

**2.** Cut a 19" x 7½" rectangle light aqua print.

**3.** Mark the rectangle with a 1" diagonal grid as shown in Figure 1.

Figure 1

**4.** Sew the marked rectangle on the bottom of the tea towel with the right side of the marked rectangle on the back side of the tea towel; press the rectangle to the right side of the tea towel with seam at the bottom edge. Baste top edge of rectangle in place to hold.

**5.** Stitch along the marked lines of the grid through both layers.

**6.** Using a straight pin or tweezers, separate the fabrics of one square. Carefully cut a square in the top layer ⅛" from the stitched lines with the sharp tip of your scissors.

**7.** Repeat step 6, cutting alternating rows of the top layer as shown in Figure 2.

Figure 2

**8.** Stitch the rickrack over the basted top edge of the cut section.

**9.** Cut three 1½" lengths of gold pearl cotton. Clump four strands together and tie a knot around the center of the clump with the remaining length to make a bow shape. Repeat to make three bows.

**10.** Hand-stitch the bows in place on the blue rickrack.

**11.** Finish side edges of the tea towel referring to Finishing Towel Edges on page 2.

**Aqua Diamonds**
Placement Diagram 18" x 25"

## Fuchsia Fences

### Materials

- 1 purchased or self-made tea towel in desired color
- 1 fat quarter pink/white print
- Thread to match fabric
- 3 (1") circle flower motifs with fusible web already bonded to the wrong sides
- 19" length orange rickrack
- Very sharp, small, pointed-tip scissors
- See-through ruler

### Instructions

**1.** If using a purchased tea towel, remove the finished edge from one short end.

**2.** Cut a 19" x 7½" rectangle pink/white print.

**3.** Mark ½"-wide grid lines 1¾" apart on the diagonal of the print rectangle as shown in Figure 3.

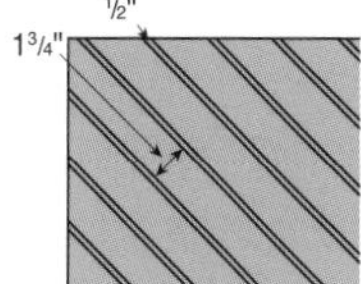

Figure 3

Figure 4

**4.** When the entire rectangle has been marked repeat step 3 on the opposite diagonal of the rectangle as shown in Figure 4.

**5.** When the entire rectangle has been marked again, draw vertical lines ½" apart at the intersections of the square corners formed from the diagonal grid as shown in Figure 5.

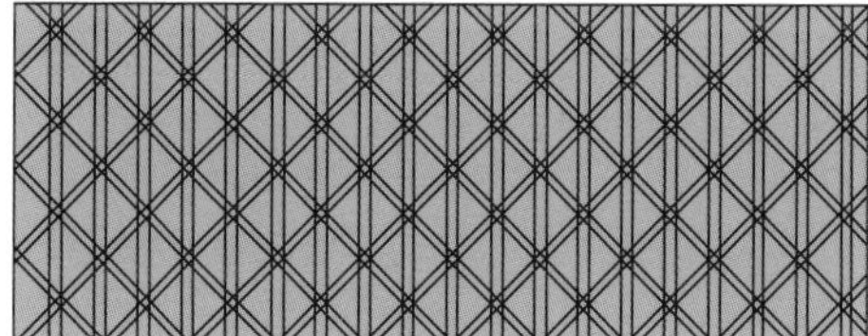
Figure 5

**6.** Repeat steps 4 and 5 of the Aqua Diamonds tea towel.

**7.** Using a straight pin or tweezers, separate the fabrics of one square. Carefully cut a triangle in the top layer ⅛" from the stitched lines with the sharp tip of your scissors as shown in Figure 6.

Figure 6

**8.** Repeat step 7, cutting out each triangle shape on the entire gridded rectangle.

**9.** Stitch the rickrack over the basted top edge of the cut section.

**10.** Remove paper backing from the circle flower motifs. Center and fuse a circle to the gridded section referring to Figure 7 for positioning; machine-appliqué each shape in place.

Figure 7

**11.** Finish side edges of the tea towel referring to Finishing Towel Edges on page 2. ❖

**Fuchsia Fences**
Placement Diagram 18" x 25"

# Faced Appliqué

## General Instructions

Faced appliqué shapes are finished on both sides. By facing the shapes, it is possible to extend them beyond the hem or to stitch only parts of them to the background to add a 3-D flavor to a tea towel. Faced appliqué adds dimension and creates more interesting border edges.

Choose 100 percent cotton, tightly woven fabrics for faced appliqué.

### Supplies & Tools

- Scissors—small, very sharp point
- Pencil or air-soluble marking pen
- Tracing paper or lightweight template plastic
- Fine-line permanent marker or pencil
- Long, thin straight pins
- All-purpose thread to match fabrics

### Preparing Faced Appliqué Shapes

The patterns given in this chapter feature a solid outside line. This will be the sewing line for joining two layers together.

Using tracing paper or lightweight template plastic, make templates using patterns given. Place the paper or plastic on the pattern drawings and carefully trace along the solid line with a pencil or fine-line permanent marker. Cut out the template on the marked lines.

Reverse the templates and place them on the wrong side of the fabrics as directed on the patterns for color and number to cut. Trace around the templates with a pencil or an air-soluble marking pen. If more than one shape is being cut from the same fabric, be sure to leave at least ½" between pieces when drawing for seam allowance beyond the stitching line.

With right sides together, pin the marked fabric to the backing fabric—that is, the facing fabric. Cut through both layers approximately ¼" from the marked line as shown in Figure 1.

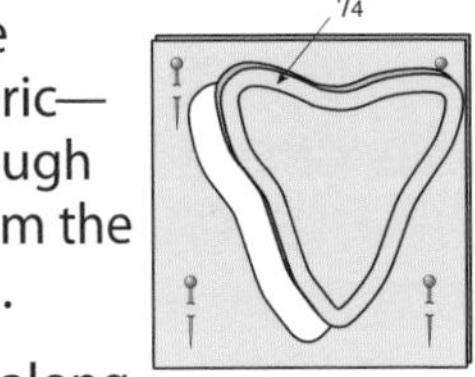


Figure 1

With the sewing machine, stitch along the marked line through the pinned layers. Trim the seam allowance to ⅛" from the stitched line. Cut perpendicular lines in the seam allowance and clip the inside corners as shown in Figure 2.

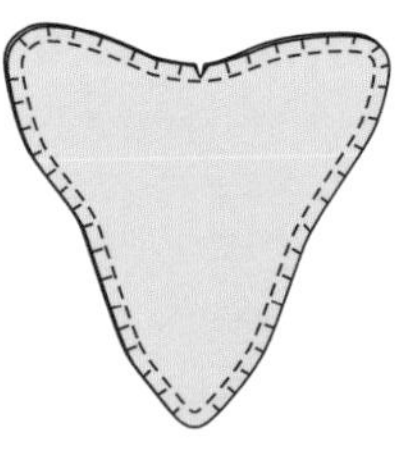

Figure 2

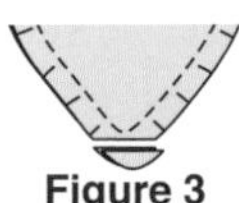

Figure 3

Trim the excess fabric from the outside corners as shown in Figure 3.

Carefully cut a diagonal line in the center of the back layer or facing piece as shown in Figure 4, being careful not to cut through the top layer.

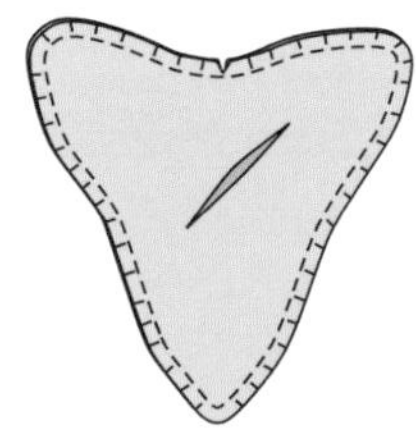

Figure 4

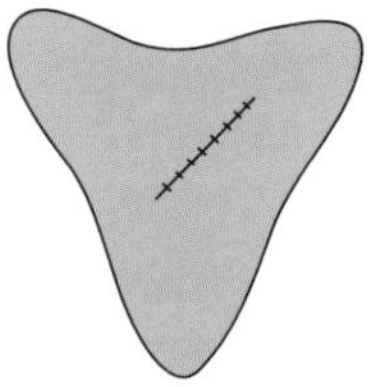

Figure 5

Turn the shape right side out through the cut opening. Use a pin to pull the seam to the outside edge and press. Slipstitch the diagonal opening closed as shown in Figure 5.

Some images are made from pieced fabric. This is accomplished by using a straight seam to machine-stitch contrasting fabrics together as shown in Figure 6.

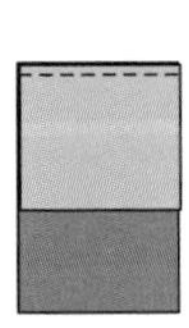

Figure 6

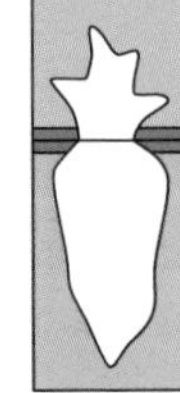

Figure 7

Press the seam allowance of these pieced sections open and place the template on the wrong side of the fabric. Align the straight, positioning line on the pattern with the seam on the piece as shown in Figure 7.

Some images are made with layered shapes. Make each shape separately and then layer them as indicated on the pattern. Slipstitch the top shape to the bottom shape with thread to match fabrics.

### Appliquéing Shapes in Place

Pin the prepared faced shapes in place on the tea towel referring to project instructions, photo of the project or the Placement Diagram for positioning suggestions.

Using a sharp needle and matching thread, knot the thread end and bring the needle up from the wrong side of the background fabric (tea towel. Pierce the pressed edge of the shape and slipstitch in place with small, evenly spaced stitches as shown in Figure 8.

Figure 8

Most of the projects in this chapter combine faced appliqué with embroidery. Complete the appliqué first and then refer to the Embroidery chapter for instructions for specific stitches. ❖

# Pastel Pretties

### Project Note

Refer to Preparing Faced Appliqué Shapes (facing page) for completing selected motifs. Refer to Stitching the Design (page 24) for stitch instructions.

## Tulips

### Materials

- 1 purchased or self-made tea towel in desired color
- 1 fat quarter each pink dot and green solid
- 3½" x 19" strip blue check fabric
- 6-strand embroidery floss: dark pink and green

### Instructions

**1.** Cut one 2¾" x 21" strip pink dot and one 1¾" x 21" strip green solid. Cut one 3¾" x 21" facing strip pink dot.

**2.** Join the 2¾" pink and 1¾" green strips with right sides together along length; press seam open.

**3.** Prepare a template for the tulip/leaf pattern using the pattern given on page 80.

**4.** Trace the pattern onto the wrong side of the pieced strip, aligning placement line between the tulip and leaf on the seam of the strips.

**5.** Finish five tulip/leaf motifs.

**6.** Remove the finished edge from the bottom of the prepared towel. Measure up 1¾" from the trimmed edge and draw a line from side to side on the right side of the towel.

**7.** Place the 3½" x 19" strip blue check right sides together matching raw edge to the marked line; stitch the strip to the towel. Press the strip to the right side.

**8.** Finish edge referring to Finishing Towel Edges on page 2.

**9.** Arrange and pin the five prepared tulip/leaf shapes on the towel with the seam between the leaf and tulip shapes aligned with the seam between the towel and the blue check strip, with the tips of the tulip flowers touching as shown in Figure 9.

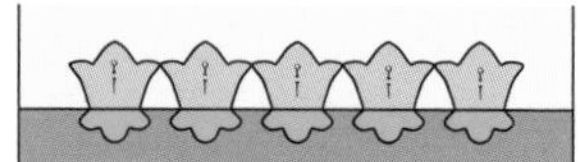

**Figure 9**

**10.** Hand-stitch shapes in place.

**11.** Add embroidery details referring to the patterns for stitch and color suggestions.

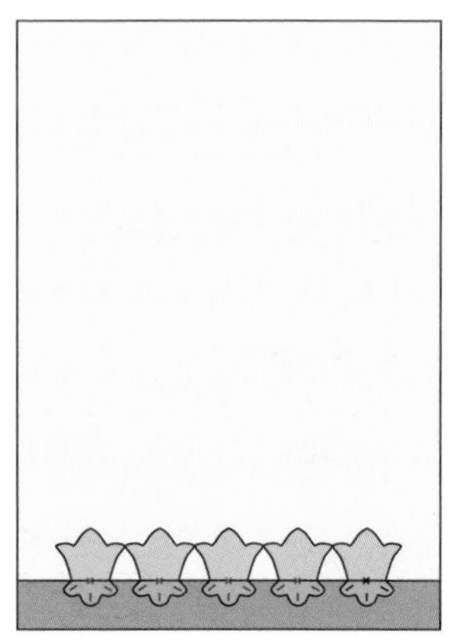

**Tulips**
Placement Diagram 18" x 25"

**Pears**
Placement Diagram 18" x 25"

## Pears

### Materials

- 1 purchased or self-made tea towel in desired color
- 1 fat quarter yellow mottled
- 1 fat eighth green solid
- 3½" x 19" strip pink-with-white dots fabric
- 6-strand embroidery floss: brown and cream

### Instructions

**1.** Cut two 1½" x 21" strips green solid, and one strip each 3½" x 21" and 4½" x 21" yellow mottled.

**2.** Sew a 1½" green strip to the 3½" yellow strip with right sides together along length.

**3.** Complete five pear/leaf motifs using the pear/leaf pattern given on page 80 and the 4½" strip yellow mottled for the pear/leaf facing referring to steps 3–5 for Tulips.

**4.** Repeat steps 6–8 for Tulips except use the 3½" x 19" pink-with-white dots strip.

**5.** Repeat steps 9 and 10 for Tulips except align top of pear with the seam between the strip and the towel referring to Figure 10.

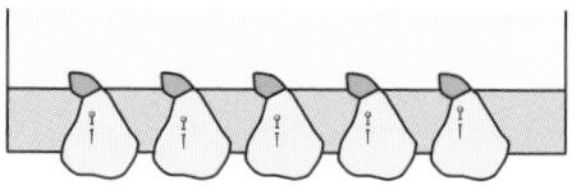

**Figure 10**

**6.** Prepare five leaf shapes using the remaining 1½" x 21" green strip for the facing.

**7.** Arrange and hand-stitch a leaf to each pear/leaf motif referring to the pattern for positioning.

**8.** Add embroidery details referring to the patterns for stitch and color suggestions.

## Baskets

### Materials

- 1 purchased or self-made tea towel in desired color
- 1 fat quarter each light blue solid and white-with-blue print
- Fat eighth red solid
- 3" x 19" strip brown solid fabric
- Blue 6-strand embroidery floss

### Instructions

**1.** Cut one strip each 1" x 21" and 3½" x 21" white-with-blue print, three 2½" x 21" strips light blue solid, and two 1½" x 9" strips red solid.

**2.** Using basket pattern given on page 80, trace the handle shapes on the wrong side of one strip light blue solid; place it right sides together with another strip light blue solid and stitch on the marked lines, leaving the short ends unstitched. Clip and trim.

**3.** Turn right side out through open ends and press flat to make five basket handles.

**4.** Make five red circles using the 1½" x 9" strips red solid, referring to Preparing the Faced Appliqué Shapes on page 76. Satin-stitch a circle in the center of the red circle with 2 strands of blue embroidery floss.

**5.** Sew the 1" white-with-blue strip to the remaining 2½" strip light blue strip with right sides together along length; press seam open.

**6.** Trace the basket shape on the wrong side of the stitched strips, aligning line on pattern with seam between strips.

**7.** Pin a prepared handle shape on the right side of the traced basket shape referring to pattern for positioning; pin the 3½"-wide white-with-blue strip right sides together with the pinned handle and basket layer, and stitch on the marked lines. ***Note:*** *The ends of the handle should be between the facing and the basket front when turned right side out.*

**8.** Complete five basket motifs.

**9.** Center and hand-stitch a red circle on each basket referring to the pattern for positioning.

**10.** Repeat steps 6–8 for Tulips except use the 3"-wide brown solid strip and measure up 1¼" from trimmed edge before marking line.

**11.** Repeat steps 9 and 10 for Tulips except align top of basket shapes (not handle) ⅜" below seam between the towel and the strip with the sides of the baskets touching referring to Figure 11 to finish.

Figure 11

**Baskets**
Placement Diagram 18" x 25"

# Bows

## Materials

- 1 purchased or self-made tea towel in desired color
- Fabric scraps: medium blue and aqua solids
- 2¼" x 19" coral solid fabric
- 3½" length aqua rickrack
- ⅝" white button
- 6-strand embroidery floss: light blue and pink

## Instructions

**1.** Complete two bow motifs using the medium blue scrap for top and facing sides. Slipstitch the bow shapes to the tail shapes.

**2.** Add embroidery details using 2 strands of embroidery floss as directed on the pattern.

**3.** Cut two 1" x 2" rectangles aqua scrap. Fold the long sides of each rectangle to the wrong side ⅛" and press.

**4.** Wrap a folded rectangle around each bow motif; hand-stitch together on the back side, pulling the rectangle a bit to slightly gather the bows.

**5.** Repeat steps 6–8 for Tulips except use the 2¼" x 19" coral strip and measure up ¾" from trimmed edge before marking line.

**6.** Center and hand-stitch a bow motif ¾" from the seam between the towel and the coral strip.

**7.** Repeat with the second bow motif 2" above the first motif.

**8.** Center and sew the 3½" length of rickrack between the two stitched motifs. Sew the button in the center of the rickrack strip to finish. ❖

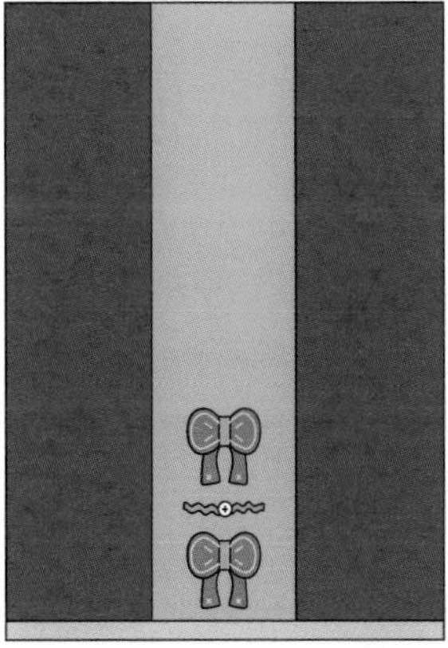
**Bows**
Placement Diagram 18" x 25"

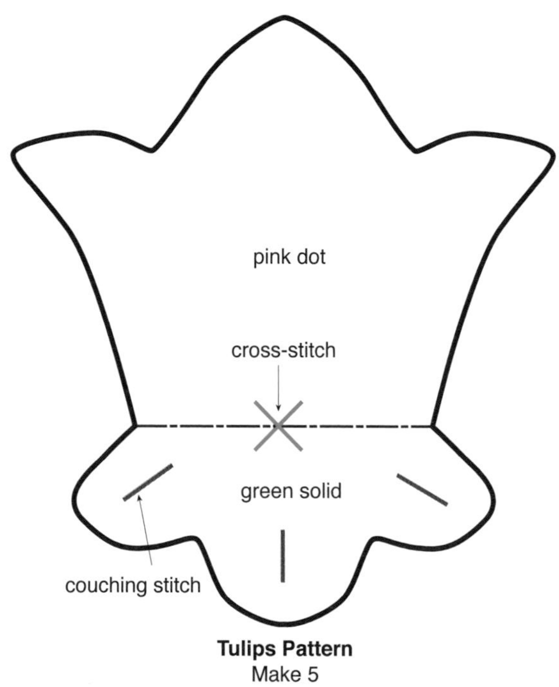


**Tulips Pattern**
Make 5

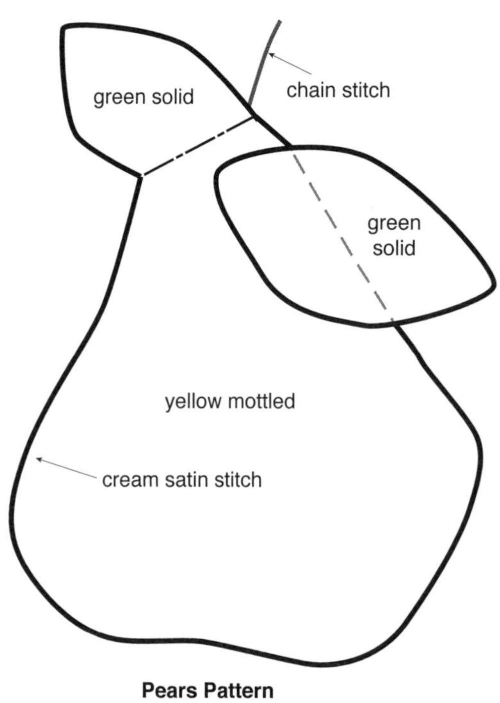


**Pears Pattern**
Make 5 of each piece

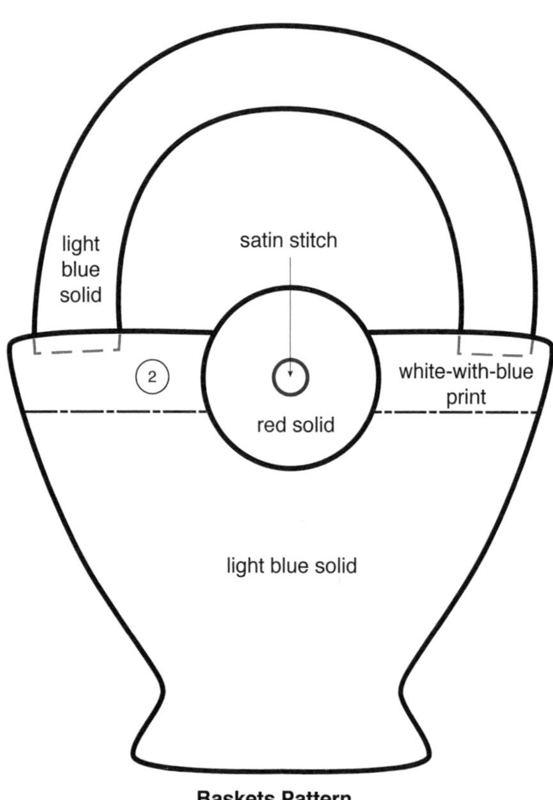


**Baskets Pattern**
Make 5 of each piece

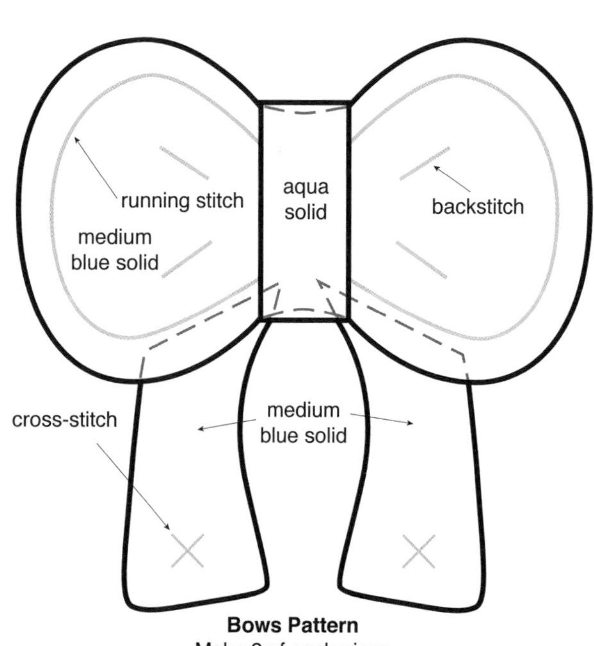


**Bows Pattern**
Make 2 of each piece

# Dimensional Dryers

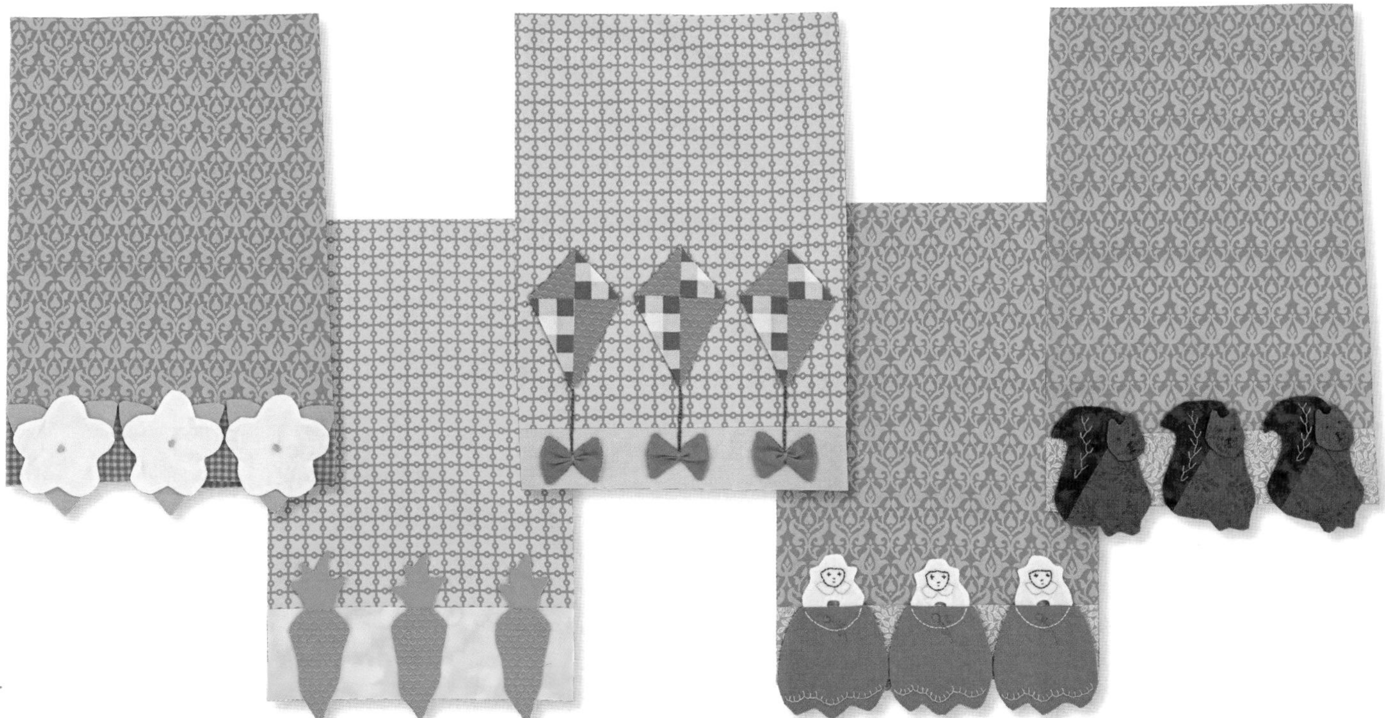

## Project Note

Refer to Preparing Faced Appliqué Shapes (page 76) for completing selected motifs. Refer to Stitching the Design (page 24) for stitch instructions.

## Carrot Crop

### Materials

- 1 purchased or self-made tea towel in desired color
- 1 fat quarter each orange tonal and bright green solid
- 4" x 19" strip yellow mottled fabric
- Light green 6-strand embroidery floss

### Instructions

**1.** Fold the towel in half along length and crease to mark the center.

**2.** Remove the finished edge from the bottom of the prepared towel. Measure up 2¼" from the trimmed edge and draw a line from side to side on the right side of the towel.

**3.** Place the 4" x 19" strip yellow mottled right sides together matching raw edge to the marked line; stitch the strip to the towel. Press the strip to the right side.

**4.** Finish edge referring to Finishing Towel Edges on page 2.

**5.** Cut one 2¾" x 21" strip bright green solid and one 4" x 21" strip orange tonal. Cut one 5½" x 21" facing strip orange tonal.

**6.** Join the 2¾" bright green and 4" orange strips with right sides together along length; press seam open.

**7.** Prepare a template for the carrot/leaf using the pattern given on page 85.

**8.** Trace the pattern onto the wrong side of the pieced strip, aligning placement line between the carrot and leaf on the seam of the strips.

**9.** Finish five carrot motifs.

**10.** Add couching stitches using 2 strands light green embroidery floss to complete the carrot motifs.

**11.** Pin one carrot motif on the bottom center of the tea towel with placement

**Carrot Crop**
Placement Diagram 18" x 25"

line between the carrot top and bottom aligned with the seam of the yellow mottled strip; hand-stitch in place.

**12.** Arrange and hand-stitch remaining carrot motifs in place with two on each side of the center motif and 1⅛" apart to finish.

## Kites a Flyin'

### Materials

- 1 purchased or self-made tea towel in desired color
- 1 fat quarter each blue check, green tonal and turquoise solid
- 3" x 21" strip lavender solid fabric
- 6-strand embroidery floss: turquoise and dark blue

### Instructions

**1.** Fold the towel in half along length and crease to mark the center.

**2.** Remove the finished edge from the bottom of the prepared towel. Measure up ¼" from the trimmed edge and draw a line from side to side on the right side of the towel.

**3.** Place the 3" x 21" strip lavender solid right sides together matching raw edge to the marked line; stitch the strip to the towel. Press the strip to the right side.

**4.** Finish edge referring to Finishing Towel Edges on page 2.

**5.** Cut two 3" x 21" strips each blue check and green tonal. Cut two 5" x 21" facing strips green tonal.

**6.** Sew a blue check strip to a green tonal strip along the length to make a strip set; press. Repeat to make two strip sets. Subcut strip sets into (10) 3" squares as shown in Figure 12.

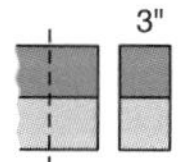

Figure 12

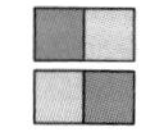
Figure 13

**7.** Join two segments from step 6 to make a Four-Patch unit as shown in Figure 13; press. Repeat to make five units.

**8.** Refer to steps 6–9 of Carrot Crop to make five kite motifs, aligning the template on the Four-Patch, matching intersections of units with template placement lines as shown in Figure 14 and using the 5" x 21" green tonal strips as the facing.

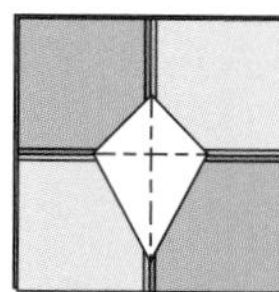
Figure 14

**9.** Repeat step 8 to make five bow motifs using turquoise solid for bows and facing.

**10.** Center and hand-stitch one kite motif with bottom point of kite 1" from the lavender border.

**11.** Arrange and hand-stitch two kite motifs on each side of the center motif with corners ⅜" apart.

**12.** Mark a straight line from bottom tip of kite to within ¾" of bottom edge of the tea towel.

**13.** Add embroidery details referring to the patterns for stitch and color suggestions.

**14.** Using 3 strands turquoise embroidery floss, wrap the floss around the center of each bow several times to pinch into a bow shape; knot to hold.

**15.** Hand-stitch a bow to the bottom of each chain-stitched line with tip of bows ¼" from bottom edge of tea towel to finish.

**Kites a Flyin'**
Placement Diagram 18" x 25"

## Snowdrops

### Materials

- 1 purchased or self-made tea towel in desired color
- 1 fat quarter each white and light green solids
- 4½" x 21" strip blue check fabric
- Turquoise 6-strand embroidery floss

### Instructions

**1.** Fold the towel in half along length and crease to mark the center.

2. Remove the finished edge from the bottom of the prepared towel. Measure up 1¾" from the trimmed edge and draw a line from side to side on the right side of the towel.

3. Place the 4½" x 21" strip blue check right sides together matching raw edge to the marked line; stitch the strip to the towel. Press the strip to the right side.

4. Finish edge referring to Finishing Towel Edges on page 2.

5. Referring to steps 6–9 of Carrot Crop, prepare five each flower and leaf motifs using matching-fabric facing pieces.

6. Layer a flower on a leaf referring to the placement lines for positioning; slipstitch together on overlapped edges.

7. Using 2 strands turquoise embroidery floss, satin-stitch flower centers.

8. Center and hand-stitch a flower/leaf motif with one leaf extending beyond the bottom edge of the tea towel referring to the Placement Diagram for positioning.

9. Stitch two flower/leaf motifs on each side of the center motifs with edges of leaves not quite touching to finish.

**Snowdrops**
Placement Diagram 18" x 25"

## Merry Maids

### Materials

- 1 purchased or self-made tea towel in desired color
- 1 fat quarter each white and dark turquoise solids
- 4½" x 21" strip pink/white print fabric
- 6-strand embroidery floss: white, dark brown, turquoise and orange

### Instructions

1. Fold the towel in half along length and crease to mark the center.

2. Remove the finished edge from the bottom of the prepared towel. Measure up 1¾" from the trimmed edge and draw a line from side to side on the right side of the towel.

3. Place the 4½" x 21" strip pink/white print right sides together matching raw edge to the marked line; stitch the strip to the towel. Press the strip to the right side.

4. Finish edge referring to Finishing Towel Edges on page 2.

5. Cut two 2¾" x 21" strips white solid and two 3¾" x 21" strips dark turquoise solid.

6. Prepare five head motifs from white solid strip using matching-fabric facing pieces, leaving bottom edges open.

7. Trace the skirt shapes as directed on the wrong side of one 3¾" x 21" dark turquoise strip. Mark the center of each skirt shape.

8. Pin a prepared head shape right side against the right side of the strip on the top edge of a traced skirt shape, aligning center of head shapes with marked center of skirt shapes referring to Figure 15. ***Note:*** *The marked skirt shape will be not be on the side of the strip to which the head shape is pinned. The marked center will be the important matching mark when positioning the head piece.* Pin the remaining 3¾"-wide dark turquoise strip right sides together with the pinned head and skirt layer, and stitch on the marked lines. ***Note:*** *The ends of the head should be between the facing and the skirt front when turned right side out.*

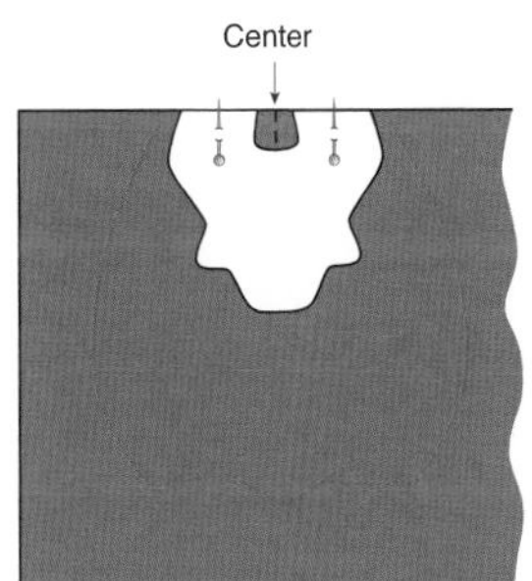


**Figure 15**

9. Referring to steps 6–9 of Carrot Crop finish five merry maids motifs.

10. Add embroidery details referring to the patterns for stitch and color suggestions.

**11.** Center a merry maid motif with head/skirt seam aligned with seam between the pink/white print strip and the tea towel; hand-stitch in place.

**12.** Pin and stitch two merry maid motifs on each side of the center motif with skirt edges almost touching to finish.

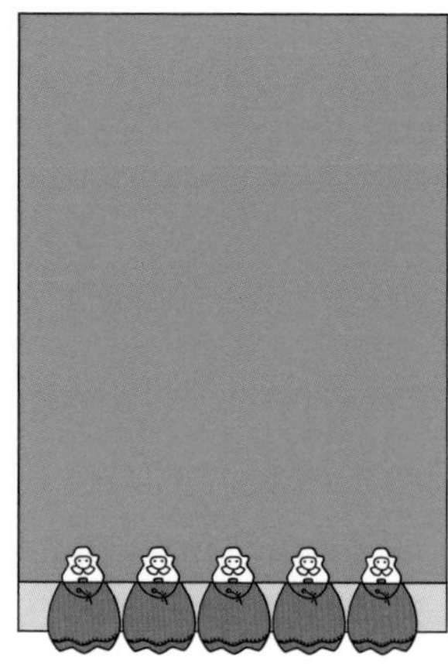

**Merry Maids**
Placement Diagram 18" x 25"

## Squirrel Friends

### Materials

- 1 purchased or self-made tea towel in desired color
- 1 fat quarter each medium brown tonal and rust/brown mottled
- 4½" x 21" strip pink/white print fabric
- 6-strand embroidery floss: tan, navy and rust/brown

### Instructions

**1.** Fold the towel in half along length and crease to mark the center.

**2.** Remove the finished edge from the bottom of the prepared towel. Measure up 1¾" from the trimmed edge and draw a line from side to side on the right side of the towel.

**3.** Place the 4½" x 21" strip pink/white print right sides together matching raw edge to the marked line; stitch the strip to the towel. Press the strip to the right side.

**4.** Finish edge referring to Finishing Towel Edges on page 2.

**5.** Cut one 2½" x 21" strip rust/brown mottled. Cut one each 2¾" x 21" and 4½" x 21" facing strip medium brown tonal.

**6.** Sew the 2½" and 2¾" strips together along length; press seam open.

**7.** Trace the squirrel body shape on the wrong side of the stitched strips, aligning pattern placement line with seam between strips.

**8.** Referring to steps 6–9 of Carrot Crop, complete five squirrel body motifs and five squirrel head motifs.

**9.** Add embroidery details referring to the patterns for stitch and color suggestions.

**10.** Place a head shape on a body shape; hand-stitch in place. Repeat to complete five squirrel motifs.

**11.** Center a squirrel motif with the tip of the tail aligned with seam between the pink/white print strip and the tea towel; hand-stitch in place.

**12.** Pin and stitch two squirrel motifs ⅜" apart on each side of the center motif. ❖

**Squirrel Friends**
Placement Diagram 18" x 25"

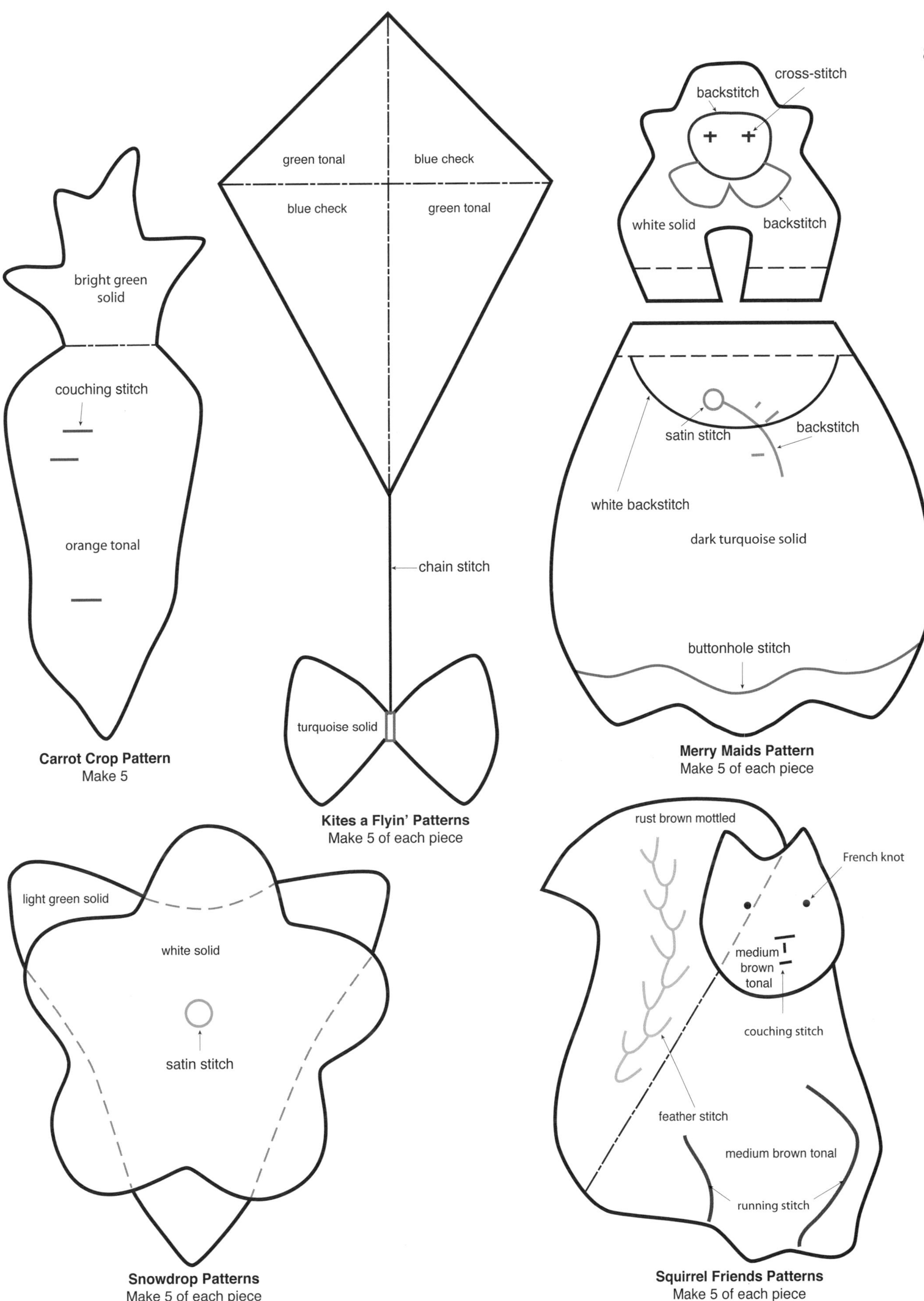


**Carrot Crop Pattern**
Make 5

**Kites a Flyin' Patterns**
Make 5 of each piece

**Merry Maids Pattern**
Make 5 of each piece

**Snowdrop Patterns**
Make 5 of each piece

**Squirrel Friends Patterns**
Make 5 of each piece

# Hand Appliqué

## General Instructions

Hand appliqué is a sort of fabric collage that allows for versatile compositions. The designs have a softer appearance than those that are pieced because of layered colors and the introduction of curved shapes. Hand or needle-turn appliqué means that you turn a narrow seam allowance under and slipstitch it to the background.

### Supplies & Tools

- Scissors—small, very sharp point
- Pencil or air-soluble marking pen
- Fine-line permanent marker or pencil
- Tracing paper or lightweight template plastic
- Long, thin straight pins
- Appliqué sewing needle—a fine needle with a sharp tip, preferably No. 11 or 12
- All-purpose thread to match fabrics

### Preparing the Appliqué Shapes

Hand-appliqué patterns are given without any turn-under seam allowance. This seam allowance will be added when cutting the shape from the fabric.

Using tracing paper or lightweight template plastic, make templates using patterns given. Place the paper or plastic on the pattern drawings and carefully trace along the solid line with a pencil or fine-line permanent marker.

Place the templates on the right side of the fabrics as directed on the patterns for color and number to cut. Trace around the templates with a fine-point pencil or an air-soluble marking pen. If more than one shape is being cut from the same fabric, be sure to leave at least ½" seam allowance area between pieces when drawing.

Cut out shapes, leaving ¼" all around for seam allowance.

The marked line is the exact line for turning edges under, and it should not be visible when the piece has been applied.

Carefully clip the seam allowances perpendicular to the marked line at concave and convex curves, and clip into inside corners as shown in Figure 1. Trim excess fabric from the outside corners.

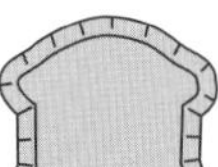

Figure 1

### Hand Appliqué

Noting the gray dashed overlap lines on patterns and numbers that indicate the order of piecing, pin the first shape (No. 1) in place in the suggested location on the tea towel. Turn the seam allowance under at the marked line and make a crease with your fingers. Knot the thread and bring the needle up from the wrong side of the background fabric. Pierce the folded edge of the shape and slipstitch the appliqué piece in place with small, evenly spaced stitches as shown in Figure 2.

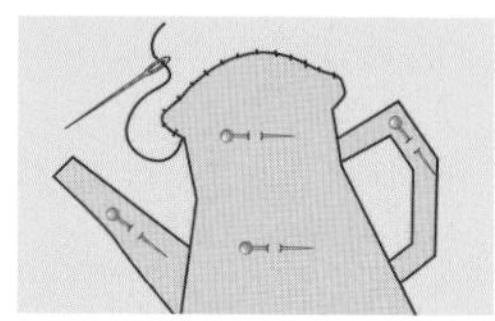

Figure 2

Do not turn under seam allowance on edges that are covered by another piece to reduce bulk.

Make smaller stitches at points and corners.

Many of the projects in this chapter combine hand appliqué with embroidery. Complete the appliqué first, and then refer to the pattern and the Embroidery chapter on page 24 for instructions for specific stitches.

### Reverse Appliqué

When the top layer of fabric is turned under and stitched to a lower fabric shape, it is called reverse appliqué. To accomplish this, the template for the underneath piece is cut with a ⅛"–¼" seam allowance all around.

The top piece is cut leaving a seam allowance in the opening to turn under as shown in Figure 3.

Figure 3

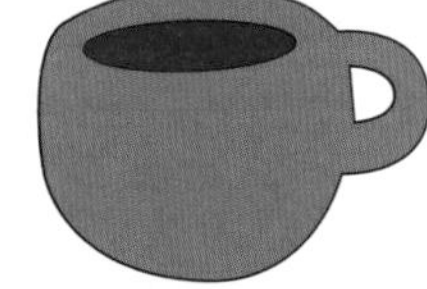

Figure 4

The seam allowance around the open area is folded to the back side along the marked line, placed on top of the underneath piece and slipstitched in place as shown in Figure 4. The black "coffee" area of the cups in the Vintage Kitchen towel set uses the reverse appliqué technique.

### General Project Instructions

**1.** Fold and crease the tea towel along length to mark the center.

**2.** Refer to Preparing the Appliqué Shapes to cut out the appliqué patterns.

**3.** Refer to Hand Appliqué section to appliqué patterns to the tea towel, layering and stitching pieces in numerical order, starting 1" from bottom edge and ½" on each side of the center crease with ½" between the top and bottom shapes.

**4.** Add embroidery details referring to the patterns for stitch and color suggestions, and referring to the Embroidery chapter for stitch instructions to finish. ❖

---

# Tea Party

## Mrs. Teapot

### Materials

- 1 purchased or self-made tea towel in desired color
- Fabric scraps: light pink and yellow/green solid
- 2½" x 7¾" rectangle cream/pink floral fabric
- 1 fat quarter medium pink solid
- 2¼" x 19" strip gold print fabric
- 4¼"-length light green rickrack
- 6-strand embroidery floss: dark pink, green, blue and brown

### Instructions

**1.** If using a finished tea towel, remove the bottom finished edge. Measure up ¾" from the trimmed edge and draw a line from side to side.

**2.** Finish edge using the gold print strip referring to Finishing Towel Edges on page 2.

**3.** Prepare templates for teapot and appliqué in place referring to steps 1–3 of the General Project Instructions above to complete the Mrs. Teapot tea towel, placing the cream/pink floral rectangle 1½" from the seam between the tea towel and the gold print strip.

**5.** Sew the piece of rickrack to the tea towel ¼" below the bottom edge of the floral rectangle.

**6.** Add embroidery details referring to the patterns for stitch and color suggestions, and referring to the Embroidery chapter for stitch instructions to finish.

**Mrs. Teapot**
Placement Diagram 18" x 25"

**Flower Friends**
Placement Diagram 18" x 25"

## Flower Friends

### Materials

- 1 purchased or self-made tea towel in desired color
- Fabric scraps: light and dark pink prints, and yellow solid
- 2¼" x 19" strip gold print
- 4¼"-length light green rickrack
- 6-strand embroidery floss: dark pink, green, blue, pink, yellow and brown

### Instructions

**1.** Refer to the instructions for Mrs. Teapot to complete the Flower Friends tea towel. ❖

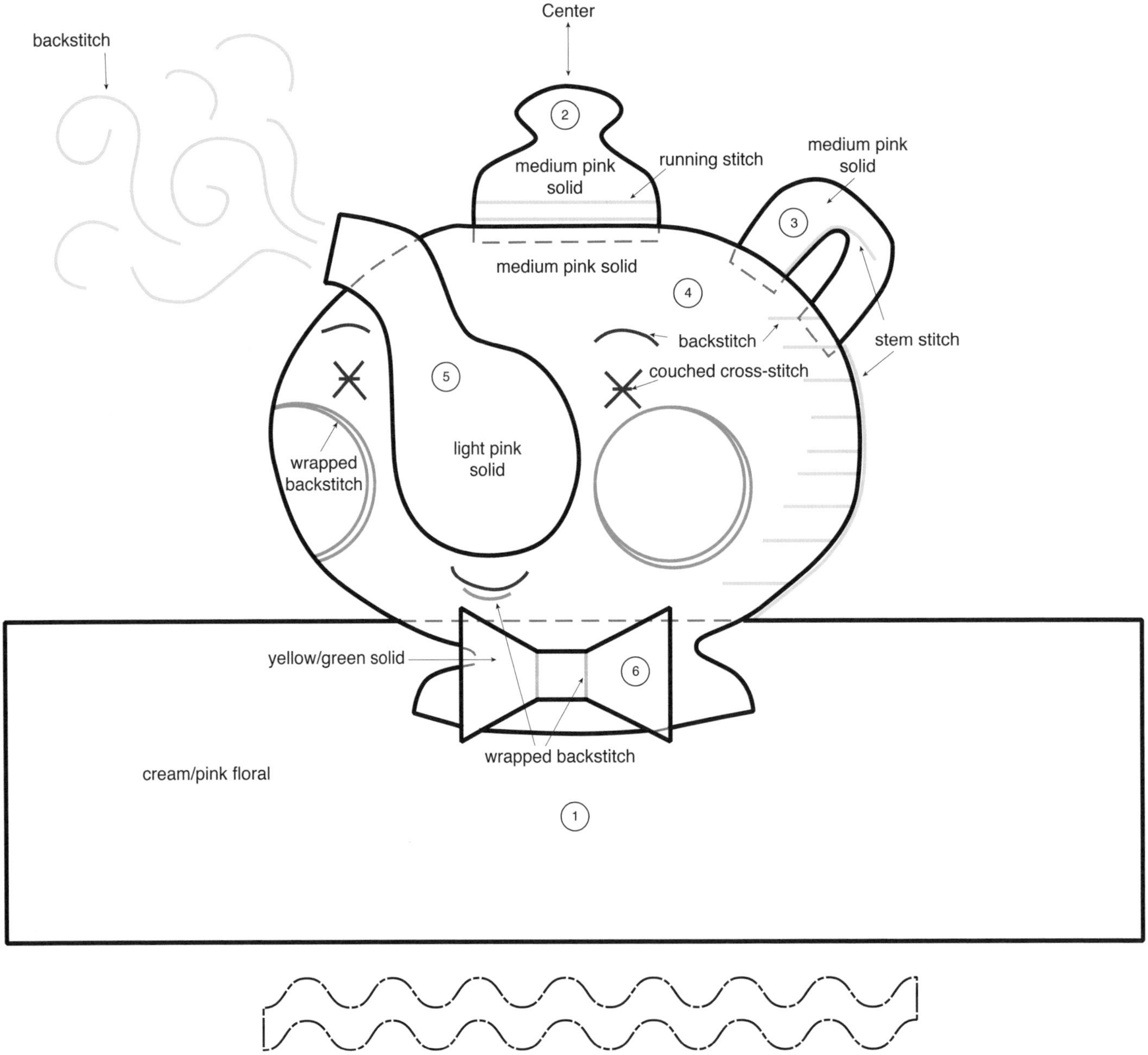

Center
backstitch
2
medium pink solid
running stitch
medium pink solid
3
medium pink solid
4
backstitch
stem stitch
couched cross-stitch
5
light pink solid
wrapped backstitch
yellow/green solid
6
wrapped backstitch
cream/pink floral
1

**Mrs. Teapot Pattern**

**Flower Friends Pattern**
All unmarked stitches are wrapped backstitch.

# Vintage Kitchen

## Salt 'n' Pepper

### Materials

- 1 purchased or self-made tea towel in desired color
- Fabric scraps: gray and black solids, and cream tonal
- 6-strand embroidery floss: black and light gray

### Instructions

**1.** Prepare templates for the salt and pepper shakers, and refer to steps 1–4 of the General Project Instructions (page 87) to complete the tea towel.

**Salt 'n' Pepper**
Placement Diagram 18" x 25"

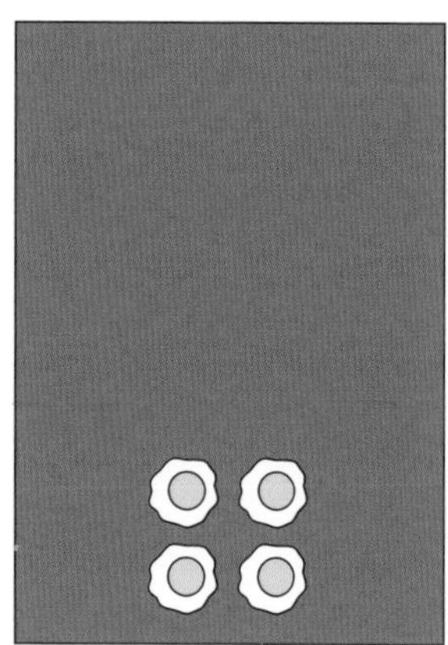

**Sunny-Side Up**
Placement Diagram 18" x 25"

## Sunny-Side Up

### Materials

- 1 purchased or self-made tea towel in desired color
- Fabric scraps: white and gold solids

### Instructions

**1.** Prepare templates for egg and yolk pieces, and refer to steps 1–3 of the General Project Instructions (page 87) to complete the Sunny-Side Up tea towel.

## Coffee Time

### Materials

- 1 purchased or self-made tea towel in desired color
- Scrap black solid fabric
- 1 fat quarter each gray and red solids
- 6-strand embroidery floss: gold, black, white and gray
- ¼" melon-color button

### Instructions

**1.** Refer to Preparing the Appliqué Shapes on page 86 to cut out coffeepot and cup shapes.

**2.** Prepare the cups for reverse appliqué, placing the red cup on top of the black coffee referring to Reverse Appliqué instructions on page 86.

**3.** Refer to steps 1–4 of the General Project Instructions (page 87) to complete the Coffee Time tea towel, except place the lower cup 1" from the bottom edge of the tea towel and remaining pieces as desired referring to the pattern and Placement Diagram for positioning.

**4.** Sew the button to the top center of the coffeepot.

**Coffee Time**
Placement Diagram 18" x 25"

**Time for Toast**
Placement Diagram 18" x 25"

## Time for Toast

### Materials

- 1 purchased or self-made tea towel in desired color
- Fabric scraps: white, cream, brown, black, turquoise and blue solids
- 1 fat quarter green solid
- 6-strand embroidery floss: purple, rust and royal blue

### Instructions

**1.** Prepare templates for toaster and small flower, and refer to steps 1–4 of the General Project Instructions (page 87) to complete the Time for Toast tea towel, placing the toaster 1⅛" from the edge of the tea towel and the flower 1" above the toast referring to the pattern and Placement Diagram for positioning. ❖

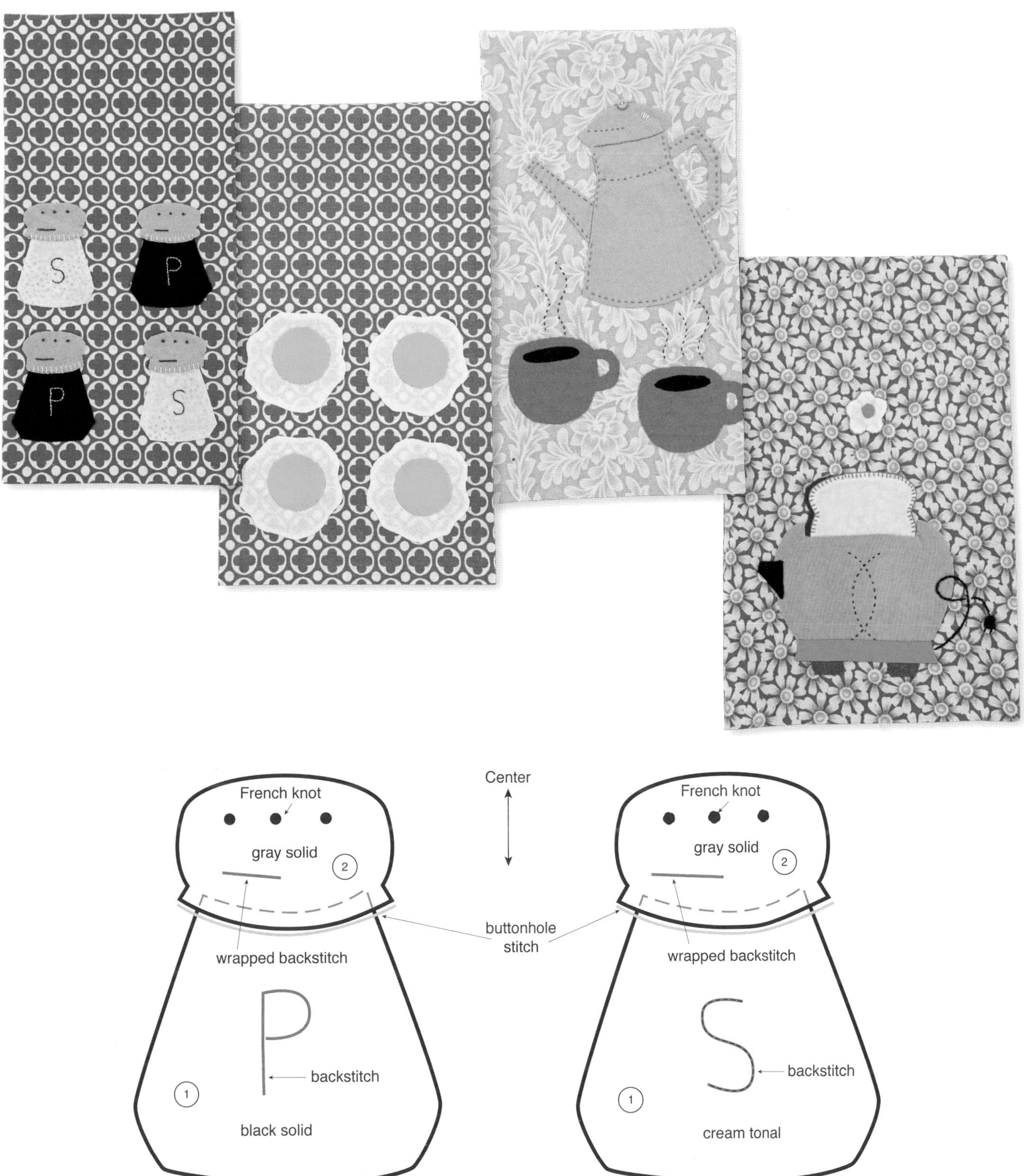


**Salt 'n' Pepper Pattern**
Make 2 of each

**Coffee Time Pattern**

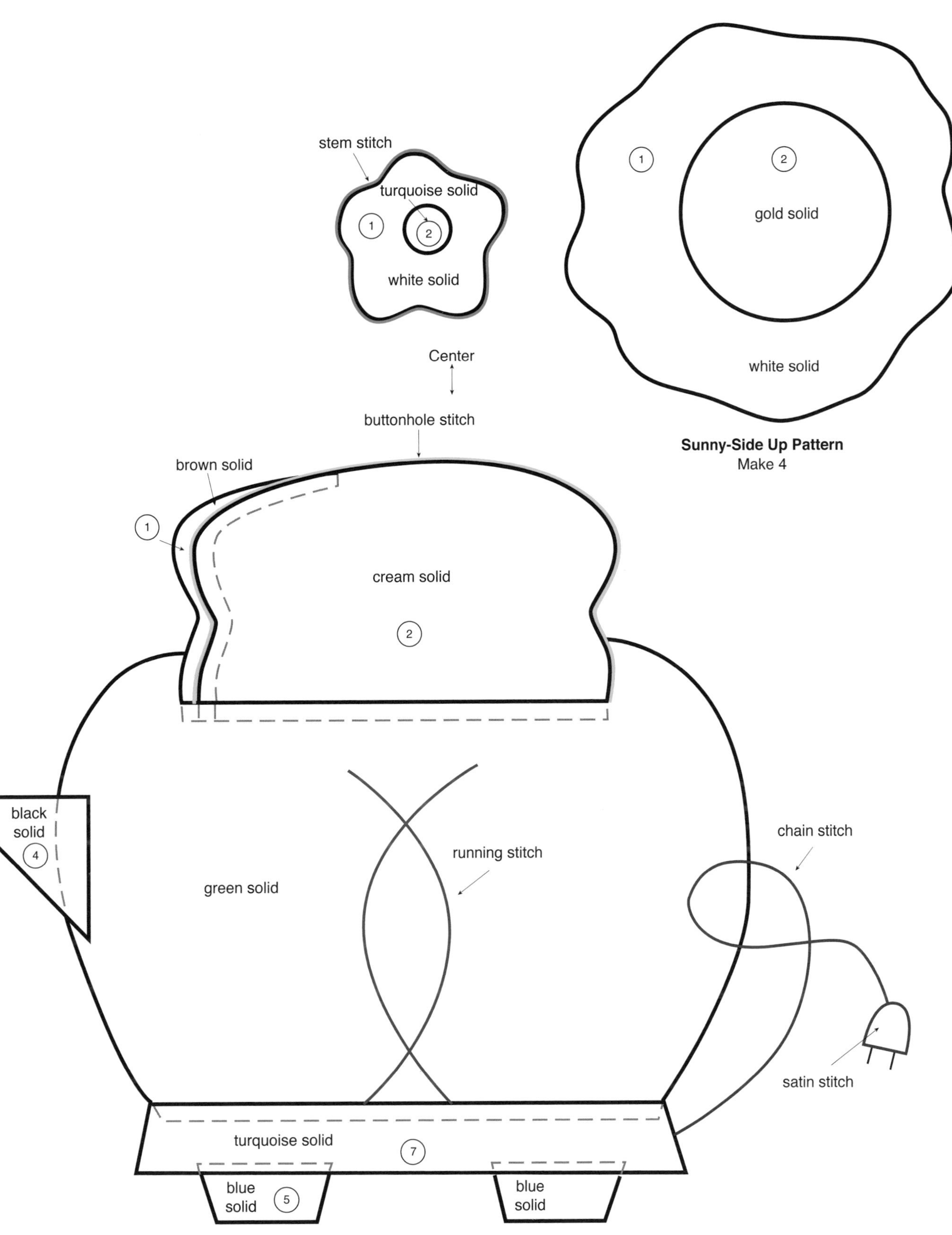


**Sunny-Side Up Pattern**
Make 4

**Time for Toast Pattern**

# Blanket-Stitch Beauties

## Golden Bows

### Materials

- 1 purchased or self-made tea towel in desired color
- 1 fat quarter each gold and tan solids
- 6-strand embroidery floss: rust and gold

### Instructions

**1.** Refer to the General Project Instructions (page 87) with ¾" between motifs and 1" between the bottom of the towel and the lower motif to complete the appliqué.

**2.** Refer to chart and Making Cross-Stitches on page 114 to complete the Golden Bows tea towel.

## Flower Basket

### Materials

- 1 purchased or self-made tea towel in desired color
- Fabric scraps: lavender, red and blue solids
- 6-strand embroidery floss: yellow, tan, and light and medium green

### Instructions

**1.** Refer to the General Project Instructions (page 87) with 1½" between the bottom of the towel and the motif to complete the Flower Basket tea towel. ❖

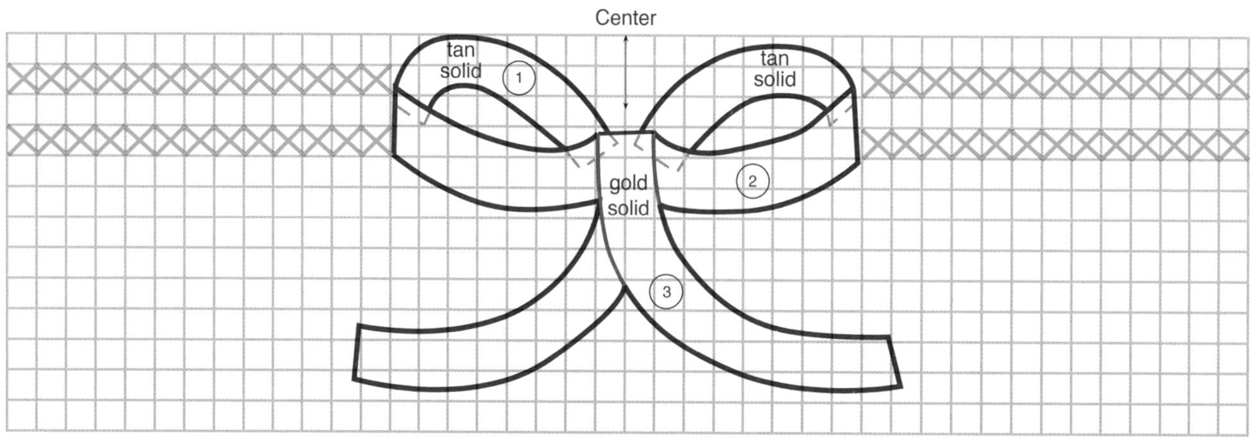


**Golden Bows Chart**
All edges of bow are blanket-stitched using rust embroidery floss.

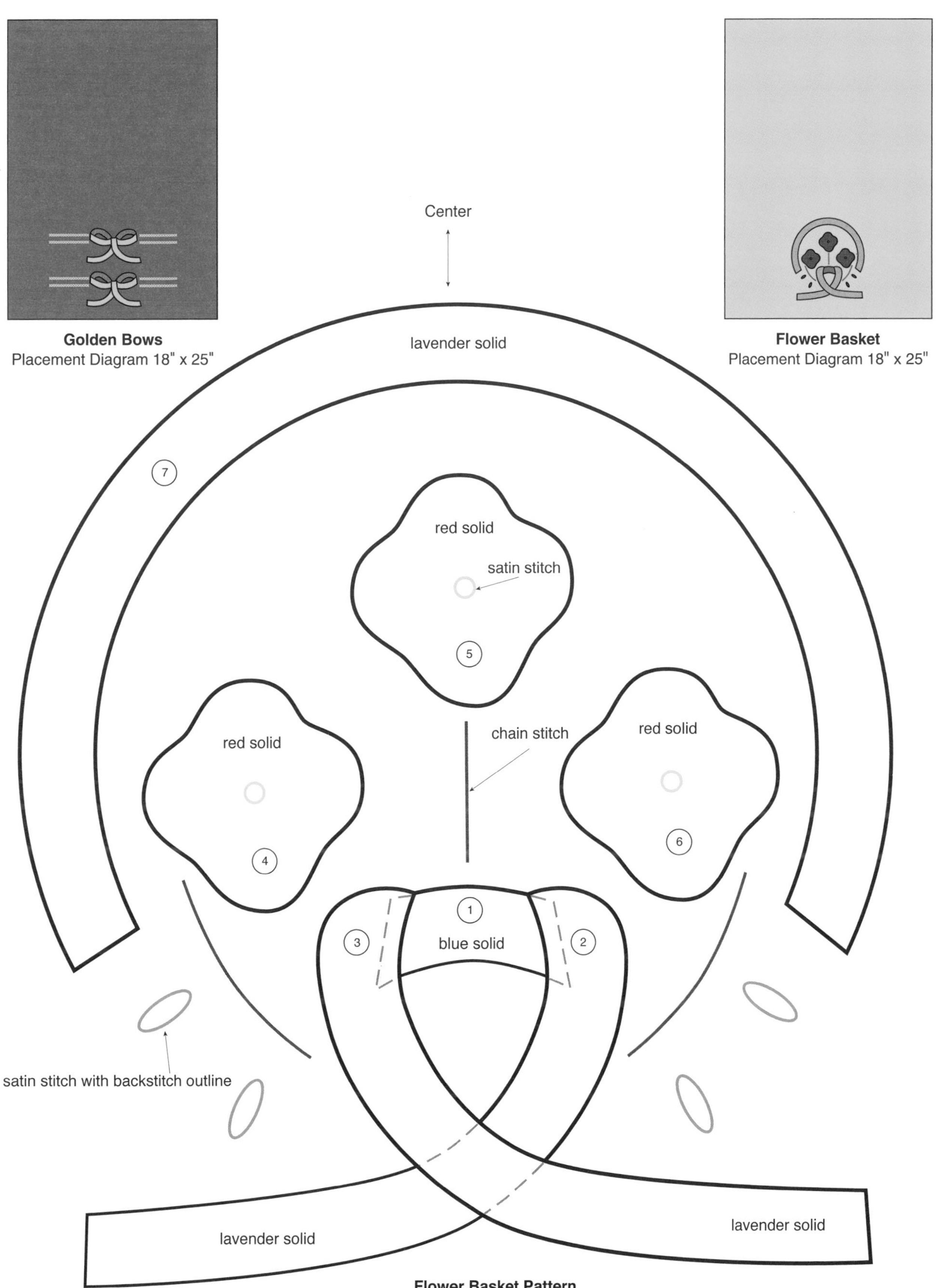


**Flower Basket Pattern**

All edges of appliqué shapes are blanket-stitched using tan embroidery floss.

# Antebellum Ladies

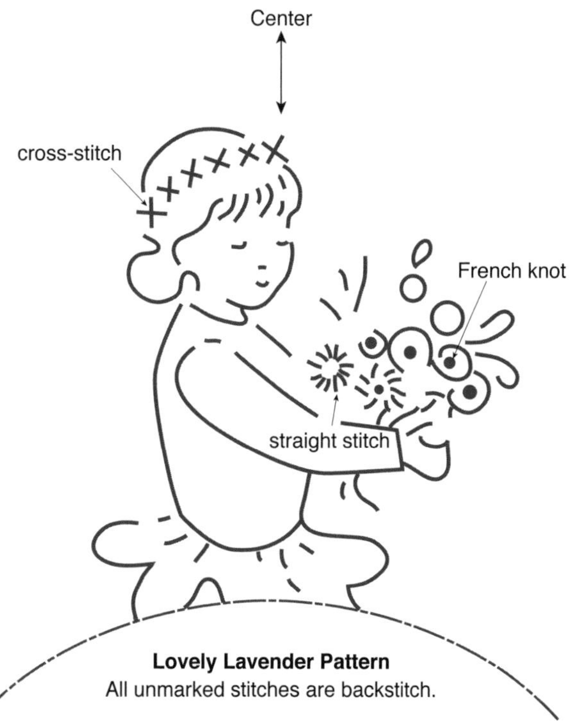


**Lovely Lavender Pattern**
All unmarked stitches are backstitch.

**Blushing Rose Pattern**
All unmarked stitches are backstitch.

## Lovely Lavender

### Materials

- 1 purchased or self-made tea towel in desired color
- 4½" x 7½" rectangle purple floral fabric
- 4½" x 19" strip green print fabric
- 12" piece blue trim
- Dark blue 6-strand embroidery floss

### Instructions

**1.** If using a finished tea towel, remove the bottom finished edge. Measure up 2¾" from the trimmed edge and draw a line from side to side.

**2.** Fold and crease tea towel along the length to mark the center.

**3.** Prepare template for skirt opening.

**4.** Center and trace the shape onto the tea towel aligning straight edge with the drawn line; cut out shape from tea towel. Turn under opening edges ¼".

**5.** Place the purple floral rectangle under the opening.

**6.** Hand-stitch the edges of the towel to the rectangle to complete reverse appliqué.

**7.** Machine-stitch trim along appliquéd edge; echo the shape with a machine stitching line ⅛" from the edge of the motif.

**8.** Trim excess rectangle on the back side even with the edge of the turned-under towel edge.

**9.** Finish edge using the green print strip referring to Finishing Towel Edges on page 2.

**10.** Center and transfer the embroidery design above the skirt motif.

**11.** Add embroidery details using 2 strands of embroidery floss as directed on the pattern and referring to the Embroidery chapter (page 24).

## Blushing Rose

### Materials

- 1 purchased or self-made tea towel in desired color
- 4½" x 7½" rectangle green floral fabric
- 4½" x 19" strip pink tonal fabric
- 12" length multicolored trim
- Dark purple 6-strand embroidery floss

### Instructions

**1.** Complete the Blushing Rose tea towel as for Lovely Lavender tea towel. ❖

**Blushing Rose**
Placement Diagram 18" x 25"

**Lovely Lavender**
Placement Diagram 18" x 25"

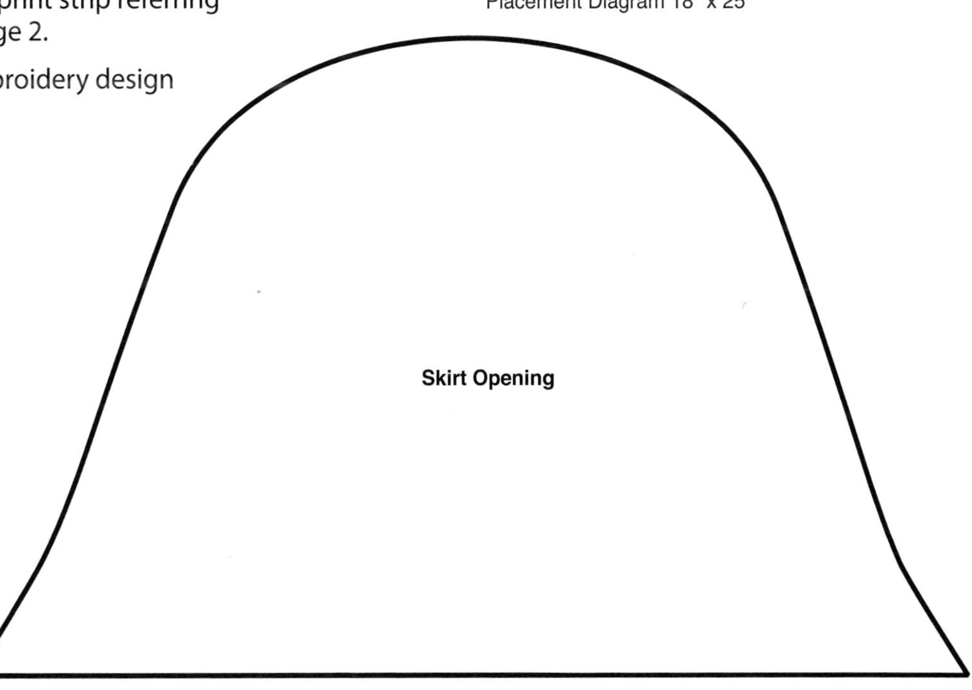

# Row by Row

## Clover Square

### Materials

- 1 purchased or self-made tea towel in desired color
- 1 fat quarter green check
- 6-strand embroidery floss: light and medium green

### Instructions

**1.** Refer to the General Project Instructions (page 87) with 1" between the bottom of the towel and the lower motifs, 1½" between top and bottom motifs, and 1" between motifs from side to side to complete the Clover Square tea towel.

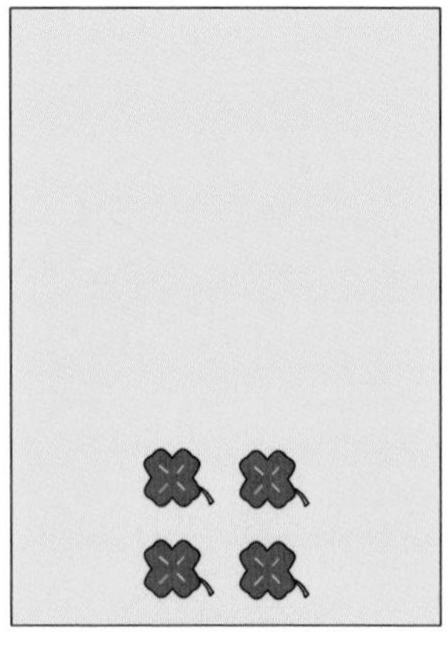

**Clover Square**
Placement Diagram 18" x 25"

**Perfect Pansies**
Placement Diagram 18" x 25"

## Perfect Pansies

### Materials

- 1 purchased or self-made tea towel in desired color
- Scrap blue solid fabric
- 1 fat quarter purple mottled
- 6-strand embroidery floss: gold, green, light blue and purple

### Instructions

**1.** Refer to the General Project Instructions (page 87) with 1" between the bottom of the towel and the lower motifs, 1⅛" between the top and bottom motifs, and ¾" between motifs from side to side to complete the Perfect Pansies tea towel.

## The Mighty Oak

### Materials

- 1 purchased or self-made tea towel in desired color
- Fabric scraps: tan and light green solids, and brown mottled
- 6-strand embroidery floss: brown and tan

### Instructions

**1.** Refer to the General Project Instructions (page 87) with 2" between the bottom of the towel and the lower motifs, and ¾" between motifs from top to bottom and side to side to complete The Mighty Oak tea towel. ❖

**The Mighty Oak**
Placement Diagram 18" x 25"

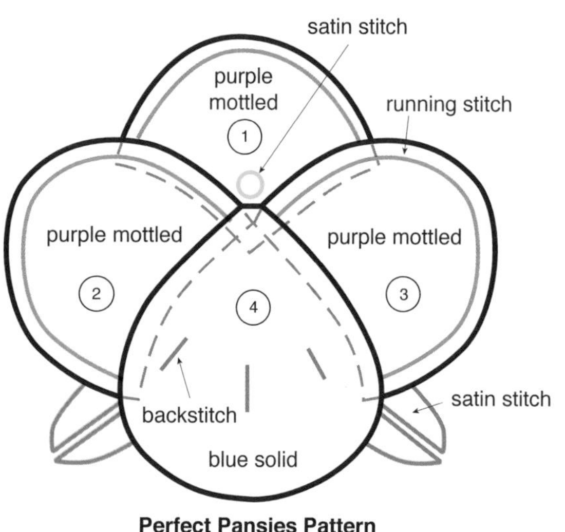


**Perfect Pansies Pattern**
Make 4

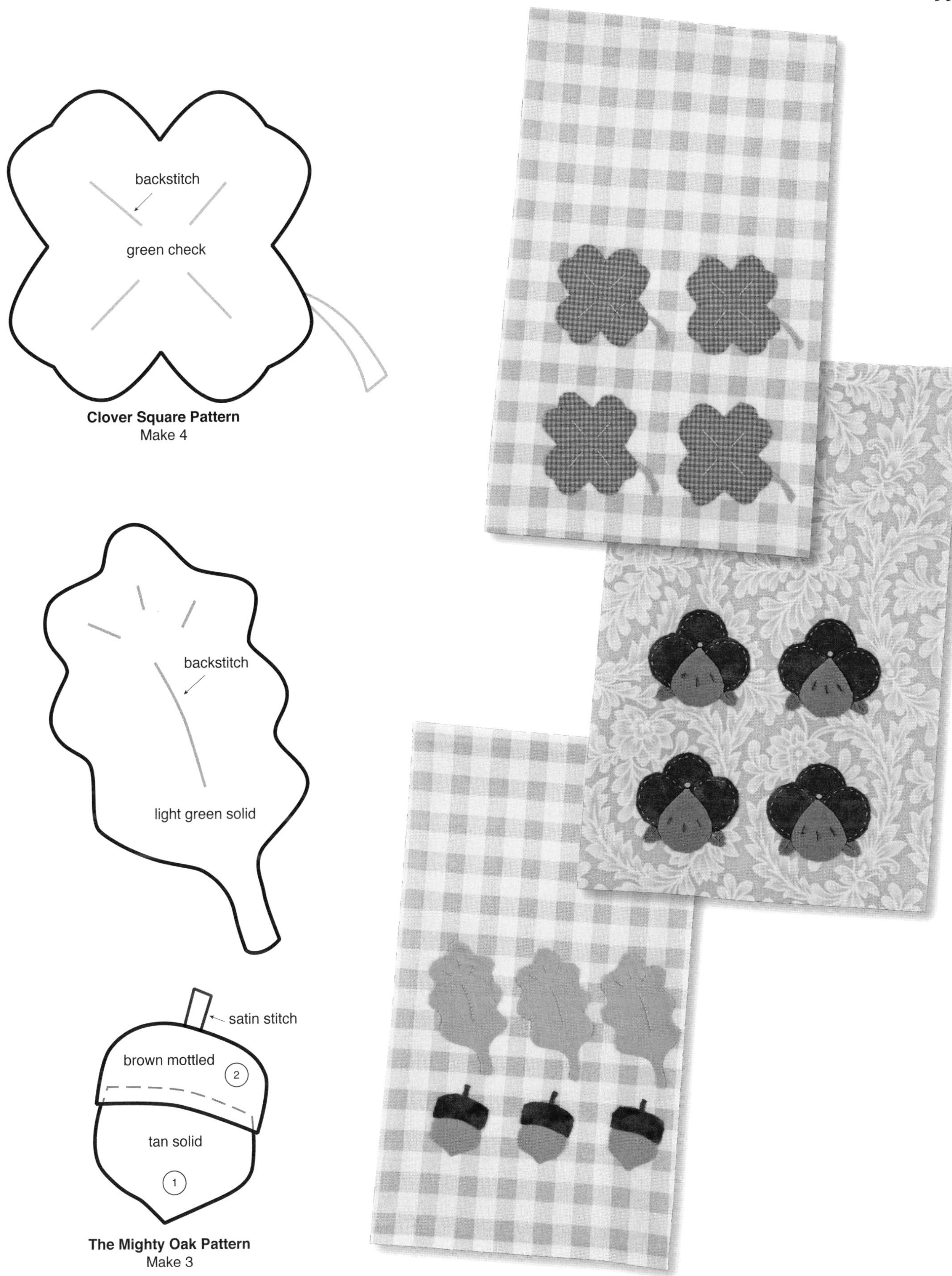


**Clover Square Pattern**
Make 4

**The Mighty Oak Pattern**
Make 3

# Old-World Charm

## Delft Bluebirds

### Materials

- Fabric scraps: light blue and dark blue solids
- 2 (6½" x 8") rectangles and 1 (18½" x 18") rectangle Osnaburg
- 6½" x 8" rectangle pink solid fabric
- 4" x 18" strip each blue plaid and blue stripe fabric
- 18½" x 25½" rectangle muslin
- Pearl cotton: dark and medium blue
- Dark blue 6-strand embroidery floss

### Instructions

**1.** Transfer the embroidery pattern to the pink solid rectangle and stitch design referring to the Embroidery chapter (page 24).

**2.** Prepare templates for the bird pieces using patterns given and cut as directed. Appliqué in place on the pink solid rectangle as marked with the embroidery design.

**3.** Sew a 6½" x 8" Osnaburg rectangle to each side of the embroidered rectangle; press.

**4.** Sew the 18½" x 18" rectangle Osnaburg to the pieced section to complete the towel top referring to the Placement Diagram; press.

**5.** Cut many 4" lengths of dark and medium blue pearl cotton. ***Note:*** *The number of lengths to cut will vary with the density of your fringe.*

**6.** To add the fringe, layer the 4" x 18" fabric strips with the right side of the bottom strip against the wrong side of the top strip; machine-baste together along one long edge adding 4" lengths of pearl cotton randomly as desired.

**7.** Pin the basted strips right sides together with the bottom edge of the towel top; machine-baste to hold.

**8.** Place the muslin rectangle right sides together with the towel top; stitch all around, leaving a 4" opening on one side.

**9.** Turn right side out through the opening; press edges flat. Turn the opening edges to the inside and hand-stitch closed.

**10.** Cut the layered strips almost to the seam area every ½" to make fringe.

**11.** Gather four or five of the cut pieces together and using the remaining cut pieces of the pearl cotton, tie a knot around the group ¾" from the edge of the towel; repeat across the strips to finish.

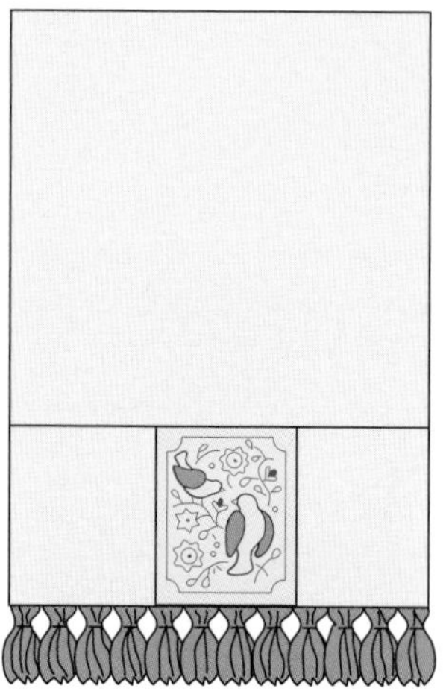

**Delft Bluebirds**
Placement Diagram 18" x 25

**Crimson Star Flower**
Placement Diagram 18" x 25"

## Crimson Star Flower

### Materials

- Scrap red solid fabric
- 2 (6½" x 8") rectangles and 1 (18½" x 18") rectangle Osnaburg
- 6½" x 8" rectangle pink solid fabric
- 2 (4" x 18") strips pink/red plaid fabric
- 18½" x 25½" rectangle muslin
- Pearl cotton: red and dark pink
- Red 6-strand embroidery floss

### Instructions

**1.** Complete the towel as for the Delft Bluebirds using the pink/red plaid strips, and red and dark pink pearl cotton for fringe.

## Nesting Dolls

### Materials

- 1 purchased or self-made tea towel in desired color
- 4" x 6" rectangle dark pink solid fabric
- 4" x 5" rectangle lime green solid fabric
- 3" x 5" rectangle blue tonal fabric
- 1 fat quarter mint green solid
- 6-strand embroidery floss: dark brown, tan, peach, red, gold, plum, orange, light green, bright pink, light pink and dark pink

### Instructions

**1.** Fold and crease tea towel along the length to mark the center.

**2.** Prepare templates for the doll and doll background shapes shown as heavy black lines on patterns. Cut as directed.

**3.** Transfer embroidery patterns to the doll shapes and stitch designs referring to the Embroidery chapter (page 24).

**4.** When all stitching is complete, turn under edges of each doll shape ¼" all around and center the large one on the dark pink rectangle, the medium one on the lime green rectangle and the smallest one on the blue tonal rectangle.

**5.** Hand-appliqué each shape in place.

**6.** Trim the back fabric layer ½" from the edge the appliquéd shape.

**7.** Turn under ¼" all around each back fabric shape; baste to hold.

**8.** Center the medium-size doll 2" from the bottom edge of the tea towel and hand-appliqué in place. Repeat with the large doll shape 2½" from bottom and nearly touching the appliquéd center doll. Repeat with the small doll 1½" from bottom edge to finish. ❖

**Nesting Dolls**
Placement Diagram 18" x 25"

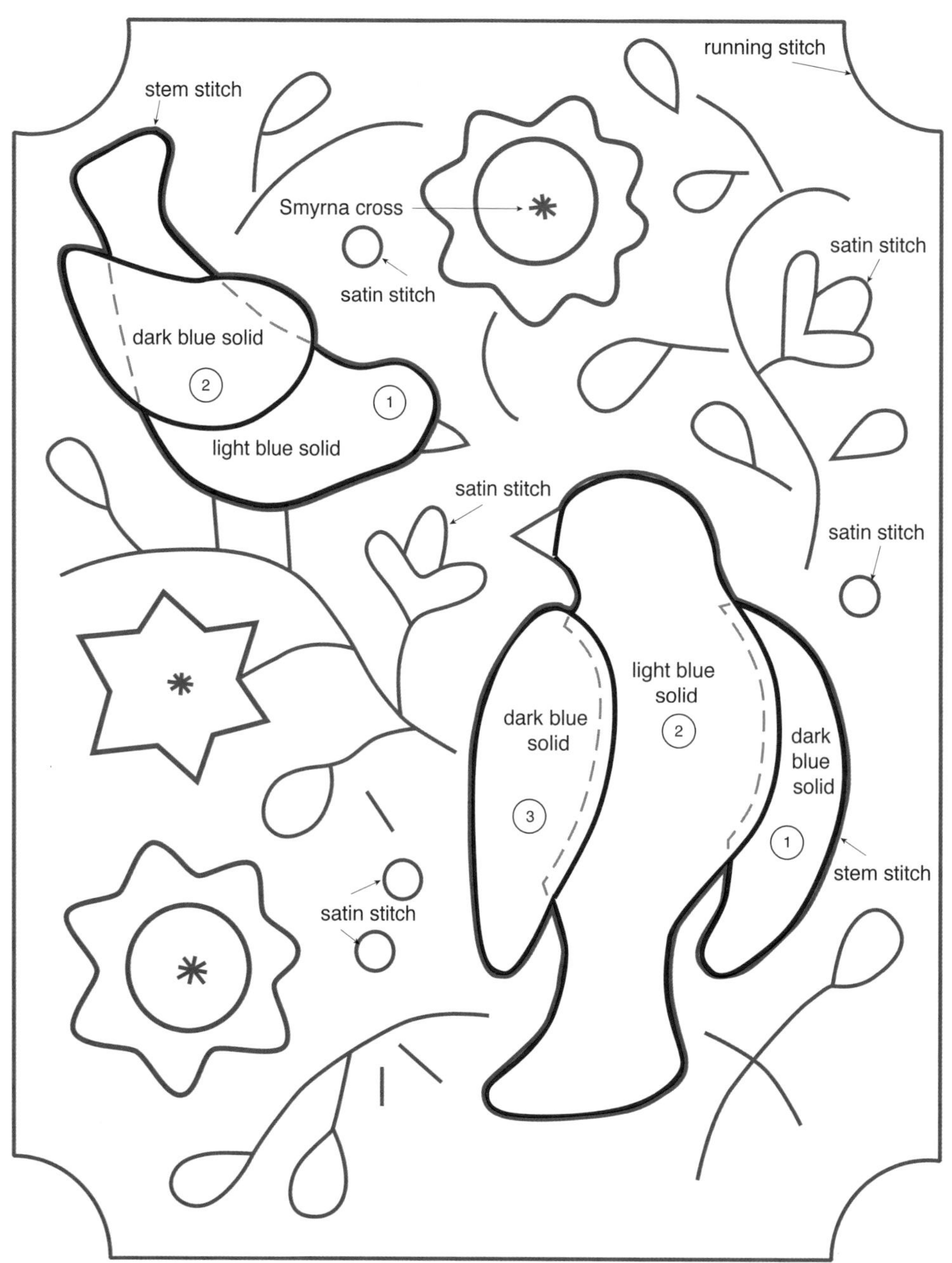


**Delft Bluebirds Pattern**
All unmarked stitches are chain stitch.

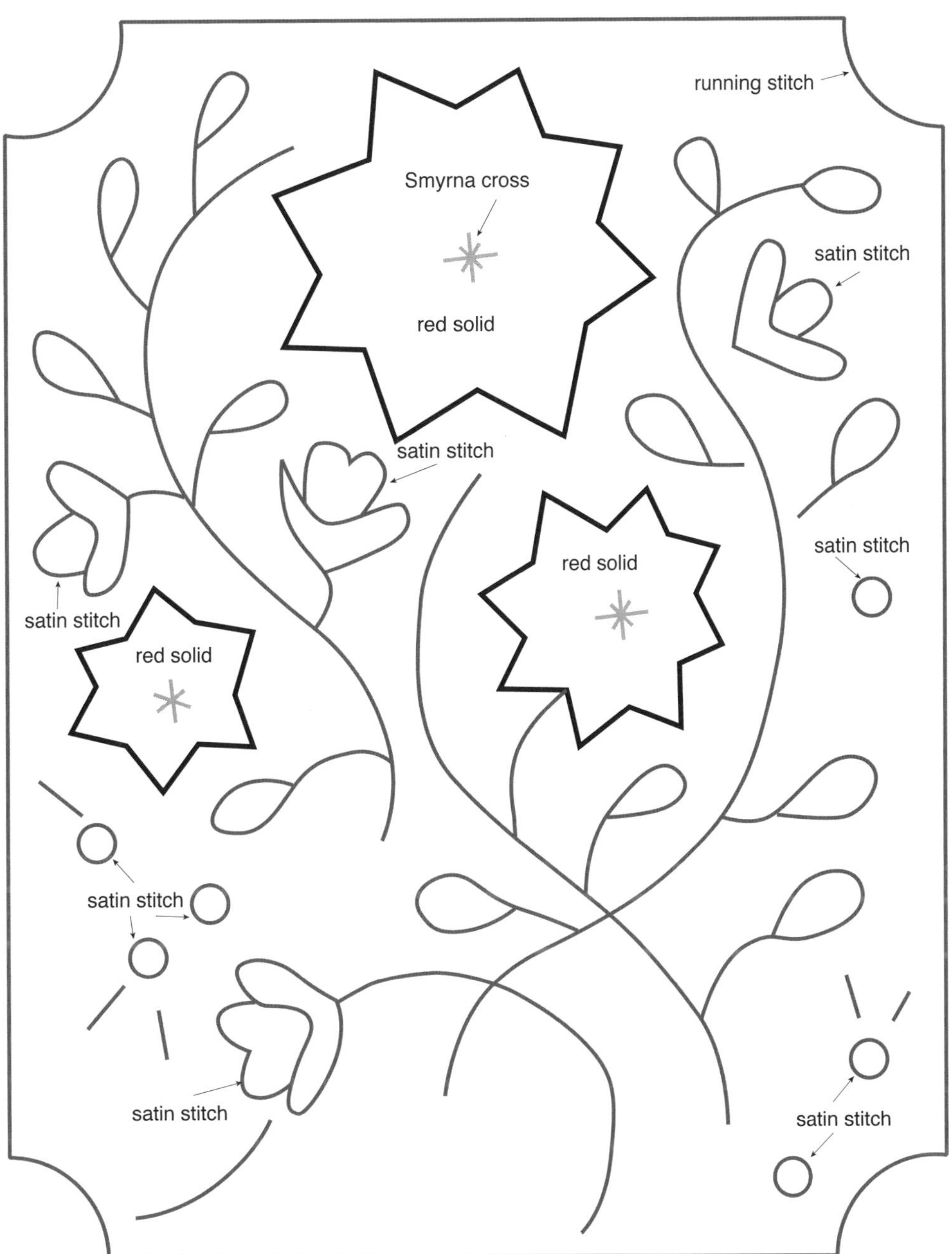


**Crimson Star Flower Pattern**
All unmarked stitches are chain stitch.

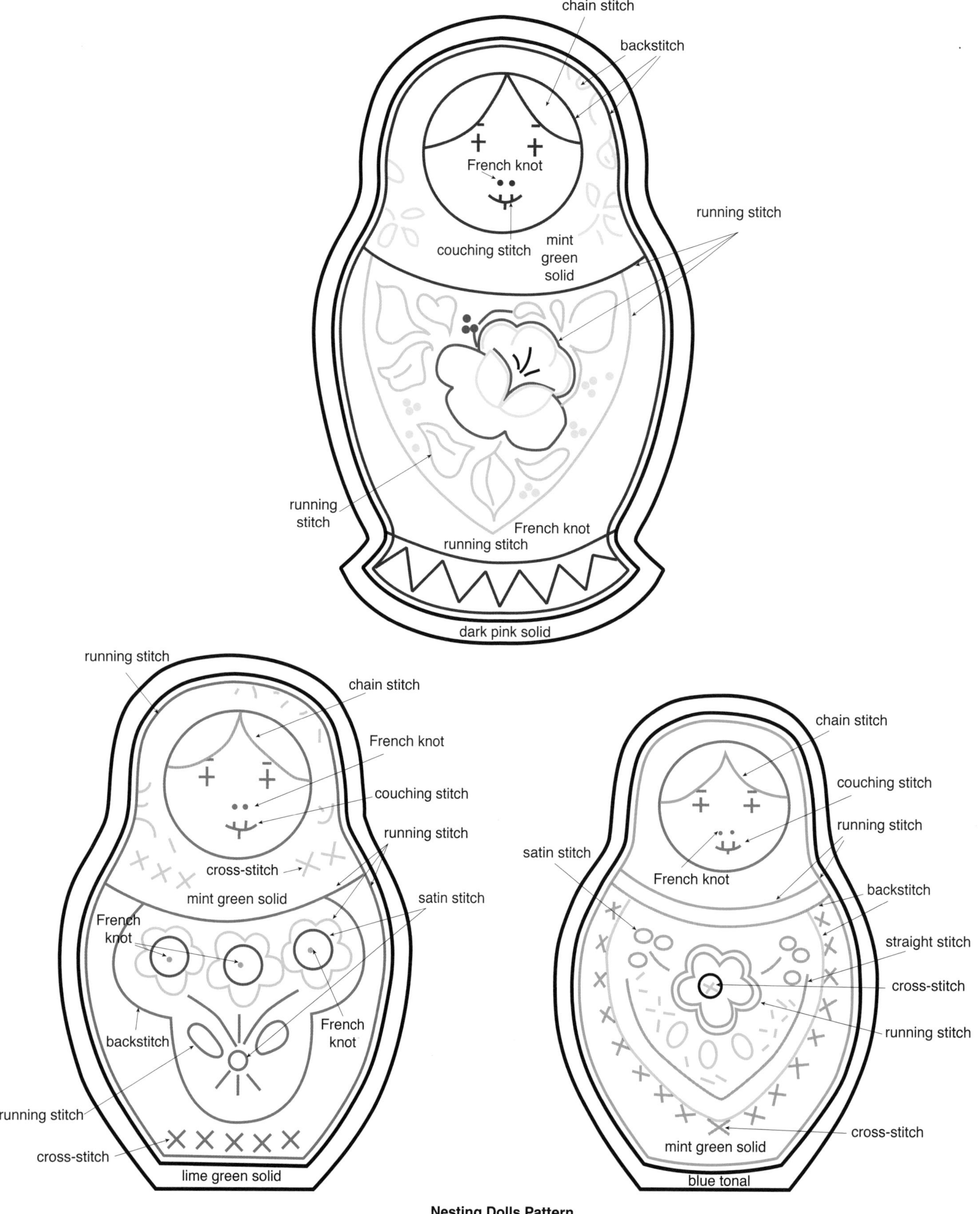


**Nesting Dolls Pattern**

# Animal Friends

## Spotty Dog

### Materials

- 1 purchased or self-made tea towel in desired color
- Fabric scraps: gold, navy, red and tan solids
- 2¼" x 19" strip pink/white print fabric
- 6-strand embroidery floss: blue, gold and pink

### Instructions

**1.** If using a finished tea towel, remove the bottom finished edge. Measure up ½" from the trimmed edge and draw a line from side to side.

**2.** Finish edge using the pink/white print strip referring to Finishing Towel Edges on page 2.

**3.** Prepare templates and appliqué pieces in place referring to the General Project Instructions (page 87) with 2" between the bottom of the towel and the motif to complete the Spotty Dog tea towel.

**Spotty Dog**
Placement Diagram 18" x 25"

## Purrfect Kitty

### Materials

- 1 purchased or self-made tea towel in desired color
- Fabric scraps: lavender, green and white solids, and gold dot
- 2¼" x 19" strip pink print
- 6-strand embroidery floss: dark brown, purple and orange

House of White Birches, Berne, Indiana 46711 Clotilde.com

### Instructions

**1.** If using a finished tea towel, remove the bottom finished edge. Measure up ½" from the trimmed edge and draw a line from side to side.

**2.** Finish edge using the pink print strip referring to Finishing Towel Edges on page 2.

**3.** Prepare templates and appliqué pieces in place referring to the General Project Instructions (page 87) with 2" between the bottom of the towel and the motif to complete the Purrfect Kitty tea towel.

**Purrfect Kitty**
Placement Diagram 18" x 25"

## Goldie Fish

### Materials

- 1 purchased or self-made tea towel in desired color
- Fabric scraps: blue, peach and gold solids
- 2¼" x 19" strip pink print
- 6-strand embroidery floss: blue, gold, navy and pink

**Goldie Fish**
Placement Diagram 18" x 25"

### Instructions

**1.** If using a finished tea towel, remove the bottom finished edge. Measure up 1¾" from the trimmed edge and draw a line from side to side.

**2.** Finish edge using the pink print strip referring to Finishing Towel Edges on page 2.

**3.** Prepare templates and appliqué pieces in place referring to the General Project Instructions (page 87) with 2" between the bottom of the towel and the motif to complete the Goldie Fish tea towel.

## Blue Bunny

### Materials

- 1 purchased or self-made tea towel in desired color
- Fabric scraps: light and dark blue solids
- 2¼" x 19" strip pink/white print
- 6-strand embroidery floss: navy, white, light blue and purple

### Instructions

**1.** If using a finished tea towel, remove the bottom finished edge. Measure up ½" from the trimmed edge and draw a line from side to side.

**2.** Finish edge using the pink/white print strip referring to Finishing Towel Edges on page 2.

**3.** Prepare templates and appliqué pieces in place referring to the General Project Instructions (page 87) with 2" between the bottom of the towel and the motif to complete the Blue Bunny tea towel.

**Blue Bunny**
Placement Diagram 18" x 25"

## Happy Hen

### Materials

- 1 purchased or self-made tea towel in desired color
- Fabric scraps: gold, red and green solids
- 2¼" x 19" strip pink/white print
- 6-strand embroidery floss: gold, brown and dark orange

### Instructions

**1.** If using a finished tea towel, remove the bottom finished edge. Measure up ½" from the trimmed edge and draw a line from side to side.

**2.** Finish edge using the pink/white print strip referring to Finishing Towel Edges on page 2.

**3.** Prepare templates and appliqué pieces in place referring to the General Project Instructions (page 87) with 2" between the bottom of the towel and the motif to complete the Happy Hen tea towel.

**Happy Hen**
Placement Diagram 18" x 25"

## Polka-Dot Pig

### Materials

- 1 purchased or self-made tea towel in desired color
- Fabric scraps: pink dot and red solid
- 2¼" x 19" strip multicolored print fabric
- 6-strand embroidery floss: brown and dark pink

### Instructions

**1.** If using a finished tea towel, remove the bottom finished edge. Measure up ½" from the trimmed edge and draw a line from side to side.

**2.** Finish edge using the brown print strip referring to Finishing Towel Edges on page 2.

**3.** Prepare templates and appliqué pieces in place referring to the General Project Instructions (page 87) with 2" between the bottom of the towel and the motif to complete the Polka-Dot Pig tea towel. ❖

**Polka-Dot Pig**
Placement Diagram 18" x 25"

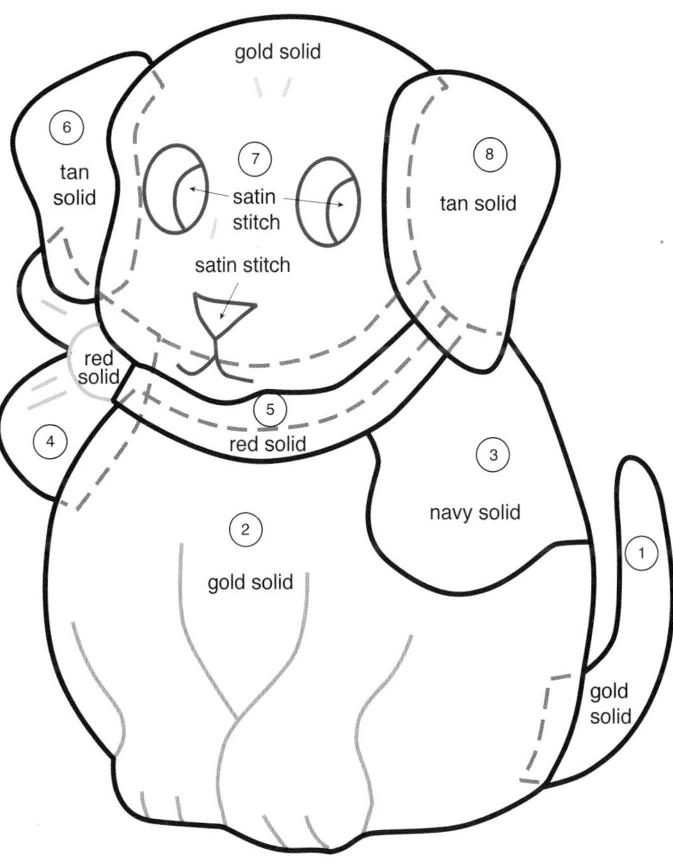


**Spotty Dog Pattern**
All unmarked stitches are backstitch.

**Purrfect Kitty Pattern**
All unmarked stitches are backstitch.

**Polka-Dot Pig Pattern**
All unmarked stitches are backstitch.

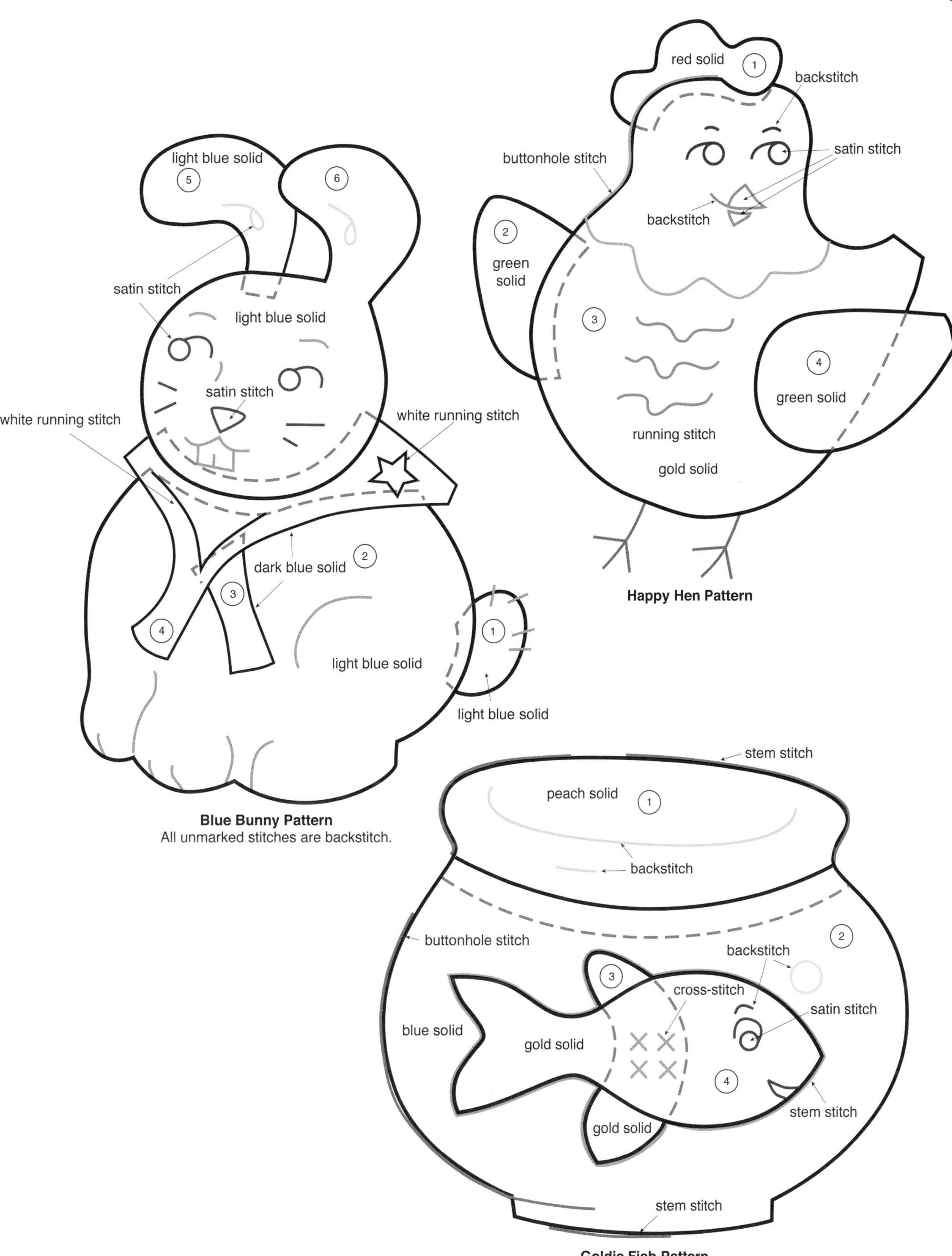


**Blue Bunny Pattern**
All unmarked stitches are backstitch.

**Happy Hen Pattern**

**Goldie Fish Pattern**

# Royal Decor

## Lady-in-Waiting

### Materials

- 19" x 26½" rectangle blue solid fabric
- 19" x 23" rectangle pink print fabric
- 19" x 4" strip tan solid fabric
- 19" length lace trim (optional)

### Instructions

**1.** Prepare a template for the Lady-in-Waiting design using the pattern given. The template should include four complete designs and a half design at each end referring to Figure 5. Mark the center of the template.

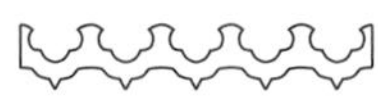

Figure 5

**2.** Fold the pink rectangle in half and crease to mark the center.

**3.** Mark a line from side to side ¼" from one short end of the pink rectangle.

**4.** Center and trace the top edge of the border design on the pink rectangle, aligning the lowest point of the design with the marked line and extending the ends of the design to the outer edges of the rectangle, as shown in Figure 6. Cut out ¼" from the marked line.

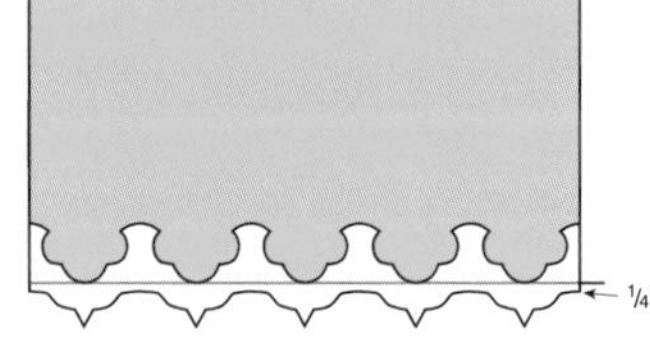


Figure 6

**5.** Align the top and side edges of the trimmed rectangle with the blue rectangle; baste layers together to hold.

**6.** Turn under ¼" along the trimmed edge of the pink rectangle and slipstitch to the blue rectangle as shown in Figure 7.

Figure 7

**7.** Repeat steps 2–4 with the tan strip, aligning the uppermost point of the bottom edge of the design on the marked line as shown in Figure 8. Cut ¼" from the marked line.

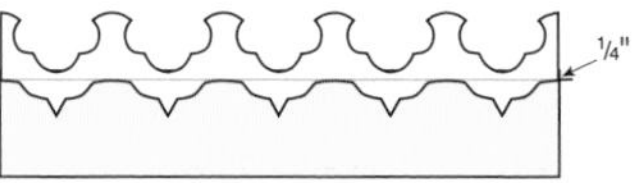


Figure 8

**8.** Align the bottom and side edges of the tan strip with the blue rectangle and baste to hold.

**9.** Turn under ¼" along the trimmed edge of the tan rectangle and slipstitch to the blue rectangle as shown in Figure 9.

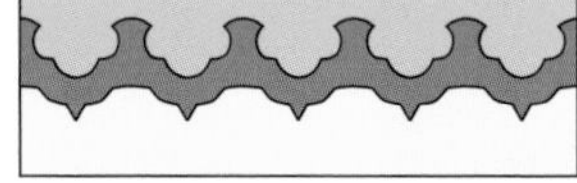

Figure 9

**Lady-in-Waiting**
Placement Diagram 18" x 25"

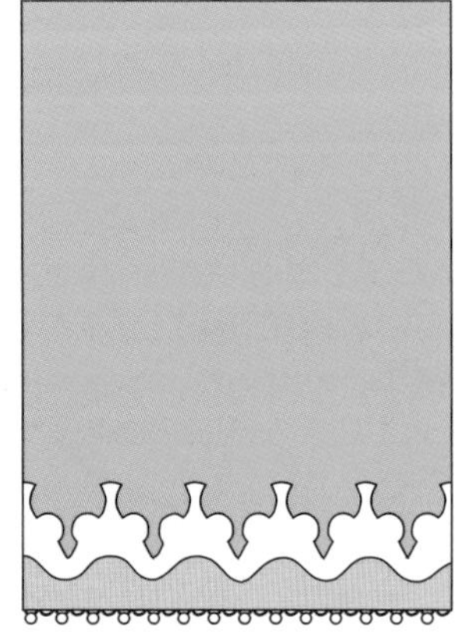

**Fit for a Princess**
Placement Diagram 18" x 25"

**Queen's Fancy**
Placement Diagram 18" x 25"

**King's Delight**
Placement Diagram 18" x 25"

**10.** Finish the edges of the tea towel as desired referring to Finishing Towel Edges on page 2. Add lace to bottom edge if desired.

## Fit for a Princess

### Materials

- 19" x 26½" rectangle white tonal fabric
- 19" x 23½" rectangle pink solid fabric
- 19" x 4" strip green print fabric
- 19" length ¾" white ball fringe

### Instructions

**1.** Repeat instructions for the Lady-in-Waiting tea towel using the Fit for a Princess pattern and referring to Figure 10.

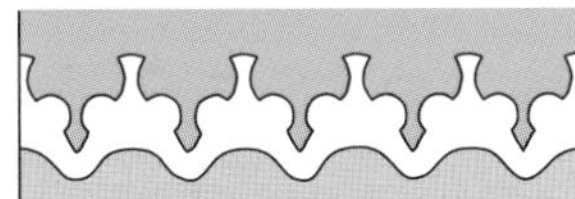

Figure 10

## Queen's Fancy

### Materials

- 19" x 26½" rectangle tan print fabric
- 19" x 22½" rectangle gold metallic print fabric
- 19" x 4½" strip pink batik fabric
- 19" length lace trim
- 19" length ½" pink ball fringe

### Instructions

**1.** Repeat instructions for the Lady-in-Waiting tea towel using the Queen's Fancy pattern and referring to Figure 11.

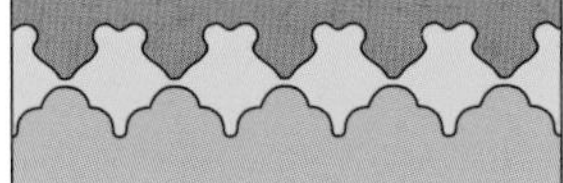

Figure 11

## King's Delight

### Materials

- 19" x 26½" rectangle peach/tan print fabric
- 19" x 23¼" rectangle red tonal fabric
- 19" x 3½" strip light brown solid fabric
- 19" length orange rickrack

### Instructions

**1.** Repeat instructions for the Lady-in-Waiting tea towel using the King's Delight pattern except repeat pattern four times in the center, and extend the top side edges of the pattern in a straight line to the ends; for the bottom edge of the pattern, repeat the bottom scallop to the ends referring to Figure 12. ❖

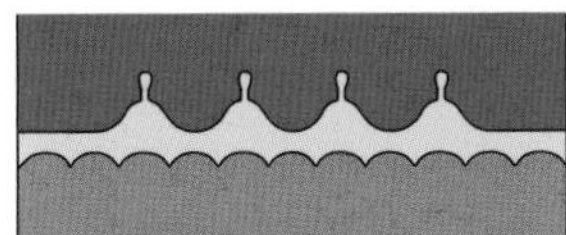

Figure 12

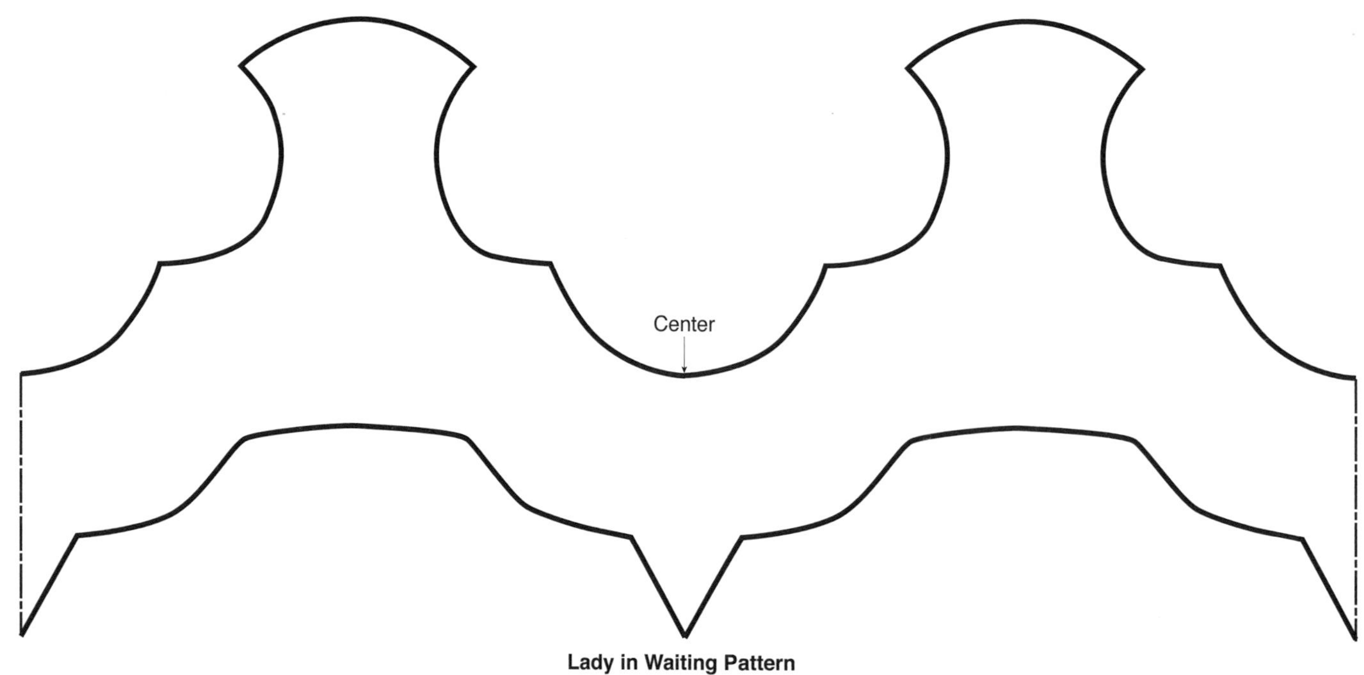


Lady in Waiting Pattern

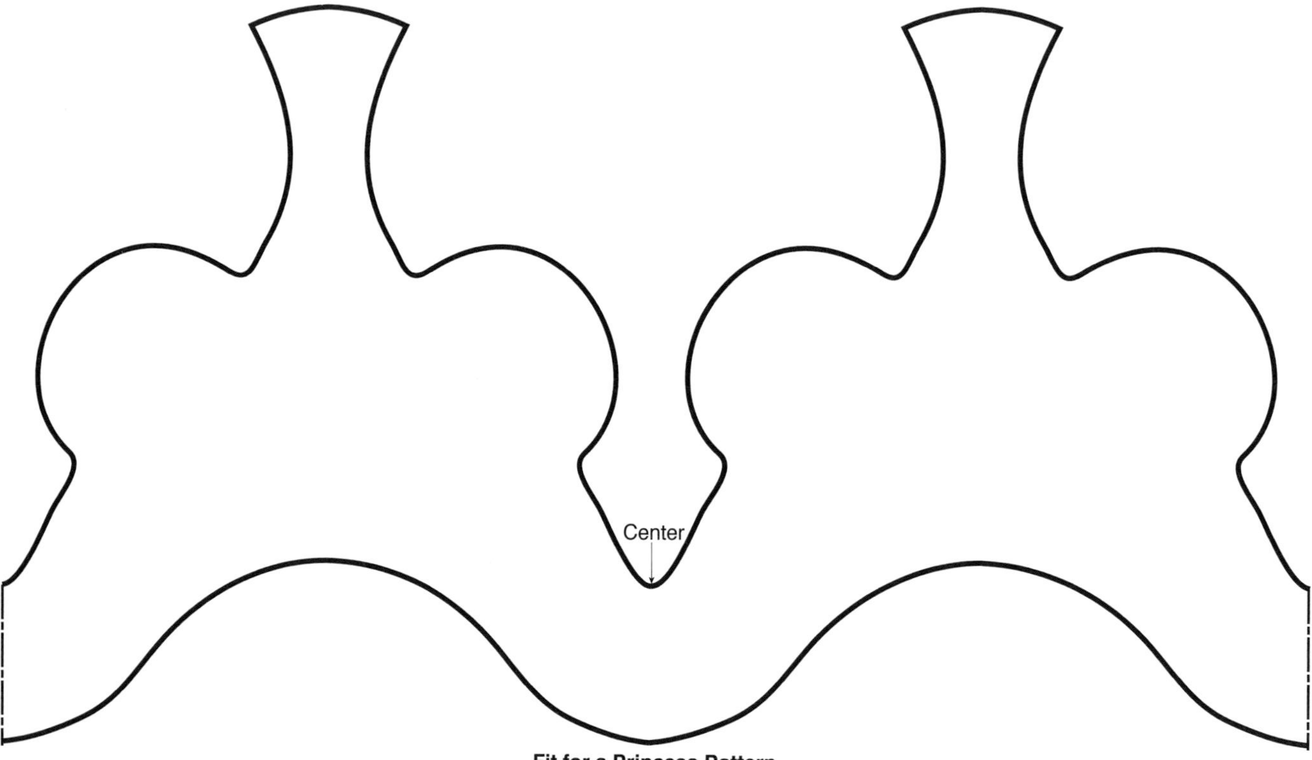


Fit for a Princess Pattern

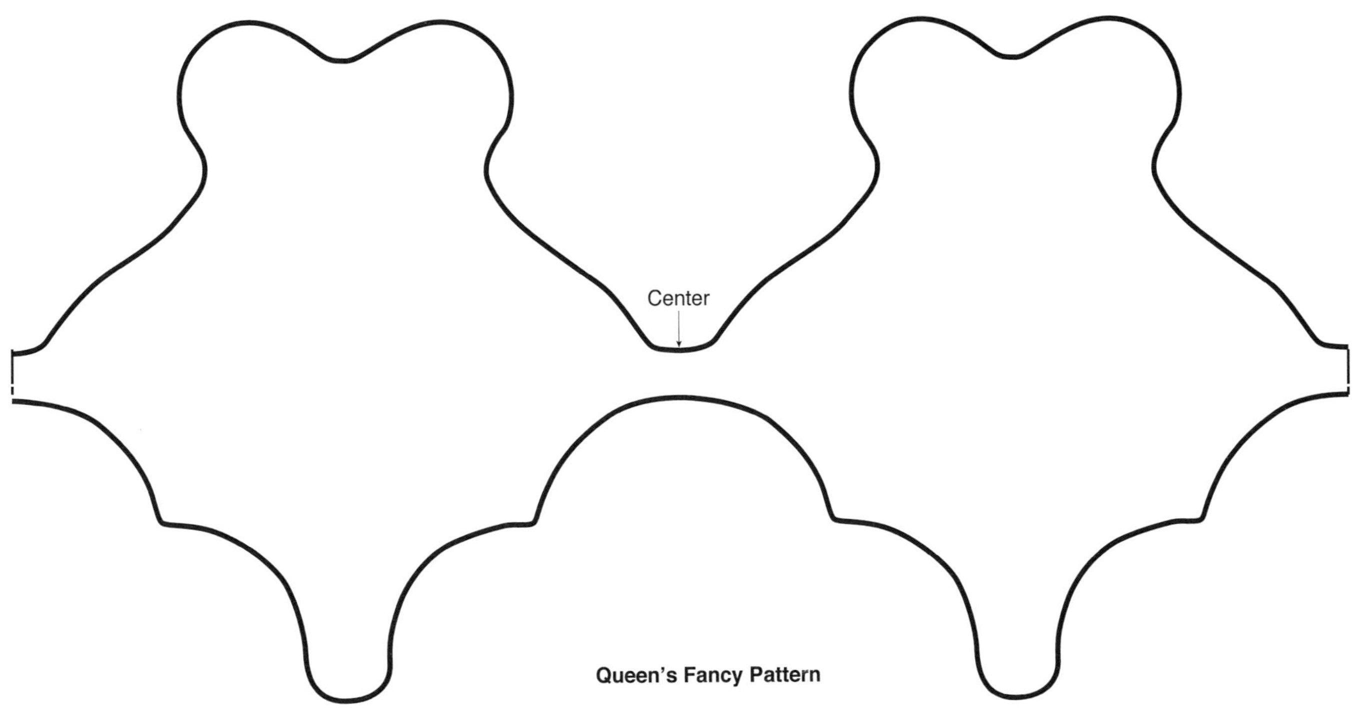


**Queen's Fancy Pattern**

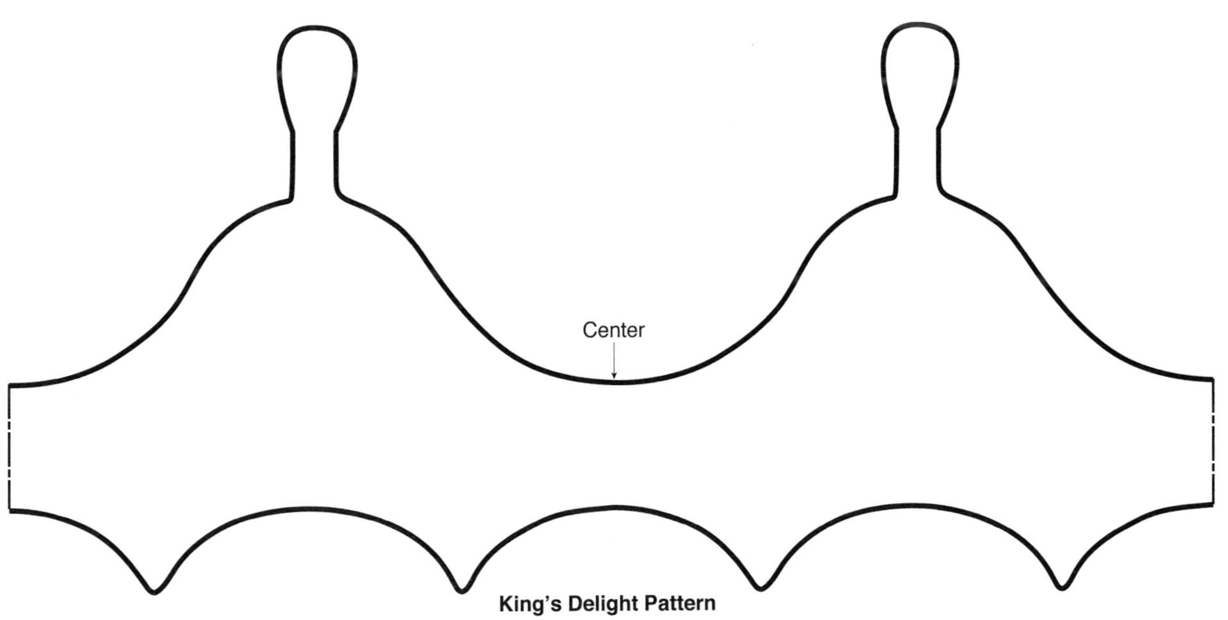


**King's Delight Pattern**

# Counted Cross-Stitch & Chicken Scratch

## General Instructions

In the same way that a photo is made of singular pixels, a cross-stitched image is made of many individual X's as shown in Figure 1. It is an easy, portable and almost foolproof way to dress up a plain-Jane tea towel.

Figure 1

### Making Cross-Stitches

This form of embroidery can be worked on any background that is countable, meaning that the insertion points make up a grid. The models in this chapter are stitched on gingham fabric, which is characterized by a pattern of light-, medium- and dark-toned squares. For the cross-stitch designs, one X will cover four gingham squares as shown in Figure 2.

Figure 2

In order for the finished design to appear harmonious, be sure that the stitches lie in the same direction. Crosses that are 3/16" wide or larger should be kept uniform with a center couching stitch as shown in Figure 3.

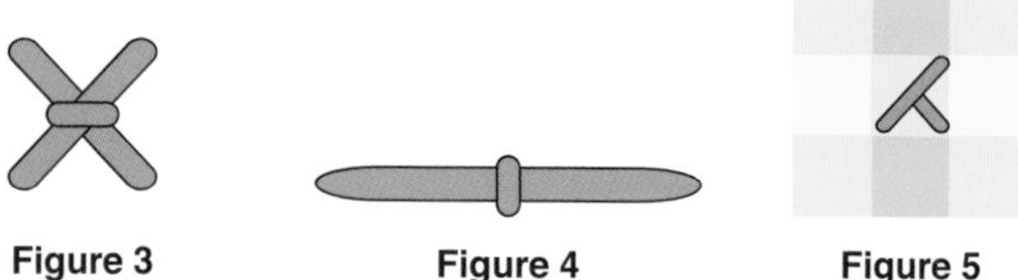

Figure 3 Figure 4 Figure 5

Straight stitches that are used for outlines and details are worked along the grid lines. Secure long stitches with a center couching stitch as shown in Figure 4.

When a full cross is too large for a specific design area, a half-cross is required as shown in Figure 5.

A more complex Smyrna Cross is a + shape worked on top of an X shape as shown in Figure 6.

Figure 6

### Chicken Scratch

A variation of cross-stitch, chicken scratch can only be stitched on gingham fabric. Usually there is one cross-stitch per square.

The designs are enhanced by covering either the light or the dark squares with decorative stitches. Along with X's and Smyrna Crosses, chicken scratch features O's that are worked into the design by weaving the thread under each of four spokes as shown in Figure 7.

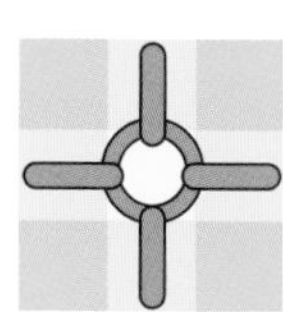

Figure 7

### Beginning to Stitch

Find the center of the design and the center of the tea towel.

Cut a 15"–18" length of embroidery floss. Separate strands, and then select 3 strands and thread through the needle as one; knot the end.

Bring the needle from the back to the front of the fabric at the beginning point.

Stitch an X in the gingham referring to the chart to count spaces. Continue a vertical row to the end of the design. Be sure that all X's are crossed in the same direction—the top of the floss should slant in the same direction on all stitches. Stitch all rows.

Knot the floss on the back side at the ending point or when floss runs out, and slide under several other stitches before trimming to finish.

### Supplies & Tools

- Scissors—small, very sharp point
- Embroidery needle—sharp and long enough to handle easily
- Embroidery hoop—An 8" wooden or plastic hoop will work with all of the designs in this book. The traditional embroidery hoop is made with two wooden rings—one smaller than the other. There is a tension screw on the side of the top hoop

which is loosened when placing the fabric in the hoop and then tightened after the fabric has been laid on the smaller hoop and the larger hoop has been placed on top. Hoops come in a variety of sizes from 4"–8" for hand embroidery and larger for quilting.
- All-purpose thread to match towel fabric

### General Project Instructions

**1.** Fold the towel in half along length and crease to mark the center.

**2.** Referring to the chart given and counting squares on the gingham, stitch the selected design starting in the center of the center motif 2¼" from the hemmed edge of the tea towel and stitching motifs on each side to center the design. ❖

# X Marks the Spot

### Project Note

Refer to Marking the Design on Fabric (page 24) for transferring and removing design. Refer to Stitching the Design (page 24) when working embroidery.

## Springtime

### Materials

- 1 purchased or self-made gingham tea towel in desired color with one 4-square unit measuring ¼"
- 6-strand embroidery floss: light green, turquoise, purple, gold, brown and pink

### Instructions

**1.** Center and transfer the flower design to the tea towel 1¼" from the bottom hemmed edge.

**2.** Stitch the design on the tea towel along marked lines referring to the pattern for color and stitch choices.

**3.** Remove transfer lines according to type of marking tool used, or as directed by the manufacturer.

**4.** To complete the cross-stitches, refer to General Project Instructions (above) except begin stitching the center design 2" from the finished bottom edge of the tea towel, using the color of floss marked on chart.

## Kitty Time

### Materials

- 1 purchased or self-made gingham tea towel in desired color with one 4-square unit measuring ¼"
- Fabric scraps: dark brown, medium brown and white solids
- 6-strand embroidery floss: blue, gold, green, orange, cream and black

### Instructions

**1.** Refer to the Hand Appliqué chapter on page 86 to prepare and appliqué the kitty/clock design to the center of the tea towel with the body 1¼" from the bottom edge of the tea towel and inserting the end of the tail under the body when stitching.

**2.** Add embroidery details to the appliquéd design as marked on pattern for color and stitches, and referring to the Embroidery chapter on page 24 for stitching instructions.

**3.** To complete the cross-stitches, refer to General Project Instructions (page 115), except begin stitching the design 2" from the finished bottom edge of the tea towel, using the colors of floss marked on chart. ❖

**Kitty Time**
Placement Diagram 18" x 25"

**Springtime**
Placement Diagram 18" x 25"

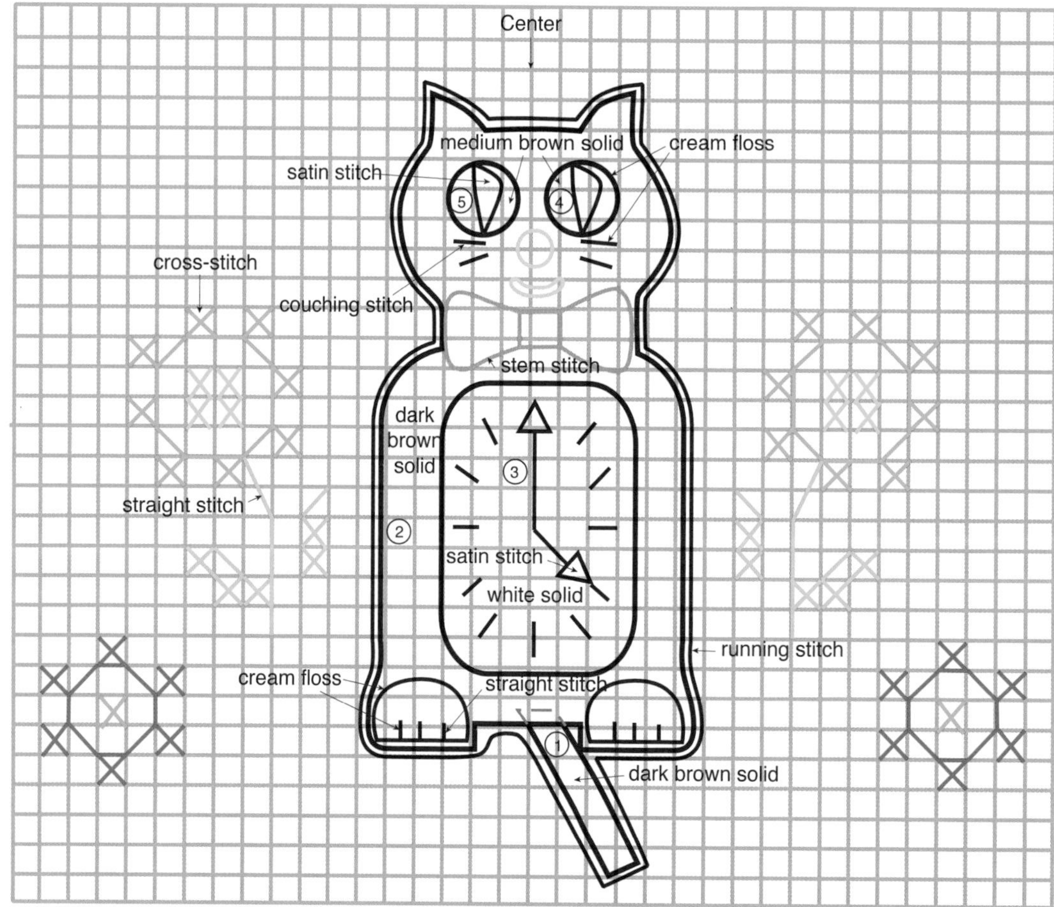


**Kitty Time Chart**
All unmarked stitches are backstitch.

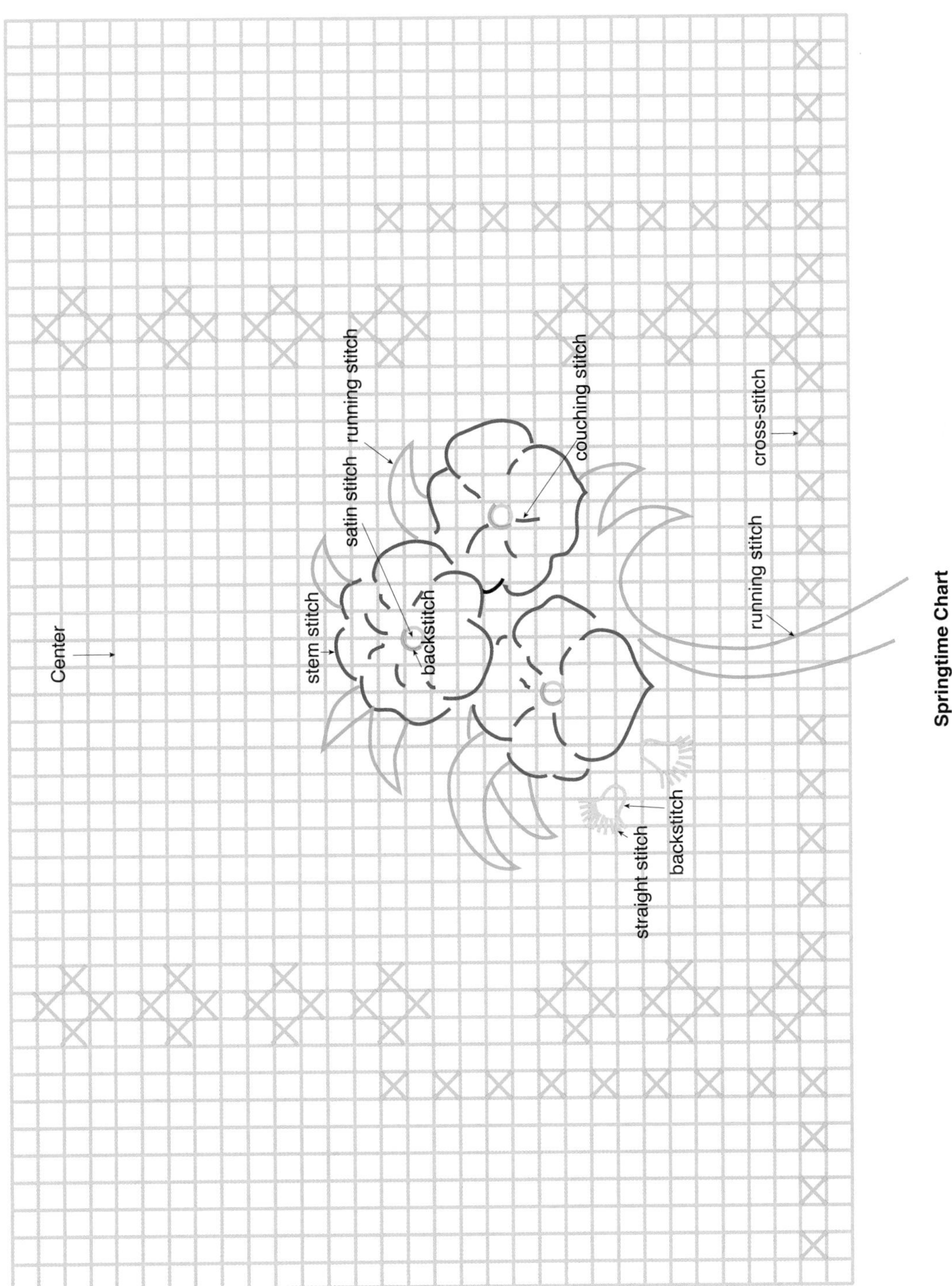


**Springtime Chart**

# Country Kitchen

## Brown Sugar

### Materials

- 1 purchased or self-made gingham tea towel in desired color with one 4-square unit measuring ½"
- 9 (½") cream buttons
- Brown 6-strand embroidery floss

### Instructions

**1.** Refer to General Project Instructions (page 115) to stitch Brown Sugar design.

**2.** Center and stitch a button to the bottom edge of the tea towel. Evenly space four buttons on each side of the center button to finish the tea towel.

**Brown Sugar**
Placement Diagram 18" x 25"

**Wildflowers**
Placement Diagram 18" x 25"

## Wildflowers

### Materials

- 1 purchased or self-made gingham tea towel in desired color with one 4-square unit measuring ½"
- 9 (½") cream buttons
- 6-strand embroidery floss: brown and teal

### Instructions

**1.** Refer to General Project Instructions (page 115) except begin stitching the center of the center design 2½" from the finished bottom edge of the tea towel and use the two colors of floss as marked on chart. ❖

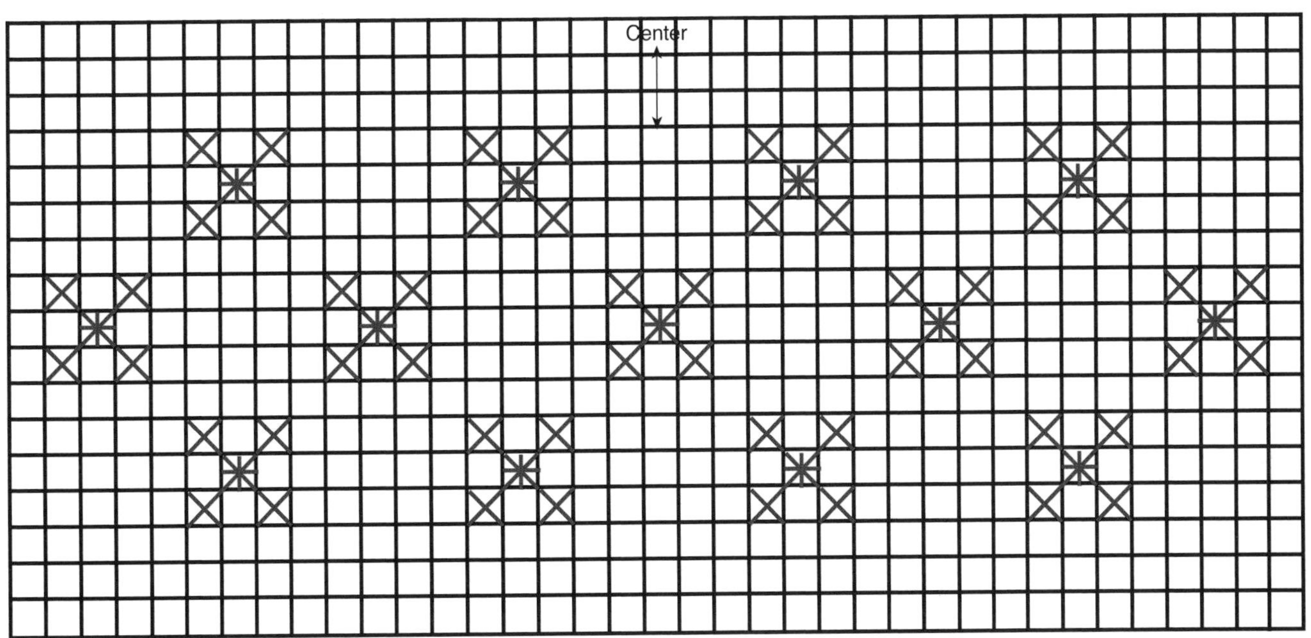


Brown Sugar Chart

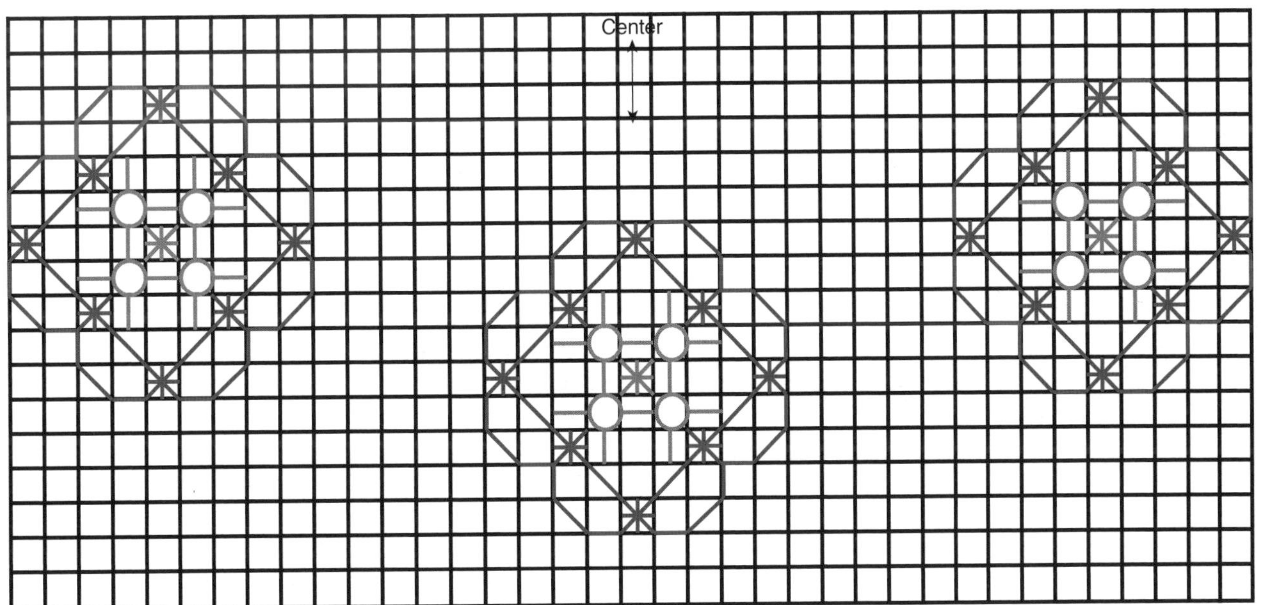


Wildflowers Chart

# Cross Checks

## Celtic Cross

### Materials

- 1 purchased or self-made gingham tea towel in desired color with one 4-square unit measuring 1"
- Red 6-strand embroidery floss

### Instructions

**1.** Refer to General Project Instructions (page 115) except begin stitching the center of the design 3" from the finished bottom edge of the tea towel.

**Celtic Cross**
Placement Diagram 18" x 25"

**Stars in a Row**
Placement Diagram 18" x 25"

## Stars in a Row

### Materials

- 1 purchased or self-made gingham tea towel in desired color with one 4-square unit measuring 1"
- 6-strand embroidery floss: red and gold
- 6 (¼") orange buttons

### Instructions

**1.** Refer to General Project Instructions (page 115) except begin stitching the center of the design 1½" from the finished bottom edge of the tea towel, using the two colors of floss as marked on chart.

**2.** To complete, stitch 3 buttons in alternating squares on each side of center square referring to chart.

## Square Dance

### Materials

- 1 purchased or self-made gingham tea towel in desired color with one 4-square unit measuring 1"
- 9 (1⅛") squares pink felt
- 9 (¼") orange buttons
- 7 pink embroidered flower appliqués
- Magenta 6-strand embroidery floss

### Instructions

**1.** Refer to General Project Instructions (page 115) except begin stitching the center of the design 1½" from the finished bottom edge of the tea towel.

**2.** Center and slipstitch a square of pink felt inside each stitched frame referring to Figure 8.

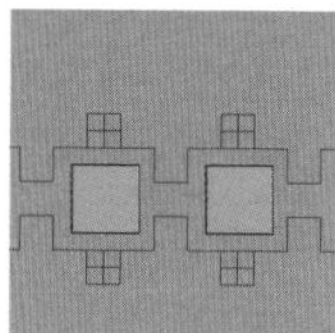

**Figure 8**

**3.** Sew a button in the center of each felt square.

**4.** Sew an embroidered pink flower above each square motif referring to the Placement Diagram for positioning. ❖

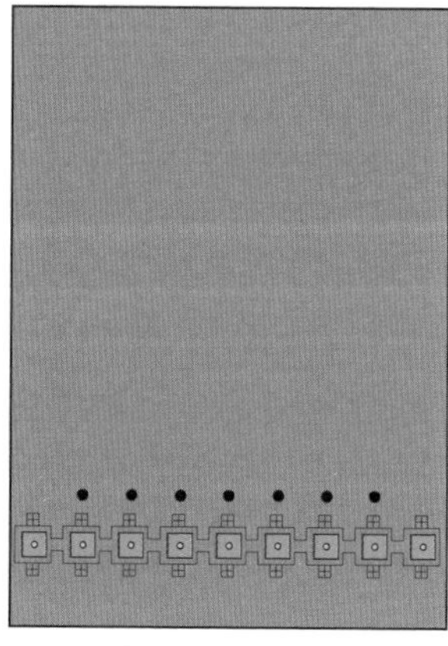

**Square Dance**
Placement Diagram 18" x 25"

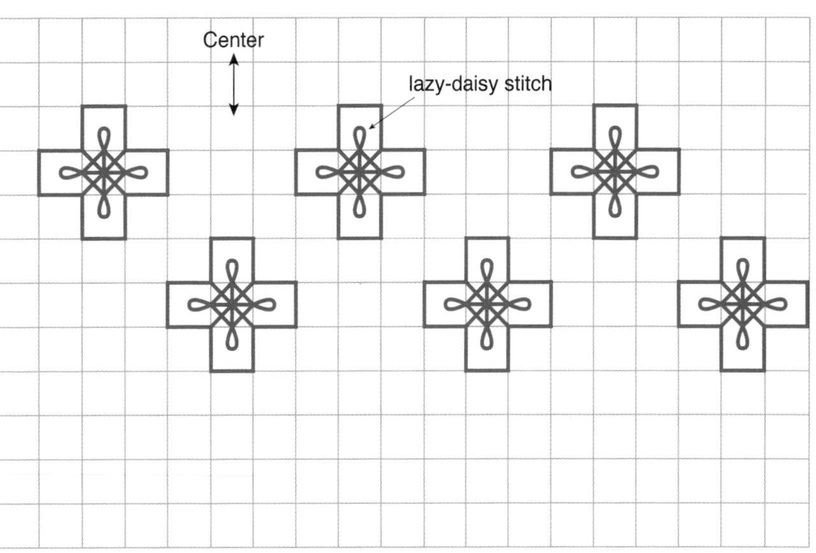


**Celtic Cross Chart**

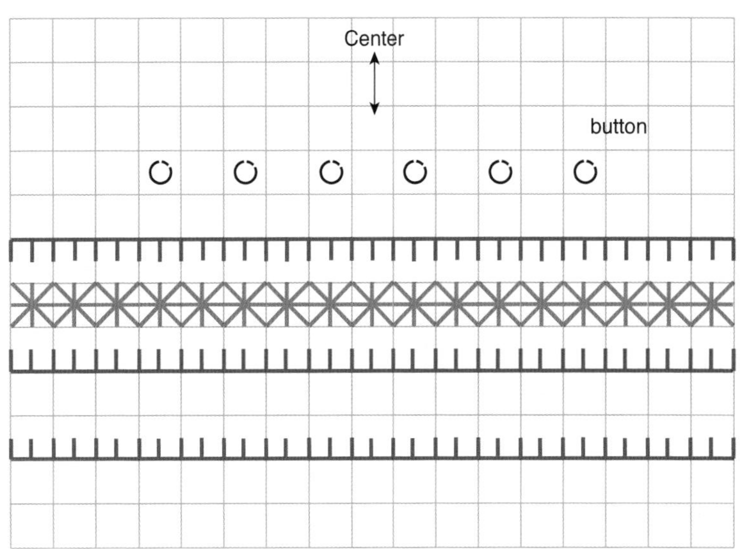


**Stars in a Row Chart**

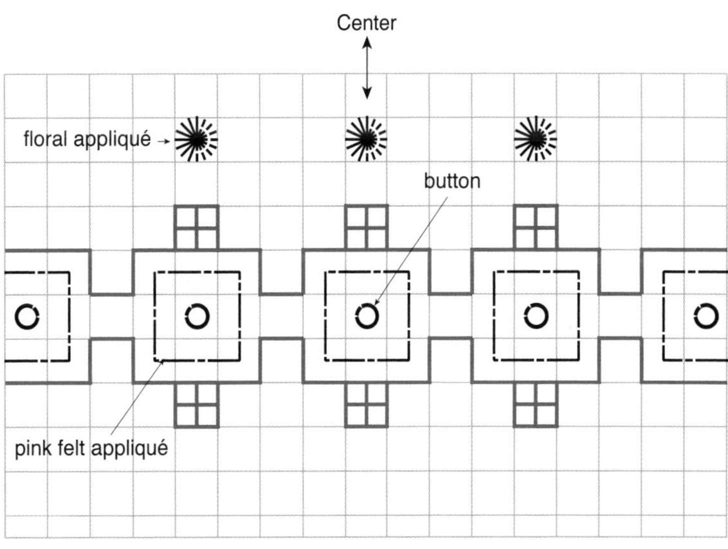


**Square Dance Chart**

# Chicken Scratch Kitchen

## Pansy Row

### Materials

- 1 purchased or self-made gingham tea towel in desired color with one 4-square unit measuring ¼"
- 6-strand embroidery floss: white, yellow and green

### Instructions

**1.** Refer to General Project Instructions (page 115) except begin stitching the center of the design 1½" from the finished bottom edge of the tea towel, using the colors of floss marked on chart.

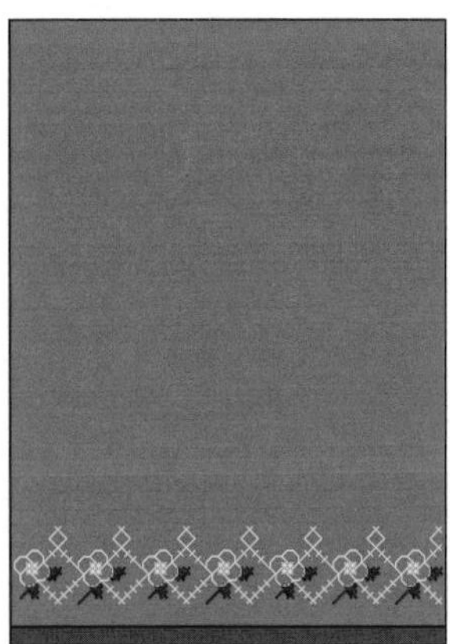

**Pansy Row**
Placement Diagram 18" x 25"

**Bless This House**
Placement Diagram 18" x 25"

## Bless This House

### Materials

- 1 purchased or self-made gingham tea towel in desired color with one 4-square unit measuring ¼"
- 6-strand embroidery floss: medium green, dark green, ivory, medium blue, dark blue and pink

### Instructions

**1.** Refer to General Project Instructions (page 115) except begin stitching the center of the design 2½" from the finished bottom edge of the tea towel, using the colors of floss marked on chart.

## Flower Blossoms

### Materials

- 1 purchased or self-made gingham tea towel in desired color with one 4-square unit measuring ¼"
- 6-strand embroidery floss: peach, orange, blue and green
- 2 (¼") white buttons
- 1 (½") blue flower button

### Instructions

**1.** Refer to General Project Instructions (page 115) except begin stitching the center of the design 1" from the finished bottom edge of the tea towel, using the colors of floss marked on chart.

**2.** Sew on the blue and white buttons as marked on the chart.

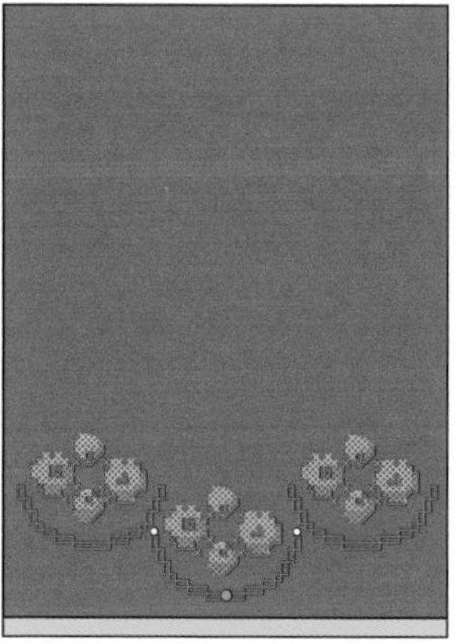

**Flower Blossoms**
Placement Diagram 18" x 25"

**Three Hoots**
Placement Diagram 18" x 25"

## Three Hoots

### Materials

- 1 purchased or self-made gingham tea towel in desired color with one 4-square unit measuring ¼"
- 6-strand embroidery floss: gold, orange, brown, light blue, dark blue and pink

### Instructions

**1.** Refer to General Project Instructions (page 115) except begin stitching the center of the design 2" from the finished bottom edge of the tea towel, using the colors of floss marked on chart.

## Cherries Jubilee

### Materials

- 1 purchased or self-made gingham tea towel in desired color with one 4-square unit measuring ¼"
- 6-strand embroidery floss: red, burgundy, tan, medium brown, dark brown, white, turquoise, pink and dark blue

### Instructions

**1.** Refer to General Project Instructions (page 115) except begin stitching the center of the design 2" from the finished bottom edge of the tea towel, using the colors of floss marked on chart.

**Cherries Jubilee**
Placement Diagram 18" x 25"

## Home Sweet Home

### Materials

- 1 purchased or self-made gingham tea towel in desired color with one 4-square unit measuring ¼"
- 6-strand embroidery floss: yellow, red, mint green, dark blue, orange and gold
- 2 (¼") red buttons

### Instructions

**1.** Refer to General Project Instructions (page 115) except begin stitching the center of the design 1¾" from the finished bottom edge of the tea towel, using the colors of floss marked on chart.

**2.** Stitch red buttons at center of flowers, referring to stitch chart. ❖

**Home Sweet Home**
Placement Diagram 18" x 25"

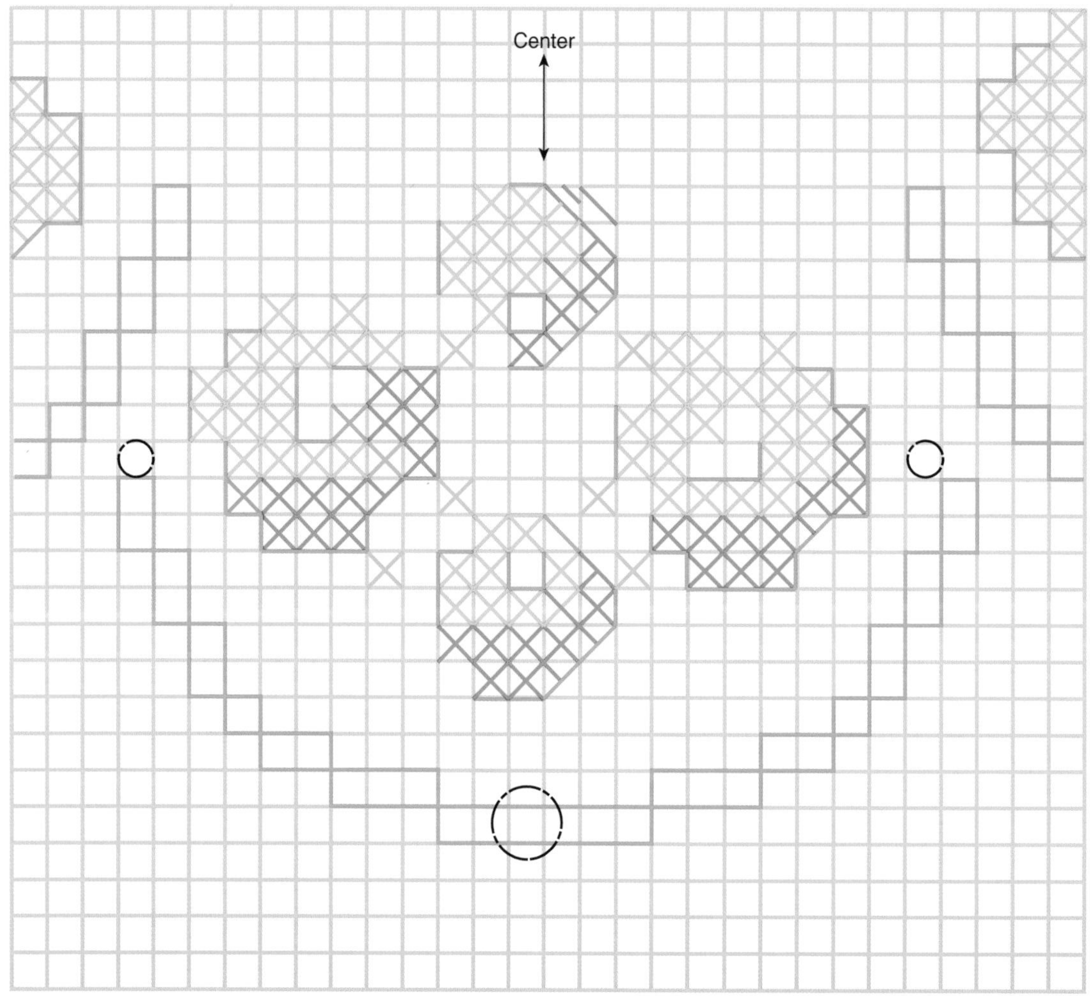


**Flower Blossoms Chart**

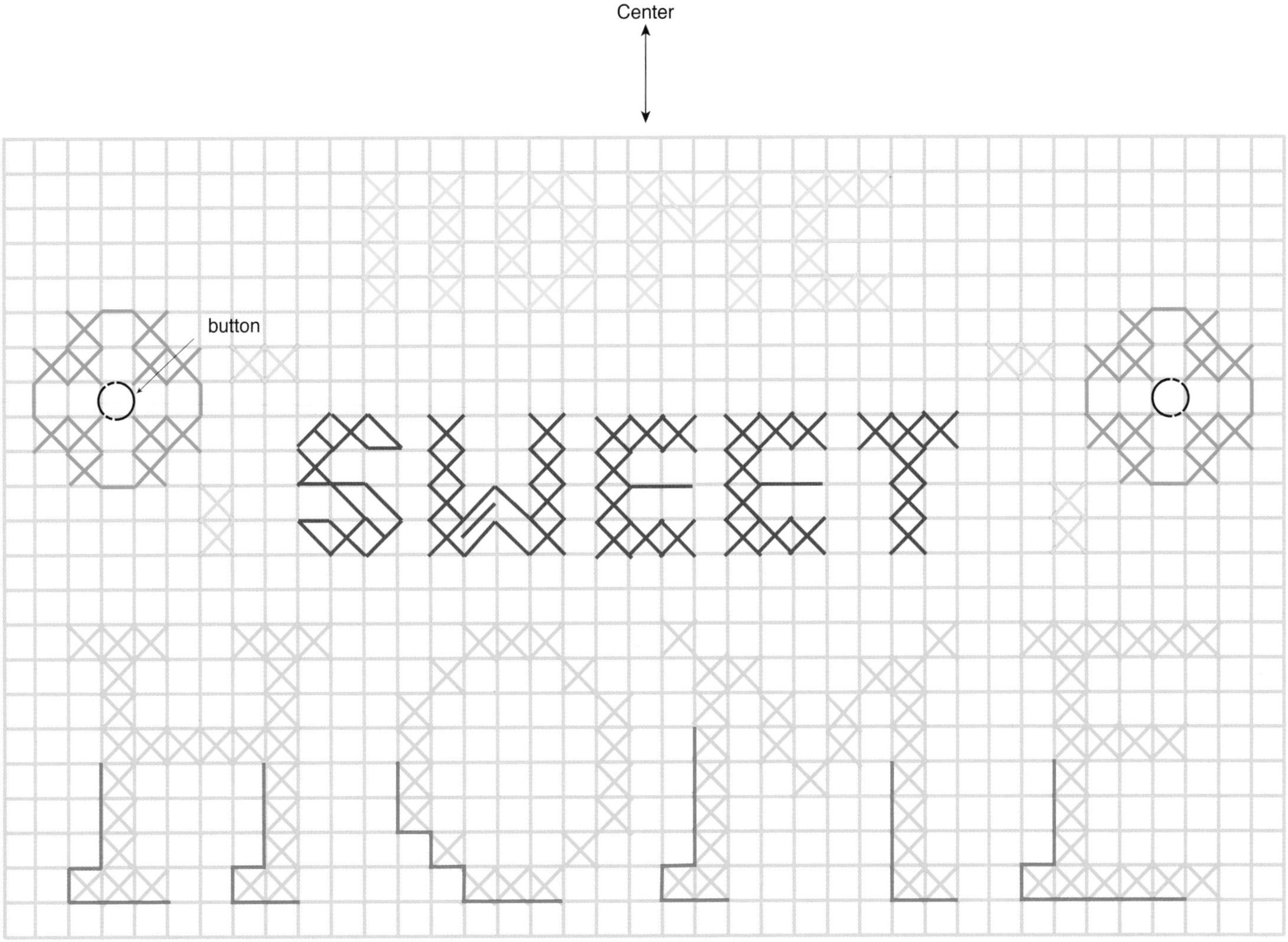

Center
button
SWEET

**Home Sweet Home Chart**

Center

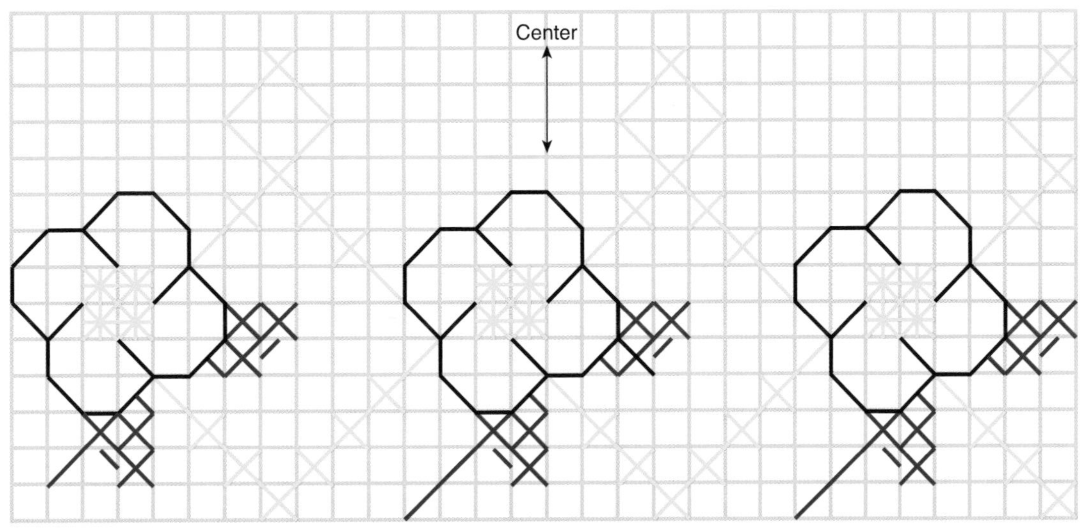

**Pansy Row Chart**
Use white floss for all black lines.

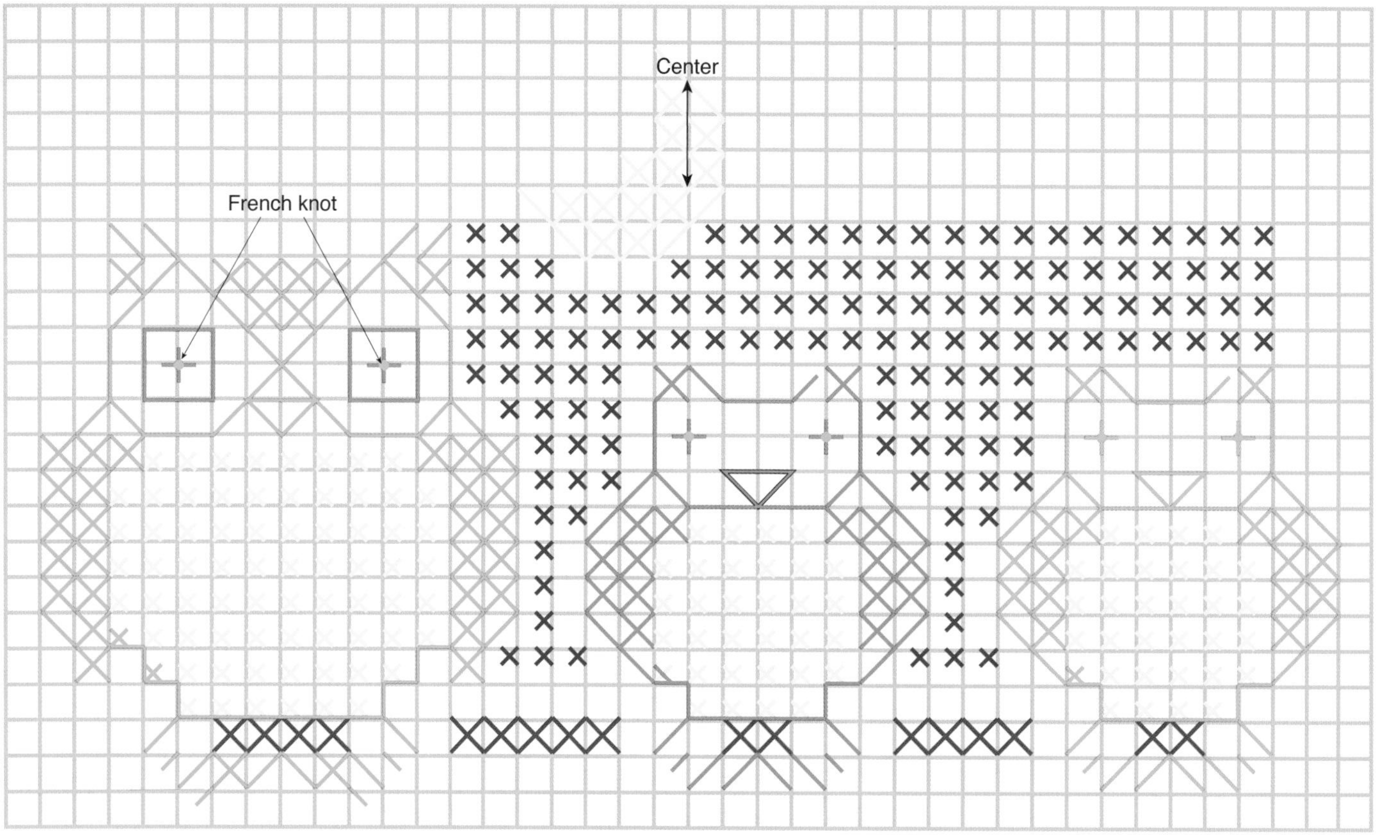

**Three Hoots Chart**
Use satin stitch for beaks and French knots for centers of eyes.

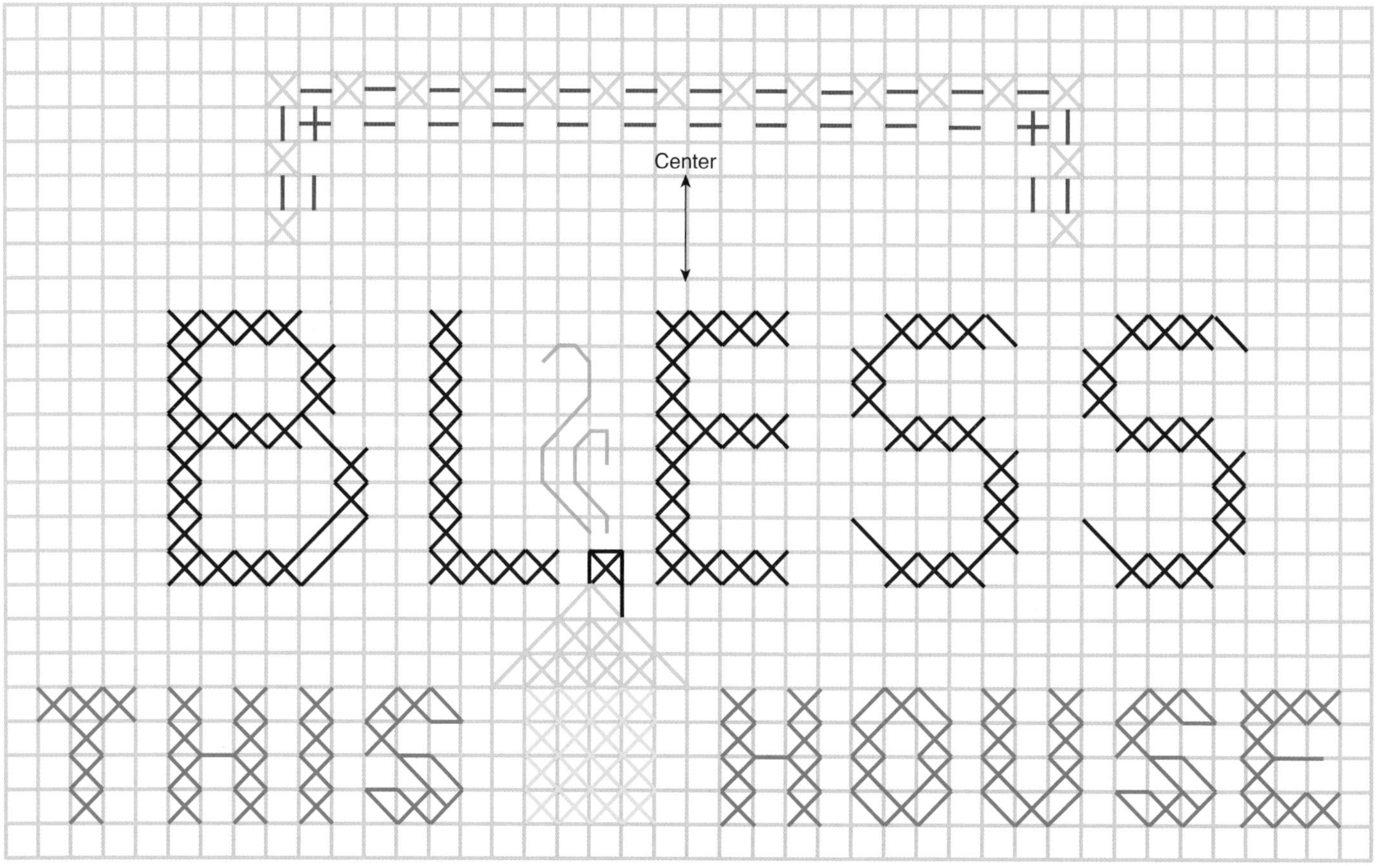

**Bless This House Chart**
Use ivory floss for all black lines.

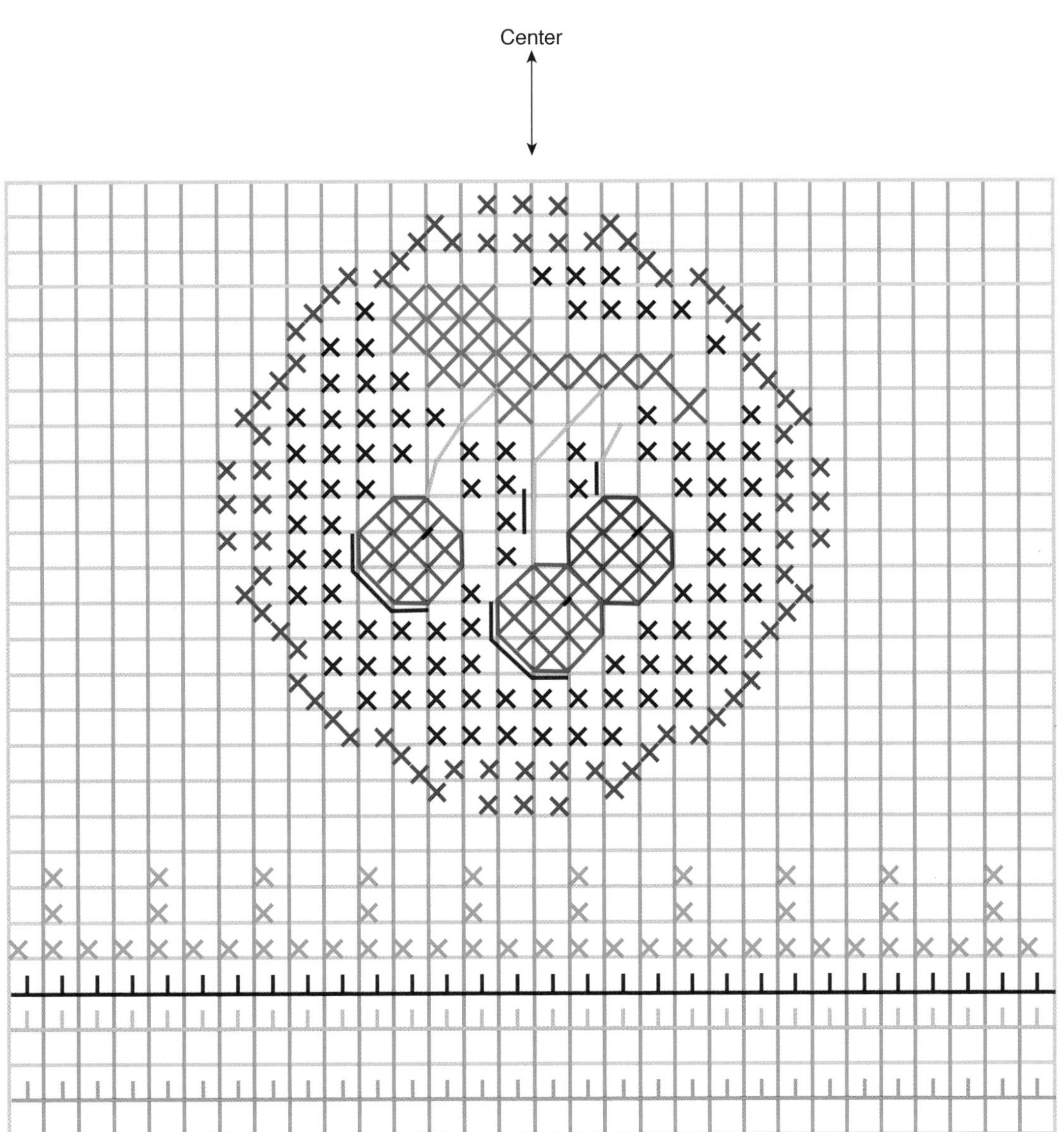


**Cherries Jubilee Chart**
Use white floss for all black lines.
Use white satin stitch for highlight on each cherry.

# Metric Conversion Charts

## Metric Conversions

| Canada/U.S. Measurement | | Multiplied by | | Metric Measurement |
|---|---|---|---|---|
| yards | x | .9144 | = | metres (m) |
| yards | x | 91.44 | = | centimetres (cm) |
| inches | x | 2.54 | = | centimetres (cm) |
| inches | x | 25.40 | = | millimetres (mm) |
| inches | x | .0254 | = | metres (m) |

| Canada/U.S. Measurement | | Multiplied by | | Metric Measurement |
|---|---|---|---|---|
| centimetres | x | .3937 | = | inches |
| metres | x | 1.0936 | = | yards |

## Standard Equivalents

| Canada/U.S. Measurement | | | | Metric Measurement |
|---|---|---|---|---|
| ⅛ inch | = | 3.20 mm | = | 0.32 cm |
| ¼ inch | = | 6.35 mm | = | 0.635 cm |
| ⅜ inch | = | 9.50 mm | = | 0.95 cm |
| ½ inch | = | 12.70 mm | = | 1.27 cm |
| ⅝ inch | = | 15.90 mm | = | 1.59 cm |
| ¾ inch | = | 19.10 mm | = | 1.91 cm |
| ⅞ inch | = | 22.20 mm | = | 2.22 cm |
| 1 inch | = | 25.40 mm | = | 2.54 cm |
| ⅛ yard | = | 11.43 cm | = | 0.11 m |
| ¼ yard | = | 22.86 cm | = | 0.23 m |
| ⅜ yard | = | 34.29 cm | = | 0.34 m |
| ½ yard | = | 45.72 cm | = | 0.46 m |
| ⅝ yard | = | 57.15 cm | = | 0.57 m |
| ¾ yard | = | 68.58 cm | = | 0.69 m |
| ⅞ yard | = | 80.00 cm | = | 0.80 m |
| 1 yard | = | 91.44 cm | = | 0.91 m |
| 1⅛ yards | = | 102.87 cm | = | 1.03 m |
| 1¼ yards | = | 114.30 cm | = | 1.14 m |

| Canada/U.S. Measurement | | | | Metric Measurement |
|---|---|---|---|---|
| 1⅜ yards | = | 125.73 cm | = | 1.26 m |
| 1½ yards | = | 137.16 cm | = | 1.37 m |
| 1⅝ yards | = | 148.59 cm | = | 1.49 m |
| 1¾ yards | = | 160.02 cm | = | 1.60 m |
| 1⅞ yards | = | 171.44 cm | = | 1.71 m |
| 2 yards | = | 182.88 cm | = | 1.83 m |
| 2⅛ yards | = | 194.31 cm | = | 1.94 m |
| 2¼ yards | = | 205.74 cm | = | 2.06 m |
| 2⅜ yards | = | 217.17 cm | = | 2.17 m |
| 2½ yards | = | 228.60 cm | = | 2.29 m |
| 2⅝ yards | = | 240.03 cm | = | 2.40 m |
| 2¾ yards | = | 251.46 cm | = | 2.51 m |
| 2⅞ yards | = | 262.88 cm | = | 2.63 m |
| 3 yards | = | 274.32 cm | = | 2.74 m |
| 3⅛ yards | = | 285.75 cm | = | 2.86 m |
| 3¼ yards | = | 297.18 cm | = | 2.97 m |
| 3⅜ yards | = | 308.61 cm | = | 3.09 m |
| 3½ yards | = | 320.04 cm | = | 3.20 m |
| 3⅝ yards | = | 331.47 cm | = | 3.31 m |
| 3¾ yards | = | 342.90 cm | = | 3.43 m |
| 3⅞ yards | = | 354.32 cm | = | 3.54 m |
| 4 yards | = | 365.76 cm | = | 3.66 m |
| 4⅛ yards | = | 377.19 cm | = | 3.77 m |
| 4¼ yards | = | 388.62 cm | = | 3.89 m |
| 4⅜ yards | = | 400.05 cm | = | 4.00 m |
| 4½ yards | = | 411.48 cm | = | 4.11 m |
| 4⅝ yards | = | 422.91 cm | = | 4.23 m |
| 4¾ yards | = | 434.34 cm | = | 4.34 m |
| 4⅞ yards | = | 445.76 cm | = | 4.46 m |
| 5 yards | = | 457.20 cm | = | 4.57 m |

**101 Tea Towels** is published by DRG, 306 East Parr Road, Berne, IN 46711. Printed in USA. 

**RETAIL STORES:** If you would like to carry this pattern book or any other DRG publications, visit DRGwholesale.com



ISBN: 978-1-59217-309-9
1 2 3 4 5 6 7 8 9